BOOK FINDS

BOOK FINDS

How to Find, Buy, and
Sell Used and Rare
Books

Ian C. Ellis

A PERIGEE BOOK

A Perigee Book
Published by The Berkley Publishing Group
A division of Penguin Putnam Inc.
375 Hudson Street
New York, New York 10014

Copyright © 2001 by Ian C. Ellis
Book design by Irving Perkins Associates
Cover photograph by John D. Kennedy/FPG International Corp.
Cover design by James R. Harris

First edition: January 1996
Revised Perigee edition: February 2001

Published simultaneously in Canada.

The Penguin Putnam Inc. World Wide Web site address is
http: //www.penguinputnam.com

Library of Congress Cataloging-in-Publication Data

Ellis, Ian C.
    Book finds : how to find, buy, and sell used and rare books / Ian C. Ellis.—
2nd ed.
        p. cm.
    Includes index.
    ISBN 0-399-52654-4
    1. Antiquarian booksellers—United States.   2. English literature—20th
century—First editions—Bibliography.   3. American literature—20th
century—First editions—Bibliography.   4. English imprints—Collectors
and collecting—United States.   5. American imprints—Collectors and
collecting—United States.   I. Title.

Z479.E57 2001
381'.45002'0973—dc21   00-062429

Printed in the United States of America

10   9   8   7   6   5   4   3

STILL FOR **P.M.**

Let's go buy us some more books.

CONTENTS

PREFACE TO THE
SECOND EDITION

～

I n the five years since I first wrote *Book Finds*, the world
has changed, several times. In fact, more has changed
over the past five years in the rare and used book world than
changed in the past four hundred. The Internet has caused a
revolution in book dealing and buying like nothing since Gutenberg first figured out how to make ink that could stick to
both metal and paper.

This second edition takes these new developments into account and tries to figure out where we're headed from here—
which may just be a fool's game, but I've got to give it a shot.
On the horizon are e-books, electronic paper, and computers
that jack straight into your head like a bad 1950s science fiction
novel.

But no matter what happens, we're still going to be reading
print, and people who love books will still want a *book*—paper
and ink—the most perfect piece of technology ever devised.

How much time did you spend worrying about your book-shelves being Y2K compliant?

Because we're still dealing with books, a lot of this book takes on the same subjects as before: how to care for books, what makes a book beautiful and worthwhile.

While technology has changed dramatically over the past five years, the prices of books have been rising faster than tech stocks on the NASDAQ; however, as in all markets, there have been some fairly spectacular crashes, while the blue chips—Hemingway, Faulkner, Pynchon, Updike—continue to tick along at a merry 10 percent per annum gain.

No matter which way the prices run, remember this: there is no joy like that of holding a beautiful book in your hands. We are here to spend the next couple hundred pages on the subject of books because the book is the perfect combination of form meets function, the best ever devised. Books are Good Things.

I consider myself astoundingly lucky to be one of those who, in the words of Umberto Eco, "live for books. A sweet mission in this world dominated by disorder and decay."

Here's wishing the same for you. Happy hunting.

INTRODUCTION

~

W|hen I spend a day seriously book shopping, I expect
to make at least a couple hundred dollars' profit from
the books I buy.

You can do it too.

On more casual days, when I'm moving from store to store
around town and enjoying a leisurely day browsing shelves,
finding new titles and discovering old friends long forgotten, I
expect not only to add one or two fine items to my ever-
burgeoning book collection, not only to experience the sheer
joy of buying books, but also to make at least enough money
(and, with luck, quite a bit more) to cover the cost of what I've
bought, simply by buying yet more books and selling them
again somewhere else.

I do this not by hunting out old and moldy books from centuries past, nor by searching out obscure volumes that are
rarely seen outside of libraries, but by buying modern first editions—books printed in this century. Really quite common
books, comparatively.

You can do the same.

There is no satisfaction quite like the one that comes with buying a book. There's the tactile heft of the volume, the smell of the pages, the excitement of the world held between the covers. Buying a fine book is an end in itself, and a very pleasant end it is. Collecting books—searching out fine editions in fine condition, discovering by chance a key early work of a favorite author—is one of the grand glories of life, a pastime that can become all-consuming for every lovely minute of your life as your bookcases gradually fill up.

But you can also go book shopping with ulterior motives: not only increasing your enjoyment, but making some money along the way. If you really try, and if you have a little luck, you can actually make a living buying books—even if you keep many of the best volumes for yourself. If I didn't make money by selling books, I'd never be able to afford to keep buying books for my own collection.

The market for modern first editions has boomed during the last decade. These books, usually defined as those printed since 1900, have outpaced nearly every other collectible on the market for increasing value. A copy of James Lee Burke's first book, *Half of Paradise*, which sold new in 1965 for a couple dollars, is now worth a couple thousand dollars. Randy Wayne White's *Sanibel Flats*, sold for twenty bucks upon publication less than ten years ago, is a hard find today for under a grand. That Edgar Rice Burroughs novel you enjoyed as a child could easily be worth the price of a used car now if you can find a copy in good shape. Or how about that perennial favorite, *Winnie-the-Pooh*? For one of the special editions produced when the book first came out, you're going to need a $10,000 bill. Oh, and I just sold my copy of *Where the Wild Things Are*, which I picked up for two bucks in a used bookstore, for enough to take a trip to Europe on. Authors you've probably never heard of trade regularly in the book world for hundreds, even thousands of dollars.

But despite these dramatic increases in values, books have moved quietly along in their own sedate world while collectibles such as baseball cards, fine wine, and comic books have gotten all the press. The bookselling industry is a clannish one, full of people who consider money a secondary concern to the joy of owning and handling fine books by fine authors. Time seems to stand still in bookshops.

Time may stand still, but prices don't. There are people who actually make their entire living going from one shop to another, buying and selling books. In the industry, they're known as book scouts. These lucky people spend their days wheeling and dealing, never without a book in their hands. They don't get rich, but they have a good time, and few of them would ever consider leaving books behind for regular employment (one who did was Larry McMurtry, although even now that he's a best-selling author, he owns a couple of bookstores).

What I intend to do with this book is teach you how to afford to be a bibliophile, how to make book buying a self-supporting—or perhaps even profitable—habit. I'll do this by showing the techniques the professional book scouts use, and by explaining the inner workings of used bookshops, based on my own experience and knowledge of how things work from the other side of the counter. How far you go and how much money you make is entirely up to you and the amount of effort you put into the project—and maybe how your luck runs.

Along the way, I also hope to teach you how to better appreciate the physical characteristics of a fine book, how to enjoy the hunt, and most of all, how to gloat delightedly when you find a $500 book in the dollar bin. A book scout lives the life of a treasure hunter, and there is no shortage of treasure out there.

In short, the book now in your hands is going to teach you how to shop for books, and how to sell books for their maximum value. If you're looking to improve your own collection of a favorite author, you'll discover how to do it here. You'll also discover how to pay for those expensive volumes of your favorite author by picking up other titles and reselling them. You'll learn how to deal with new and used bookshops, and how to recognize a bargain. With a bit of luck and a fair amount of perseverance, you can learn to buy books without actually spending a dime; in fact, you can easily start with nothing, and yet still buy books and actually come away with a profit.

If you have never collected books seriously before, here you'll find out where to start, and you'll discover how to avoid the costly mistakes most beginners make. If you've collected for years, now it's time to learn how to pay for this most delightful obsession.

The techniques for a good collector are the same techniques used by a professional book dealer to make a living. You have to know what to look for and be able to recognize it when you see it. You have to be able to tell the difference between the first edition of Tom Clancy's *The Hunt for Red October* and its book club edition, and you must have a fair idea of the book's market value.

As in any other field, information is power. The more you learn, the more treasures you'll find, and the more you'll enjoy the experience of book shopping. The book you're now holding is the jumping-off point: welcome to the world of the book collector and the book scout.

Chapter One

∾

GETTING STARTED

The used and collectible book market divides into three relatively neat categories: reading copy, antiquarian, and modern first edition.

READING COPIES

Reading copies are books you can take to the beach or into the bathtub. They're the largest part of the book market, and they're everywhere. If you buy a book with anything in mind other than collecting, don't particularly worry what shape it's in, you're buying a reading copy.

ANTIQUARIAN AND MODERN FIRSTS

Antiquarian book lovers seek out classic old volumes—editions of Scott, Wordsworth, Shakespeare, the Bay Psalm Book, examples of fine printing and binding from centuries past, such as books from the Doves or Ashendene Presses.

Modern first edition collectors tend to limit themselves to books published after 1900, to the writers who have defined the times we live in, such as Steinbeck, Hemingway, and Faulkner. But modern first collectors not only have the greats to choose from, they also have the works of all the wonderful, popular genre writers to search for and collect. These are the writers you curl up with over a long weekend just to enjoy entering the worlds of their books. It can be a blurry line between a reading copy and a modern first edition; when you get down to it, there are only two real differences: edition and condition, both of which will be covered in greater detail later in this book.

While the antiquarian collector is working from a larger time frame—say, from the time Gutenberg printed his first Bible in 1455 to the Industrial Revolution and the introduction of mass-produced books (which is not to say that original manuscripts of the type produced in monasteries are not collected; they are, and heavily)—the modern first collector actually has a much larger variety of material to choose from, to search for, and to deal in. The development of modern printing methods has caused a flood of books; there are probably more books printed in a year now than there were in all the centuries leading up to this one.

The antiquarian must also cope with the inevitable ravages of time, with books that have been eaten away by age and damage, that have been stored in attics until their pages crack with brittleness. True, these same problems affect the modern first collector, but to a less severe degree.

There are other advantages for the collector of modern firsts. While the antiquarian has to be intimately familiar with the minutiae of binding and printing details to avoid being taken in by a forgery, mass-produced modern books define themselves easily. Forgeries are rare, and the basic setup is easy to learn. While a true first edition of *Gulliver's Travels* may come in any one of a dozen different bindings, a first of *Gone With the Wind* comes in one (although there is a dust jacket *point*, or difference, between the first and second issue, which can mean big bucks; this wouldn't be fun if it was too easy).

Ironically, modern firsts currently tend to be more expensive than many classic older books. It is much easier to find a collector avidly seeking Dick Francis's first novel than it is to find someone looking for a fine copy of Hakluyt's travel works. The prices attained may not seem quite right, either. Sue Grafton's *"A" Is for Alibi* goes for around the same as three Joseph Conrads or two minor Charles Dickenses. The modern age is one in which historical perspective is limited, and a classic may be only a year or two old. Authors with successful second or third novels can watch their long-forgotten first novel appreciate from $1.98 in the remainder bin to several hundred dollars in just a few years.

We are going to concentrate on modern firsts in this book. While you'll learn a few things that will increase your knowledge of antiquarian books and fine printing, that's really another specialty, and in chapter 12, on reference sources, I'll point out a few books that will help you move along that path. But for our purposes here, we're moderns.

THE MODERN MARKET

What is the market for moderns? Aside from the big-name authors, there are hundreds of lesser-known literary lights whose books are avidly sought and collected. Genre writers tend to be the most consistent sellers: mystery, science fiction, and horror account for a large portion of the collectible market. Writers of modern literature—from Louise Erdrich's books set on Dakota Indian reservations to W. P. Kinsella's baseball stories to the complex works of Nobel Prize winner Gabriel García Márquez—are hotly collected and sought after. In fact, there's very little in the world of books that isn't considered collectible. Over the course of this book, you'll be introduced to the depth and breadth of the book market: it's much bigger than you may realize.

The more you learn about modern firsts, the more there is to learn. This is a great part of the fun, a lot of what makes the job of a book scout not only profitable, but also satisfying and challenging: you get to make money by learning things most people don't know. There's always another point to track down, another author heading for the hot and collectible list. But as I'll show throughout this book, you only need to go in as deeply as you want.

The most important factor in making the techniques of this book work for you—whether you want to make a living buying books or just improve your collection—is to pick a specialty and stick with it. You'll likely never know the whole range of collectible books. But you can easily become an expert on your own area of interest, be it railroad books, mystery novels, or modern women writers from Oklahoma.

One quick example: although I collect in several genres, for years I dealt mostly in modern women writers. On a recent trip to a favorite store, one that specializes in mystery, I came across an advance copy of Rosellen Brown's *Before and After*, marked down to $4. I can take that advance and sell it off for an easy $50 to the right collector. When I found the book, I was dealing from my strength; Ms. Brown is not a mystery writer, so for the mystery store, where they miss nothing in their genre, Rosellen Brown was "outside" for them. They either weren't interested, or didn't know the value of the book. Another quick example: a friend was looking through a catalog of nature books. Included was a fine copy of Rick Bass's first book, *The Deer Pasture*. The dealer, way out of his specialty, thought it was a book about deer. My friend knew that it was a $200 modern must, and was quite happy to pay the dealer $20 for it.

There's no other thrill quite like it in the world: the thrill of buying books. Especially when you know that the book you just paid a couple of bucks for is worth a couple of hundred.

TAKING STOCK

The first step to being a good book scout is to take a look at your own bookshelves at home. This is going to be your opening stock, so take a minute to appraise what you own. Do you have a lot of paperbacks with cracked spines and tattered covers? Or do you have a nice selection of good hardbacks neatly cared for, books you bought as soon as they came out? The fact that you own books at all shows that you're a lover of books, which is the first step to becoming a serious collector.

Collectors come in all forms, but what all collectors have in common is a kind of happy dementia. To a book collector, it actually makes sense to pay $600 for a first edition hardback of a book after reading the $5.95 reading copy. She may never read that $600 first edition, but owning it, being in some way closer to a much-loved author, is often satisfaction enough. I've gone into shops to scout and walked out having spent serious money on things that will never leave the shelves of my own collection. The collecting impulse is probably stronger in most people than the buying and selling impulse.

But the collecting impulse does change. Fifteen years ago, I built a serious collection of books on Central Asia; today, I have only a few left, having sold off the rest. So take a look at your books. What did you buy that you're not interested in anymore? What have you outgrown, passed by? These titles are going to be important when you start trading books in shops.

THE RULES

There are a few basic points to keep in mind as you read this book; they are the glue that holds the process together, so I'll outline them briefly here, developing them each in more detail in later chapters.

RULE ONE: SPECIALIZATION

You're never going to know everything. This is the most important rule, and ultimately, the one that will offer up the most enjoyment. As you become more involved in your chosen area, you'll discover new worlds to appreciate. Do you collect travel books? If not, you may not realize how Bruce Chatwin's *The Songlines* was strongly influenced by Robert Byron's *The Road to Oxiana*. But a specialist knows and catches the echoes. Reading one book becomes, in a sense, reading history. Sue Grafton named the city her alphabet novels are set in Santa Teresa; this came from Ross Macdonald's earlier novels set in a town of the same name. Ross Macdonald was really living in Santa Barbara, the model for Santa Teresa, and he was really named Kenneth Millar. His wife was Margaret Millar, a formidable novelist in her own right. Perhaps this is why Grafton named her character Millhone. Specializing allows you to enjoy tying facts like these together, and it gives you the information you'll need to deal in highly collectible but lesser-known writers. The more depth you have, the more fun it is.

RULE TWO: CONDITION

For value, condition is everything. A trashed book is trash, no matter how rare it is. But if you find an uncommon title with the jacket shiny and neat, the pages unbent, and the spine clean and tight, you have found a treasure.

RULE THREE: THE RULE OF THREE

How do you define a treasure? Rule Three, which will be referred to often throughout this book as the Rule of Three, is: *A book has to be worth three times what you just paid for it in order to make a profit on it.* This is a lot easier than it sounds. For example, suppose you buy a book for $10, knowing it's worth $20. When you take it in to sell it to a shop, the shopkeeper has his markup to consider, and so will offer you, on average, $10 in trade (which gets you nowhere), or $6 in cash. Unless you hold it and the book starts to climb in value, you've lost money. If it's a $30 book—that Rule of Three—then you'd be offered $15 in trade or $12 in cash. At least it's profit. Of course, where you make money is not in nickel-and-dime trades like this, but in scoring $30, $50, or $500 for books that you paid pennies for. The Rule of Three also works on a sliding scale when you get into seriously pricy books: there's nothing wrong with paying $500 for a book and turning it around for a quick $750 to the right buyer, or better yet, paying a grand to make two. But always keep the Rule of Three in mind. Forgetting it is the quick road to failure.

RULE FOUR: KEEP LOOKING

Make the rounds of the shops often. You never know when a book will be missed. Like Larry McMurtry said, anything can be anywhere. To be a good, successful book scout, you'll need a regular route of stores that you go into frequently. A methodical approach is needed, because although finding the treasure book is a matter of luck, you can find yourself having a lot more luck if you keep putting yourself in the right position to have it—that is, combing the shelves of the local used bookstores. Try to find out when new stock hits the thrift stores; try to be out looking before the other scouts beat you to the good stuff.

There's a corollary to Rule Four, which is to find the hits and misses. What is a bookstore's strength? What is its weakness? Do they love mystery and hate horror? Buy horror there; it's likely to be bargain priced. You never know when the treasure will be unburied. Learning the store's personality will help you know if it is a store that should be included on your route; knowing that will help you be in the right place at the right time.

RULE FIVE: TRADING

Finally, Rule Five for the successful book scout is never neglect trade fodder. Never pay cash for a book when you can trade for it instead. Never be so blind looking for the great book you'll strike it rich on that you forget the B-list items that can pay your daily bills. Never sneer at a good reading copy, a copy no one will collect, but any reader would love to have out by the pool. There's money to be made here. The margins are lower, the glamor considerably reduced, but it can keep you going. The Rule of Three still applies here, but in trade fodder, there is a lot of money to be made with more marginal books—here is where quantity is more important than strictly quality.

These points will all be discussed in detail later on; for now, just keep them in mind to see how everything in this book fits into these five rules. Knowing them and keeping them in mind puts you well on the road to success as a book scout.

What can be more fun than buying books? Buying books and making money doing it.

Chapter Two

❧

THE BOOK

Before you start to seriously go out and buy books, you need to learn some terminology and become familiar with the book publishing and production process. For example, while most people think of book collecting only in terms of the final product as it appeared in the bookstore, there are other elements of a book that are more valuable, more elusive, and more heavily collected. Plus, the more you know about the history of books and how books are constructed, the more finely tuned your critical senses will be, and the more you'll appreciate finding a truly good book.

THE DEVELOPMENT OF THE BOOK

In the earliest stages of written culture, books weren't, of course, books as we think of them. The Sumerians scratched figures onto clay tablets at the dawn of writing; around 2500

B.C., the Egyptians improved this process by writing on papyrus scrolls, and there things pretty much stayed for a few thousand years, with people rolling and unrolling unwieldy manuscripts. Although papyrus was more durable and texturally pleasing than virtually any paper made today, the scroll concept had its limitations. While scrolls were easy to store, all the rolling and unrolling of the scroll was hard on the manuscript, and the length of the scroll was limited by how long a piece of papyrus you could make that was easy to handle. Sixty feet was about the upper limit, with the average scroll length closer to twenty feet long and eight to twelve inches wide.

CODICES

Papyrus scrolls actually consisted of sheets of papyrus laid end to end and glued to form one long roll. In other words, in order to make a scroll, the scribes did everything necessary to make the pages of a book. This led to the next innovation: cutting the scrolls back into sheets (of different sizes than the raw papyrus sheets) and combining the loose sheets into codices, the forerunner of the modern book. Not long after that, someone realized sheets weren't such a bad thing in and of themselves, and the bookmakers started producing actual pages of the desired size. Codices from the first or second century C.E. are extant in Europe; others, from the second, third, and fourth centuries, have been found in Egypt, which goes to show how quickly the scroll concept was abandoned when something better came along.

PARCHMENT AND VELLUM

These early codices were primarily made of papyrus, but before the introduction of paper, use of papyrus, made from a plant of the same name which grew only in a very limited part of the world and was guarded jealously by those who grew it, started to fade away, and Europeans used parchment and vellum for the production of books.

Parchment is split sheep- or goatskin (with occasional other skins used); vellum is unsplit skin. The very best vellum is made from the skins of stillborn sheep. These stretched, hairless skins were soaked in lime, rubbed with chalk, and finally polished smooth with a pumice stone. While vellum is rather prettier than parchment—it has a translucent quality—parchment is a little more durable. Sheets from books written on parchment or vellum often appear for sale; single, nicely decorated pages can easily run a hundred dollars and up. Thanks to the durability of the material, it's not hard to find such pages in excellent condition, better, in fact, than pages from books printed only decades ago.

Parchment and vellum had another great advantage over papyrus: you could erase on them. Once a mark was made on papyrus, that was it; with vellum or parchment, you could simply rescrape the skin, creating a new, smooth writing surface.

Of course, it did take a fearful amount of skin to make a single book. If you were growing big sheep and didn't care that much about the pure quality of the skin, you might get four pages of book per sheep. To make, say, a Bible, you were looking at a whole hillside of sheep, obviously something only the truly rich could afford.

EARLY BOOKBINDING

One problem with both parchment and, especially, vellum, was the material's tendency to bow and wrinkle. The solution to the problem was the development of bookbinding. Bindings ranged from simple leather covers (the earliest surviving ones date to the third century C.E.) to more decorated covers, to finally the medieval innovation of wooden boards covered with tooled leather. Richer people might have their books bound with hammered gold or silver covers, or might have the family crest worked into the cover with rare jewels as decoration. To keep the bowing and wrinkling to a minimum, the boards, or covers, of these early bindings were fastened with locks, straps, chains, buckles, and a variety of implements that might have looked more at home in a dungeon. Even with such precautions, the integrity of the flat sheets was nearly impossible to maintain.

In the long centuries before the development of type, books existed only in a few copies at any given time, with each copy handwritten. Because of the tedious nature of bookmaking—from scraping the skins to hand copying the text to strapping down the binding—books were the property only of the nobility or of the clergy. Besides, the upper classes and clergy were the only ones who knew how to read. Here we have an image of monks huddled in their scriptorium, working away at preserving culture and knowledge letter by carefully decorated letter. Just read Umberto Eco's *The Name of the Rose* for a wonderful look inside a medieval copy house and the politics of books in their earliest stages.

PAPER

Meanwhile, across the world in Asia, things were moving along faster. Paper as we know it was developed in China in the second century C.E. (its invention is attributed to Ts'ai Lun, in the year 105). Papermaking was slow to develop in Europe; one source places paper in Spain no sooner than 1150 (about a hundred years before the travels of Marco Polo). The first paper mill in North America was built in 1690.

BLOCK PRINTING

The Asians were also centuries ahead of the Europeans in the development of printing. Printing in China can be dated back as far as the second century C.E. In the ninth century, the empress of Japan commanded miniature pagodas to be built, with printed sutra copies placed inside, and the pagodas and sutras to be distributed throughout the nation; this while most Europeans lived in mud huts and England was nothing more than a tribal area where some of the tribes liked to paint their naked bodies blue before heading into battle.

But the printing in early Asia was not quite what we consider printing today. The Eastern bookmakers did not have movable type. Instead, they took blocks of wood, smoothed and planed down, then carved on the block the entire page to be printed. This was great for turning out multiple copies, and may be one of the first examples in the world of true mass production, but it still presented some difficulties. First, carving out a new page was a nuisance; second, it was nearly impossible to store all the huge blocks of wood with single pages carved on them. For a copy of, say, the Tibetan *Tripitaka*, you would literally need a warehouse full of carved wooden blocks.

Blocks did have some advantages—beautiful combinations of text and illustration could be easily made, since there was no real difference between carving an image and a letter—but the blocks were inherently limited, and there was a serious need for something else.

MOVABLE TYPE

That something else was movable type, the development of which is attributed to Johannes Gutenberg (although there is some evidence that the Koreans had hit upon the same idea about four hundred years earlier).

Gutenberg was born in Mainz, Germany, around the year 1400. Although block printing had finally caught on in Europe about a thousand years after its appearance in Asia, what Gutenberg did was revolutionary. Using the latest in milling technology and high standards of tolerance previously unknown in his day, he created identically sized lead and antimony bits, each with a single letter carved on one end. This made it possible to rearrange the letters to form any word. A page could be constructed and broken back down, without massive storage problems. Like the tiles in a Scrabble game, the letters could be reused endlessly.

Movable type is as much responsible for the development of our modern world as any other single factor. Even the television station A&E recognized this when they named Gutenberg the most important person of the millennium. With movable type was born the Information Age.

Suddenly book production became inexpensive, easy, and most of all, unlimited. The stage was set for mass literacy and a huge outgrowth of culture and education. No longer handmade, books became affordable and accessible to almost anyone. (That's not to say that all had time to read; most Europeans were still simple peasants, knee-deep in mud fields. Developing time to read took a few more centuries.)

The first book Gutenberg finished was his famed edition of the Bible (we have records, but no copies, of some broadsides and one-sheets that he tried before he took on a project as big as the Bible). About fifty complete copies exist today; there are also numerous loose leaves of the book which appear on the market from time to time. A complete Gutenberg Bible would auction off today for several million dollars, but one's not likely to show up—they're all in institutions. The last time half a copy, just the New Testament, appeared at auction, it went for $5.25 million. In the twentieth century, two damaged copies of the Bible have been broken apart into single sheets; one of these sheets can easily bring $30,000 or more.

Although he was inventing the form himself, Gutenberg's pages look remarkably modern, and you'll find no shortage of book scholars who will say that the very first book made remains the very best made book ever printed. The Bible is printed in two neat columns, with justified type—that is, each line ends at the same point on the page. There is light decoration around the edges, most of which was added later by hand. But there is also a certain handwritten quality to the page: it seems crowded, with minimal space between ending punctuation and the next word; the typeface Gutenberg made would give even a serious Latin scholar a headache to read now, and even within the typeface, he was trying to imitate the handwritten book—there are several different shapes of the letter *e*, for example.

This was truly the birth of modern culture, as the development of movable type spread throughout Europe. Printing reached Italy in 1465 and France by 1470. It finally arrived in England in 1476, when William Caxton brought type and press to London. Caxton's books are rather workmanlike. He made no great innovations and did little to further the cause of book design. Still, he was the first printer in England, and his books are heavily collected. He brought us the first printed edition of Mallory's *Morte d'Arthur*, source for many of the King Arthur legends, and possibly the first novel ever written expressly for the printing press.

EARLY LIBRARIES

By the beginning of the seventeenth century, an estimated twenty thousand different editions of books had been printed with movable type. The modern world of books and collecting began sometime around the 1700s. This is the time when Horace Walpole, Daniel Defoe, James Boswell, and Samuel Johnson were writing, as were the founding fathers of the United States, who were producing polemical books and pamphlets at a fantastic rate. A larger class of cultured, leisured landowners was also developing, and owning a library became a symbol of a well-rounded person—whether any of the books had actually been opened or not. By the turn of the nineteenth century, literacy had spread to the masses, and lending libraries became the vogue in Europe.

One of the most popular draws for a lending library was a large collection of Gothic novels, imitations of Walpole's *The Castle of Otranto*. With a focus more on mood and gloom than story, these early Gothics, with their mossy stones, dank grave-yards, huge abandoned castles, and secrets in shuttered rooms, drew new audiences to the world of books. The libraries would rent these popular pieces out until the books were literally fall-ing apart; anything left when the craze died down was fit only as fuel for the fire, and as a result, few collectible works remain from this time period.

SERIALIZATION

If your local penny library didn't have a book you were looking for, you could read it in serialization. Dickens, Thackeray, and hundreds of other authors first had their works printed in monthly magazines. One or two chapters of the book would be printed each month—which is why when you read, say, *Nich-olas Nickleby* today you find so many cliffhanger endings. The last page was supposed to keep you breathless until the next installment came out. Only after the entire book appeared would it be collected into a single volume (or, considering bind-ing techniques and the length of many of these books, several volumes).

It's much easier to find books by British authors from these years than ones by American authors. The United States did not recognize copyright laws throughout most of the nine-teenth century. Books were imported from England, quickly reprinted in pirated editions, and shipped around the country. Since no royalties were paid, the pirate editions sold for con-siderably less than a U.S. author's works. Until after the Civil War, writers in this country found it difficult to establish them-selves, because of these cheaper British works.

A side effect of this is that from, say, the Civil War up to the passage of the International Copyright Act in 1891, books became truly ugly, appalling things, as publishers struggled to put out the cheapest editions possible. With the postwar rise in literacy, there were more and more people wanting more and more books, and the publishers were happy to oblige with editions that make today's beach books look like fine craftsmanship. An 1884 letter in *Publishers Weekly* said that the postwar book trade was demoralized, that "in the rage for cheapness, we have sacrificed everything for slop."

Most books were not sold in bookstores at this time, because there was really no such thing. Books were primarily sold by the printers who produced them. If you wanted a book in the year 1805, you would most likely walk into a print shop, where the book, in loose pages, would be sitting on a table. You'd make your purchase and then order a binding for the book. Unlike today, when bindings are uniform, you could custom-order virtually any kind of binding on your book. If you were rich, this could get into gem-encrusted leather; if you were poor, simple cloth might have to do. Because of the wide variety of bindings employed, there are collectors and dealers who work with nothing but fine bindings. Their interest lies strictly in the outside of the book, and they really couldn't care less about what is inside.

That books were sold in loose pages for so long before they were bound has affected even the way the modern book looks. Have you ever wondered why books so often have two title pages? The first one, where there is just the title, is called the *bastard title*, or the *half title* page. When booksellers first started laying out their wares, this was absent. However, customers started to complain that wind or handling had damaged the book's actual title page while the book was in the shop. To protect the title page, yet still let people know what this pile of pages consisted of, the bastard title was developed. The binderies didn't particularly mind an extra page in the mix, and it kept the customers happy—and the lower pages free from drip marks when someone chose to browse the shop on a rainy day.

BINDING

One interesting sidelight of this period of bookmaking was an extension of fine binding: *fore-edge painting*. Here, an artist would take the front edge of a book (the long side where the book opens), fan the pages slightly, and then paint a design on the edge. Pastoral scenes were especially popular. When the pages were un-fanned, the scene disappeared. Artists could actually paint two scenes on a single book, fanning the pages first one way, then the other. This in no way disrupted the other main decoration of the outside of a book, *gilt edges*. Fore-edge painting was most popular in England from the mid-1600s into the 1700s, when methods of mass production took over. It's not terribly uncommon to "discover" fore-edge paintings on antiquarian books because no one ever bothered to fan the pages before.

By the mid-1800s, many printers were encasing their books in rough paper covers; these were meant to be temporary, until you could take the book to have it bound, but many people found the paper covers to be enough. Also around this time, standardized bindings appeared. However, unlike today when there will be a single binding style for a book, there might have been several, in varying colors or qualities, for a novel at mid-century. When *The Adventures of Huckleberry Finn* was published, it was bound in both blue and green cloth; in London, it first appeared in a red cloth binding. Some collectors will want a copy in all three bindings; others will simply be interested in the first state, the binding in which the book first appeared—which is the London red binding.

The book as we know it—a mass-produced item printed and bound in a uniform manner—can be dated to around the Civil War. Other methods still continued, but with the increasing industrialization of our society, and with the increasing literacy rate, a means to supply the demand for books was necessary. The rise of the middle class, the growth of cities, and the development of more leisure time caused a boom in book production, one that has continued over the past century.

Of course, since the Civil War, methods of book production have only become faster, helping to fulfill that increased demand for printed matter. Techniques of mechanical printing were developed, and soon it was no longer necessary for someone to hand set each and every letter on a page.

OFFSET PRINTING

When you have movable type like Gutenberg used, a method known today as *letterpress*, each and every letter is set into a tray, then the tray is pressed against the page. Therefore books produced with the letterpress method actually have indentations on them: you can run your fingers over the page and feel where type met paper.

Modern books do not have this tactile feature. Most modern books have been printed with a method called *offset printing*, in which the image is transferred from the printing plate onto a different surface—usually a rubber blanket—and then transferred to the paper from there. The printing plate itself is made through photographic processes, and the rubber blanket is treated chemically to allow the smooth reproduction of the image. There is no physical type to move about, and there is no raised impression on the pages. Unlike the wood blocks used in Asia long ago, the printing plates stack and store easily, and unlike movable type, you don't have to either use up all your type and store it, or disassemble and then reassemble each page to print another edition. With computer typesetting, storing a book for later editions is as easy as making a floppy disk—in fact, I'm writing the second edition of this book over the disk used to make the first edition.

In the modern age of printing, it has become feasible to reprint books easily, quickly, and economically. More than anything else, this has influenced the quantity of the modern first
edition. Publishers don't need to take a risk and print a lot of
books of an unknown; they can run off a few thousand, see
what happens, and then if need be, get the plates back out and
reprint the book. The widespread use of photo offset printing
dates the arrival of the modern first edition.

THE MODERN WORLD OF BOOK PUBLISHING

What has brought us from the world where printers sold their
own unbound books, to today's book industry, a multibillion-
dollar-a-year market producing more than fifty thousand new
titles annually? What has brought us to a time when a best-
selling author can sell more books in a single year than might
have been produced in the entire annals of history up to the
beginning of this century? (In 1993, 27 million John Grisham
books were sold; think how many monks, scribbling furiously,
for how many years it would have taken to produce those.)

The answers are true mass production, distribution, and a
leveling of culture that makes mass literacy the norm. Further
influences are an increase of leisure time and an increase in
the pressure to keep ever informed. The computer revolution,
despite the vast changes it has brought upon all forms of business and commerce (including the book industry), has not yet
found its way into every nook and cranny of the world; most
people still get information from the printed page—it's just that
the information on the printed page was probably first written
on a computer.

To meet the ever-increasing demand for printed information, new technologies, such as CD-ROM, have been developed
that have changed the very nature of the book. Fear not for the
demise of printed paper, though. Even on *Star Trek*, they admit

there is no pleasure like that of holding a book. Books have a tactile sensation that can never be fully replaced. No sane person wants to drift off to sleep while staring at a computer screen.

Movable type, one of history's most important inventions, however, is as much a dinosaur as the monk's quill. The only places you're likely to find the direct descendant of Gutenberg's little pieces of lead are in fine art shops and very small presses, more concerned with beauty than commerce (and we praise each and every one of these anachronistic souls). Even photo offset printing is becoming passé. Books today are printed almost directly from data bits that have been edited on a computer screen. No longer can an author deliver a trunk full of handwritten pages to his editor, as Thomas Wolfe did, and expect a book to appear. Today, more likely, the author composes on a computer screen and e-mails the file to his publisher, where it is edited on another computer screen, then typeset and sent to the printers. Most of the work happens in the world of little blinking lights.

Still, other things have not changed. A book still originates with an idea, which is then fleshed out by the author during long hours of composition. Along the way, endless revisions are performed and drafts are refined until the book is ready to be sent to the publisher.

Publishing a Book

Many elements of the publishing process affect a book's collectibility. Therefore, let's trace the production of an average book, from original manuscript to the bookstore shelf.

MANUSCRIPT

Whether the author is writing on a legal pad (the way Scott Turow wrote most of *Presumed Innocent*) or on the latest high-tech hardware and software (the way this book was written), everything begins with the manuscript.

This is also where collectibility begins: the author's original manuscript, preferably with a few hand corrections on the pages (or better yet, entirely written in hand; this is known as a *holograph* manuscript). These, understandably, do not come on the market very often, and when they do, they are priced beyond the reach of most ordinary collectors and dealers. Consider that single-page letters from notable authors can go for well over a thousand dollars, and you get an idea of what an original manuscript is going to run.

Before the dawn of the computer age there would be several stages of manuscript extant, as the book was written and revised, but now, with most revisions done on screen, these intermediate versions are few and far between. Libraries and scholars are mourning the loss, since different stages of a page allow one to see the thought process behind the work, how the author developed his ideas.

After the author finishes the book to his satisfaction, he prints out a clean copy, one with no mistakes or corrections noted on it. Today, the author will most likely print both a *hard copy*, or what most people think of as a *typescript*, and a copy stored on computer disk. These are then sent on to the editor.

Editors are rarely, if ever, satisfied with what the author has produced, and so the next stage of composition ensues, a dialogue between the author and the editor, seeking to improve the quality, the smoothness, and, yes, the salability of the manuscript. A good editor can be an author's greatest blessing, since the author is usually too closely involved with the manuscript to be able to look at it objectively. As mentioned above, Thomas Wolfe was inclined to bring in entire steamer trunks of handwritten pages; it was up to his editor, Maxwell Perkins (the patron saint of editors), to turn this morass into a coherent book.

What this means for the collector is that there are pages of manuscript with both the author's and the editor's notes on them. Again, these come onto the market very rarely, and when they do, they are extremely expensive. Depending on the amount of reworking the book undergoes in the publishing process, there can be five or six complete versions of the manuscript, each at a different stage of the revision process. Don't count on finding an example of this from your favorite author; odds are, a university library already owns it (although Clive Cussler liked to put single early pages in books he signed). The very few copies that do appear on the market are priced sky high. Again, with the advent of the computer age, these pages are becoming more and more rare; while the physical book itself is in no danger of extinction, early stage manuscript pages may soon be as rare as dodos.

Eventually the editor and author finish their work, the manuscript exists in a form both are happy with, and it's time to send the book to the production department, where the manuscript is designed and typeset, taking on the appearance of the book it is to become.

PROOFS

However, before actual printing and binding begins, these typeset pages, called *proofs* or *galley proofs*, are sent to the author for final revisions. Unlike the two states mentioned above, which exist in at most two or three copies, proofs are usually run in multiple copies, with some going to the author and some to the editor, proofreaders, publicists, and sales managers in the publishing house. Copies may also be sent to book reviewers. Again, there is frequently a state of the proofs with the author's comments on them, and this, of course, is more collectible than someone else's copy.

Sometimes the publisher will print several hundred copies of the proofs, bind them in plain paper wrappers, and send them to bookstores, hoping to generate the interest of buyers.

ARCS

One step later in production, after the author has made changes
to the proofs, the publisher may print *advance reading copies*,
or *ARC*s. These differ from proof copies in that they are a later
version of the text, and they are usually bound in paper covers
(or *wrappers*, as paperbacks are called among collectors) that
are printed with the same design the final book will have. The
ARCs are distributed at book conventions or distributed by the
publisher's salesmen to bookstores, hoping to generate advance
publicity and sales. Booksellers tend to grab every ARC they
can to help them decide what to order.

Although there can be significant differences between a
proof copy and an ARC, the term ARC is used frequently for
either state. However, you should still be aware of the difference between the two.

For the collector, the ARC is a rich world. Although the ARC
is usually printed up after the proofs have been corrected, there
are still commonly found textual differences between the ARC
and the final book. In fact, virtually every ARC has a disclaimer
on it, stating that all quotes for review should be taken from
the final book, not from the ARC. For someone seriously interested in a particular writer, these differences between the ARC
and the final version of the book can provide a great deal of
insight into the creative process. ARCs aren't as avidly collected
as they were five years or so ago, but a completist will still want
them, and anyone seriously interested in the author and the
author's working processes will still want them.

Also for the collector, the bound proofs or the ARC can honestly be considered the real first edition. Remember, primacy
is everything. These are the first versions of the book distributed to the world at large, and good quality copies of proofs
or ARCs will always have a ready market. Sue Miller's *For
Love* was produced in both a plain-wrappered proof and a

decorated-wrapper ARC; as far as primacy goes, the plain one has priority, but both versions would be sought after by collectors. Most books promoted this way will have only one or the other version.

Investing much money into advance copies of unknown writers—and sometimes known writers—that you may find for sale around town can be a risky business. It's very hard to tell this far in advance what books are going to really hit big. Gretel Ehrlich's little-known *The Solace of Open Spaces* can sell for nearly $400 in an advance copy; on the other hand, one of Paul Theroux's more recent novels might go for $20 or $30 in an ARC. While you'd expect the Theroux to hold its value longer, the Ehrlich is rare beyond belief, and it's considered a classic in nature writing. If you had a copy of each, you'd sell the Theroux a lot more easily, but when you hit the right dealer, the right buyer for the Ehrlich . . .

On the other hand, I have half a shelf full of ARCs of writers who I thought might someday be somebody. So far, they're not. I keep the books, but if there's a crunch on shelf space, these will be among the first to go.

One thing to watch out for with advance copies: they are very difficult to find in good shape. They're given to booksellers as advance promotion for the forthcoming book. ARCs are usually not made with the highest grade of materials. They're passed around by the shop's staff, they're handed out to favored customers, salesmen write notes on them. As with any other book, condition is everything. A wrinkle in the cover can knock off 10 percent; a cracked spine can mean 50 percent; and a salesman's notes scribbled on the half title can trash the book. I just threw out a proof copy of Paul Theroux's *The Consul's File*, a $100 book in good shape, that I had kept around for years, hoping the salesman's doodles on the back cover would somehow magically disappear. They didn't.

On the other hand, if you've got a good advance copy and you can get it signed by the author, you're looking at a treasure beyond compare. Dan Simmons's *Lovedeath* is a $65 item in its advance state; double that if you can get it signed, despite the fact that Simmons makes himself regularly available to conventions and readings. If you want a signed Stephen King advance copy from one of his first two or three books, be prepared to mortgage your house.

What's a median price for an advance copy on the open market? For a good, popular author who is not on the A-list, $20 to $40 for a mint condition advance. For the A-list authors (genre writers—remember, general fiction is not heavily collected)—Sue Grafton, Anne Rice—a hundred and up. For the current flavor-of-the-month writers—say, James Lee Burke when people were just discovering him—closer to $200. And the rare classic books that show up in advance copies are pure gold. I've seen an advance of *Brave New World* for $300; *Hyperion*, the first book in Dan Simmons's masterful *Hyperion Cantos* can run you $350 in a hardback first edition, or around $600 in an ARC. An advance of Sylvia Plath's *The Bell Jar* appeared in a catalog for $2,500 not long ago. Thomas Pynchon's *V.* has shown up in advance state twice in my memory. I'll leave you to guess the price.

PRINT RUNS

Now we are ready to produce the actual book itself, the hardback first trade edition, which is going to find its way onto the shelves of bookstores around the country. The author and the editor have done their work, the publicity people are gearing up (the author hopes), the book has been mentioned in the publisher's catalogs and maybe one or two of the trade journals, and advance orders are placed by bookstores around the country. The major wholesalers and retail book chains have copies on order as well, and this gives the publisher a fair idea of what the initial demand for the book is going to be. First printings of a million copies are not uncommon for some of the biggest authors; a hundred thousand to two or three hundred thousand is practically the norm for anyone who has made the best-seller list twice. There were 3.8 million copies printed for the first U.S. edition of the fourth *Harry Potter* book.

But such huge print runs are still the exception. Most first editions are quite tiny—five or ten thousand copies. This means it's quite possible that when advance word is good and creates a demand for the book, even before the book hits the shelves it will be in its second or third printing. On the first edition of this book, demand far outstripped the original supply; even my own box of free copies, sent direct from the publisher, were second printings. Again, thanks to modern printing methods, it's really cheaper to print a few more books than to store a lot, so the publisher simply goes back and prints more on demand. For the collector, this can mean a boon, if you can swoop up a few copies of the first. As a general rule, the smaller the first print run, the more valuable each individual book is going to be for a collectible title.

Just a quick note here of something that I'll go into in depth later: print runs of first edition hardbacks in England tend to be a fraction of what they are here. If you pick an author who's popular on both sides of the Atlantic and compare the print runs, you'll find the U.S. run is frequently easily ten times larger than the run in the United Kingdom. There aren't as many people there, and the book industry is run quite differently. This can make quite a difference in prices between the two countries, and having a good relationship with a dealer on the other side of the Atlantic is always a valuable asset.

DISTRIBUTION

There is a regional pattern for the distribution of most books: they hit the East Coast first. In fact, on some books that have gone to press a second or third time before publication, you can almost bet you won't see many of the first printing west of the Mississippi. It's something to be aware of if you live on the left side of the country. Here in the West, I've even had publishers send me second editions of books for review, long before the book ever hit the stands. Toni Morrison's *Beloved* is a good example: nobody west of the Mississippi saw a first of that in the original market.

One final note about regions: if a book is published in England before it is published in the United States, the British edition will always be more valuable. It's the demands of primacy again. The copy of the book that appeared first is considered to be the best edition.

And one final note about print runs: as mentioned above, sometimes you'll see a notation along the lines of "second printing before publication" on the copyright page of a book. As with the first edition of the book in your hands, the original demand of these books is greater than expected, so the publisher fires up the presses a second time before the book's release date. Many novices fall into the trap of believing that, since these second printings appeared before the book was actually published, they're as good as first printings. But no, sorry. They're still second printings, and will never be as good as a first. When I got my box of second printings of this book, I went around to stores owned by friends and swapped out seconds for firsts. It just didn't seem right to me to not even have a first printing of my own book.

The Language of the Book

Already we're probably starting to confuse you with some terminology here: printing, edition, release date. When you first get into book collecting and dealing, it seems as if everyone is speaking a foreign language. Paste-down, endpaper, free endpaper, bastard title—what does "hinged" mean?

But it's all very simple.

Take a book in your hands, a new hardcover. What greets your eye is the *dust jacket*, or *dust wrapper* (don't confuse dust wrapper with *wrappers*, the term for a paperback cover like the one on this book). If you're collecting or dealing, the dust jacket is the single most important factor on a modern first edition, being worth as much as 80 percent of the book's total value. Tears are money lost, as are chips (pieces missing), and price clips—where some thoughtful gift-giver has chopped out the book's printed price with a pair of scissors. *Any* damage to the dust jacket lowers the value of the book.

On the front and back of the dust jacket, tucked inside the covers of the book, are the *jacket flaps*; usually, there's the author's photo on the back flap, and a teaser on the front flap, enticing you to buy the book. The price—hopefully not *clipped* (whacked off by scissors)—also usually appears on the front flap.

Next, take the jacket off and lay it carefully aside. You're now looking at the actual cloth covers of the book, which are known as the *boards*. Boards are made up in many ways: *full cloth* (or leather), *half-bound*, and *quarter-bound*. This refers to how much of the front and back boards are of a particular material. A full binding is just that: the entire cover of the book is made of the same material. Half-bound books are leather (not seen much anymore, and certainly not on mass-produced books) or finer cloth across the spine and to about the one-third point of the cover (yes, it's still called half-bound); quarter-bound, by far the most common type found in better books, wraps the spine and the edges of the covers in better material. There is also *three-quarter bound*, which has the corners in the same better material as the spine. Fewer and fewer books and binderies are even trying to maintain that illusion of old craftsmanship now, and the odds are when you take the jacket off, you'll see one kind of cloth on the cover only. This is not quite even, technically, a bound book; with a bound book, the spine is an integral part of the book's architecture. Modern books are *cased* or *case-bound*, a process in which the book is dropped into an already created binding made of a single material. This is cheap, easy to make, and it gives the illusion of a real binding, but actually the only thing holding these books together is the strength of the paper gluing the *text block*—the actual pages of the book—to the case.

The back edge of the book is called the *spine*. The front edge of the book, where it opens, is the *fore-edge*. You've also got the *top edge*, or *head*, at, obviously, the top of the book. A lot of publishers like to put colors on the fore-edge or the top edge, and these are called *stains*. On older or finer editions, these may not be color stains, but *gilt*.

Where the spine meets the top edge, you have the *headband*, a thin strip of cloth running across the spine. The headband used to serve as an integral part of the binding, to reinforce the book's top edge. It's one of the most abused parts of the book, because it's what people grab when they're pulling the book off the shelf. The modern headband is just glued in, and while it helps protect the book a bit, mostly it's just decoration now. The headband is usually colored, and in older titles it's often missing, giving you a look down the spine into the binding itself. There can also be a *footband* at the bottom of the book, but this doesn't get nearly the abuse the headband does.

Now we're ready to open the cover. If you've opened the front of the book, what you're now looking at on the left side is the *front paste-down* or *paste-down endpaper*, and on the right side the *front free endpaper* or *flyleaf*. The paste-down is where the book actually attaches to the boards. On a casebound book, this is what is holding the entire book together and keeping it intact. At the back of the book the *rear paste-down* serves the same function. On antiquarian and finely made books, there is an entire art to endpapers: they are often heavily decorated, marbled, printed with fancy designs. On modern, mass-produced books, they tend to be plain and cheap, with the flyleaf made of some colored paper to get your attention. Functionally, the flyleaf is just a decorative page, subject to much abuse from people writing inscriptions in books. (If you're getting an author to sign a copy of your book, have him do it on the title page.)

Where the flyleaf meets the paste-down is the *hinge* or *gutter*. This is a point of structural weakness in books, and the hinge is something that should be carefully checked when grading the condition of a book. The hinge should be good and tight, with no sign of looseness. When it is loose, it's said that the book is *hinged*. That can mean a fair amount of money down the drain on a collectible book. "Hinged" runs from just starting, to fully opened, when the binding materials of the book start to show. When the hinges get bad enough, the boards actually separate from the text of the book. As an interesting little side note, bookstores often have to ship books to prisons; prisons do not allow hardback books, so all you have to do to turn a hardback into a paperback is zip a razor along the gutters. The case detaches, and what's left is the equivalent of a paperback book. Do not try this at home.

The page after the front flyleaf is the *half title* or *bastard title* page. As mentioned before, this was an innovation from the time when books were sold unbound; it was just a protective page. Now it's a structural anachronism.

Next is the *title page*, which doesn't say much more on most books than the bastard title page says, except it has the author's name. As mentioned above the best place to get an author to sign a book is here, on the page where the name appears.

Later, when we start talking about first edition identification, there will be more to say about the title page.

We will also be discussing in detail what usually comes on the back of the title page, the *copyright page*. This page contains the publisher's information, the Library of Congress information, and all of the disclaimers and copyright notices that keep lawyers happy. But this is also the most important page for the book dealer and collector working with modern firsts, because this is where the edition is identified, in any one of a myriad of ways (including by not identifying anything at all). An alternative to the copyright page is the *colophon*, which accomplishes the same thing at the end of the book.

And finally, we are into the text itself, the reason people buy the book to begin with. Although much of the book now in your hands works like a dissection—taking apart a book to show why it's worth buying—always remember that no book is worth anything if the text isn't going to move people in some way. Books are, in their own way, living things, breathing and interacting with the world around them. Never get so caught up in the details that you forget the book's own intrinsic life, how it came into the world, and why. To my way of thinking—and most book collectors will agree—there is nothing sadder than a mediocre book that's being eagerly sought after strictly on a speculative basis. You must allow the book its life, and appreciate it for what it is. Not money waiting to happen, but a miraculous way of transmitting thoughts and ideas.

All these wondrous thoughts and feelings are printed onto the pages—the *leaves* of the book. The leaves are then folded into *gatherings*. When a printer is making a book, he uses large sheets of paper, onto which some multiple of four pages of the book is printed. Once the paper comes off the press, it is folded, so that the pages fall into the proper page order. The most common forms of this are the *folio* (abbreviated *fo*), in which the page is folded a single time, making four pages, a *quarto* (*4to*), with two folds making eight pages, and an *octavo* (*8to*), with three folds making sixteen pages. The great majority of modern hardback books are considered octavos. However, as with all else in bookmaking, modern technology has made these tiny gatherings somewhat obsolete: it's possible to print books today on sheets large enough to be folded into thirty-two- (*sextodecimo*, or *16mo*) or sixty-four-page sections (*tricesimosecundo*, or *32mo*).

While these designations are the technical meanings of

quarto, octavo, etc., book dealers, never ones to leave good bits of jargon lying around loose, have adapted the words to their own purposes. Allow me to quote from John Carter's invaluable and indispensable *ABC for Book Collectors*: "Most booksellers' catalogues nowadays dispense with a terminology which is increasingly unfamiliar to, and unnecessarily technical for, the majority of their readers. These know or should know—that, from the early 17th century at least, a folio is a large, upright-shaped volume and an octavo a small upright-shaped volume, while a quarto . . . is essentially squarish in shape." In other words, when you see such designations in a modern catalog, it has nothing to do with the number of folds the paper went through; rather, it is a size and shape designation. A folio works out to a book roughly twelve by fifteen inches, taller than it is wide; a quarto comes out to around nine by twelve inches; an octavo—the most common size for modern books—roughly six by nine inches. These sizes derive from what was once the standard sheet of paper used in printing—nineteen by twenty-five inches—but with modern printing methods, that's almost meaningless, and the terms are used by many dealers now strictly as measurements.

For all intents and purposes, *sheet* and *leaf* are different stages of the exact same thing: the large piece of paper that the printer uses is called a sheet; once it's folded, a book's two-sided page is called a leaf. When you have a book open in front of you, the page on the left is the *verso*, the page on the right the *recto*.

The entire piece of paper, folded however many times it is going to be folded, is called a *gathering* or *signature* when the binder gets hold of it. This isn't quite right. On many books, you'll see a series of small numbers or letters at the bottom of the page. On a 16mo, these would be spaced every thirty-two pages, and they are to show the bindery what the proper order is for putting the gatherings together. Technically, *signature* only refers to the small coding; in practice, the term is used more commonly to refer to a gathering. One other term you might run into that can be used synonymously with signature or gathering is *quire*, but this is falling out of use.

MODERN BINDING

The signatures are gathered and then *bound*. As mentioned previously, binding is a nearly forgotten art in the modern book world. Especially with antiquarian book lovers, there are collectors who collect only bindings, not particularly caring what is inside, simply luxuriating in the physical beauty of a fine binding.

Intricate binding has all but disappeared in the modern era. Hardback books are now further encased in the dust jacket, so what's the point of working very hard on the binding?

The modern book is case-bound; that is, glued into cloth-covered cardboard sheets. If there's any decoration on the boards—and even that is becoming less common—it's simply the author's name embossed on the front board. It's ironic that as modern firsts get more and more expensive, they also get uglier, in the physical sense. Mass production is slowly eliminating much of the tactile joy of a fine book: the rubbed-leather smell, the flaking of gilt coming off the top edge as you take the book down from the shelf. There are publishing houses that still make beautiful, finely crafted books, but rising production costs and mass consumption are making those houses fewer and farther between.

But there are still places that make books the old-fashioned way, and as a dealer or book scout, you'll encounter them frequently, because these are the houses that produce limited and fine editions. Limited editions and fine printing will be discussed later on.

THE FIRST EDITION OR PRINTING

And so we have before us a *Book*: case-bound, flyleaf, and jacket flaps in perfect condition, no wear on the hinges, the headband as crisp as it was the day the book rolled off the bindery floor.

Do we have a collectible book? Even if the book is by a noted author, it's a more complicated question than one might think.

While collecting and dealing modern firsts is considerably simpler than working with antiquarian books, that's not to say that we can simply rush in, check copyright pages, and get down to business. First, we have to define what a "first" is.

The term "first edition" is, in itself, something of a misnomer. "Edition" technically refers to all the copies of a book printed from a single setting of the type. This works just fine on books that are hand-set, but in modern terms, where type is a matter of plates and computer information, it has lost its exact meaning. In a traditional hand-set book, the type would usually be dismantled after the book was printed. It was simply too costly and too space-consuming to leave all of one's type set in the pages of a particular book; you needed the type for the next project.

If the type was not dismantled, but was set aside for a time, then a book had different *impressions* of the edition. Often there are very minuscule changes in impressions—corrected spellings or punctuation—but they are still considered part of the first edition, or the first setting of the type. There can be many impressions included in an edition. The first impression is obviously the most sought-after, but subsequent impressions do have a healthy collectible status.

In modern terms, however, both *edition* and *impression* are sort of meaningless in their traditional sense. Instead, we use *edition* and *printing* almost interchangeably. Still, this isn't quite correct: the book now in your hands is a second edition, a revised, changed version of a book that previously existed in a different state. Printing-wise, it might be a first or thirtieth impression.

But that ain't how we talk about things anymore. People say they collect first editions, when what they really collect are first printings.

For all intents and purposes, *printing* can be used in the same way as *impression*. The first printing is the number of books run off the press at the initial time of the book's release. It is not a matter of type, it's a matter of marketing and economics. The first printing, or impression, is a set number of copies run off the press at one time.

A popular book may go through thirty or forty printings; many other books never go beyond the first.

Because most books never make it out of the first printing, the first printing is, usually, the exact same thing as the first edition. Book dealers and collectors will use *printing* and *edition* synonymously now, and many publishers will as well. Or you can skip all the confusion and just call a first edition, first printing, first impression a *first*.

However, there are often differences between printings. Again, this usually involves text corrections; the presses will stop, the correction will be made on the plates, the first edition will continue to roll off the presses. What we have now are two different *states* of the first printing.

The matter of difference between the two states is known as a *point*. A point may be something as simple as a dust jacket price—production costs went up during printing, and so did the price of the book—or it may be a word or line erroneously printed in the volume. It may be a different paper used on the front paste-down; it could even be a different headband used in the binding.

Collectors are usually only interested in first printings and first states of printings. While you can sit down and read a fiftieth printing of a good book with every bit as much pleasure as you can a first (more, because you don't have to worry about getting fingerprints or smudges on the fiftieth) it is only the first printing, the first edition, the first state, that gains and retains maximum value. There is no real objective reason why first printings are the only ones that are collected; most people say it's because the first is the one closest to the author's hand, the first state of a new book. The first edition has a primacy that subsequent printings are lacking.

Best-sellers aside, the first printing is also usually small. Publishers tend to be cautious on first printings, especially with unknown authors. But if that unknown author later becomes famous, those few copies of the first printing of his first book become pure gold. Only ten thousand copies of Stephen King's *Carrie* were printed in the first run; now his books routinely have first printings of more than a million copies. Think of the premium that puts on the tiny first printing of *Carrie*.

And so for the purposes of this book and your collecting and dealing career, *modern first edition* or *first printing* means the first state of the book as it was produced for mass consumption some time within this past century.

Now for the trick: learning to identify first printings is only slightly more difficult than graduating *summa cum laude* from medical school. Virtually each and every publisher has its own method for identifying a first, separating it from later printings. We'll learn how to identify those in the next chapter. There is also a quick reference in the appendix.

And so, here's our book. It's gone through the manuscript phase, been edited, been produced. You've checked the points, checked the condition of the hinges and flyleaf. If it's an old book, perhaps you've even fanned the pages to make sure there's no fore-edge painting that everyone else has missed.

The book is the stock of our trade; its physicality is always mixed with the value of what's inside, and the joys of holding a book produced with care are matched only by the joys of reading a book produced with care.

Chapter Three

❧

EDITION, CONDITION AND SCARCITY

N ow that you have a good idea of how a book is put together, it's time to start looking at what you need to look for when you buy a book. This chapter is going to be heavy on details, with a lot of niggling but very important little facts. I'd suggest reading it over once, then coming back to it again after you read the rest of the book. This is the chapter where the quality of your collection will be ensured, and where your money is going to be made; these are also the details you'll have to know to work deals successfully, to upgrade your collection, or to make some spare cash.

For the collector, there are three primary things to consider when buying a book: *edition*, *condition*, and *scarcity* in this condition and edition. These are the same areas you'll need to know when you sell a book as well.

Understanding these areas is the difference between success and failure, between being able to build a collection of treasures and an assortment of reading copies, between being able to collect and sell for money and just going out and buying a lot of worthless books.

THE FIRST EDITION

As mentioned in the previous chapter, collectors of moderns want what we're going to reluctantly call the first editions of books (but remember, while I'm going along with the crowd in terminology use here, what we're really talking about are first printings). There are those who collect later editions when there is something unusual about them—a revision, for example, or new illustrations—and there are those who collect only the most beautiful editions of particular books; but as a general rule, the firsts are where the action is. Ninety-nine percent of the high-ticket items in the used book market and in the modern collectible field (there are many exceptions in the antiquarian field) are first editions.

Firsts are the way the book appeared the day it hit the shops for the first time. Ideally, that's how you want to find a first, as well: looking like it did on opening day.

There's no real logic behind the mystique of firsts. On the vast majority of books, there's no textual difference between the first and subsequent printings. The books roll off the same presses, are bound in the same machines, and are printed from the same plates.

In fact, the second edition may technically be more rare than the first. If the publisher printed a small second edition after a huge first edition, then by the normal codes of rarity and collectibility, the second should be more valuable, right? But it will never happen. There is always the primacy of the first. (Of course, it wasn't necessarily first, as we saw in the last chapter.)

This primacy is where the money is. A first edition of *To Kill a Mockingbird* in fine condition is worth approximately $4,000. A second edition, in the same condition, can probably be found for under $50 (although, thanks to the rarity of the first, there are those who will settle for a second, and still be willing to pay more of a premium; but don't expect any premiums on later editions of more common books).

IDENTIFYING FIRSTS

So obviously, you've got to learn how to identify first editions to avoid making costly mistakes. After all, if you think it's a first and you turn out to be wrong after paying a premium . . .

The problem is, nearly every publisher has its own method of identifying first editions. You can memorize the policies of every single publisher in the history of the book trade and even then you'll make mistakes, because all of the rules have exceptions. On my shelves, and on the shelves of every other collector I know, there are at least a few books that looked like a first at first, but turned out later to be just plain old books instead.

As a general rule, there are two things to look for right off the bat: a *statement of edition*, and a *number line*.

The statement of edition is exactly that: on the copyright page, the book reads "FIRST EDITION" or "SECOND EDITION" or "FIFTY-THIRD EDITION." Or if not "edition" it will read "printing." With a lot of publishers that's all you'll need to find. Unfortunately, some publishers don't remove the edition slug from subsequent printings; or sometimes a book club edition will state that it's a first; or sometimes there's nothing stated at all.

The next thing to look for is the number line. This is a sequence of numbers which, on a first, usually goes from 1 to 10. Some publishers will go from 1 to 5 and then the five years around the year of publication, with the year the book is printed on the end. For example, 1 2 3 4 5 99 98 97 96 95 94. It may be in order, or it may start with the 1 on the left, the 2 on the right, and so forth, with the 10 in the middle. Look for the 1. For every publisher employing a number line except Random House, a number line with a 1 is a first edition. Random House, just to be sure that no one can ever be sure, indicates its first editions with a 2 on the number line and the "FIRST EDITION" slug. Just to make things still more difficult, this number line, except on Harper and Row books of the seventies, usually appears on the copyright page. Harper and Row, feeling ornery, put it on the last page of the book for a while. Then they stopped doing that and moved it over to the copyright page. The only problem is remembering when they did what. You can easily miss an early Hillerman if you don't look for the number line on the colophon. A friend who taught me enough about books for it to be safe to say I'd never have known enough about the subject to write this one without him, fell into this trap early on in his buying days. He thought he was getting a first of *The Blessing Way*; when he discovered the colophon trick, he discovered that he had a fifth.

There are some publishers who indicate a first edition by *not* indicating it. If you don't see anything that says it's a second or a third, then it must be a first. There are other publishers who code the information into the book somewhere, but it isn't always easy to find.

When you pick up a book, check the copyright page first. Look for a statement either of first edition or first printing. If that's missing, check for the number line. If that's missing, look for something that says "First published in . . ." That's usually a tip-off of a first, because if the publisher lists when it was first published, they usually list reprints as well.

Those three checks will help you identify *most* books from *most* publishers, but not all. As a secondary check, compare the date on the copyright page to the date on the title page. This works especially well with books from the first half of this century. Scribner's is famous for printing an "A" on the copyright page of first editions, but they didn't start doing this until 1930. Because I did not know this, early on in my career I almost passed up a first edition F. Scott Fitzgerald. What saved me was comparing the date on the title page with that on the copyright page.

While it's of doubtful use to go out and memorize the policies of every publisher in identifying first editions, you need to know the big houses without hesitation. These are going to be the bread and butter of your scouting business. Check the appendix for a listing explaining the policies of many of the major publishers.

THE LIMITED EDITION

It's important to note that all of what is truly physically lovely about a book still goes on in a hundred small publishing houses that you've probably never heard of. One of the most noted right now is William T. Vollmann's Co-Tangent Press, which creates extremely limited editions—a dozen copies or so—of Vollmann's works in very custom-made formats. Some of the books are cased in marble, others have marker ribbons woven from the hair of prostitutes. They are not only books, but also strange and disturbing works of art, designed to complement the text to the fullest extent. For less elaborate but no less beautiful books, seek out the works of Lord John Press, which prints largely genre authors in beautiful limited editions. Or buy a hard-boiled mystery or two from Dennis MacMillan, who makes wonderfully solid books. Or take a look at books from Barry Moser's Pennyroyal Press—his Bible was just published to much acclaim, and his *Alice in Wonderland* is a masterpiece—or the Arion Press, who did a Moser-illustrated edition of *Moby-Dick* that may be the most beautiful book published in the past fifty years.

Because the small presses put such pride and craftsmanship into their works, many authors like dealing with them, creating a book that goes beyond the usual mass edition. Stephen King and John Updike both do so many fine, limited editions that they've practically become cottage industries, both in printing and in dealing. Other writers got their start with small presses, which are usually more willing to look at unknowns, and feel a debt of gratitude to them, going back to the smalls even after hitting it big. Jayne Anne Phillips has had some of the loveliest books of recent years produced on small presses, including her novella *Fast Lanes*, printed by Vehicle Editions.

One of the most famous of all small presses was the Kelmscott Press. Founded by William Morris in 1891, Kelmscott books are noted for their extremely decorative pages, fine illustrations, and bindings. The books issued by Kelmscott are all highly sought after and very, very expensive, but there are few finer examples of the art of bookmaking—or at least of books as art. Although on an idealistic level, William Morris believed in simplicity, the truth is, he was a wallpaper designer working in a time when ornate was better. The books he made are beautiful to look at, impossible to read.

For sheer beauty and simplicity, turn to the Doves Press, which is another, similar press from the turn of the century. Doves is especially noted for bindings, and its 1904–1905 edition of the Bible is considered to be one of the most beautiful books ever made. When T. J. Cobden-Sanderson, the man who founded Doves (along with Emory Walker, one of the most brilliant type designers in history) decided to stop printing, he took the type used by the press and threw it into the Thames, so no one else—and especially no machine—could ever use his fonts.

Doves, Kelmscott, Arion, and Pennyroyal are all examples of small, fine presses. The work of these usually needs to be distinguished from the idea of a limited edition. Today, virtually every major writer turns out a signed, boxed, limited edition of his or her work. More times than not, these are simply put out by the same publisher as the trade edition; sometimes the work is farmed out to a different press, but that press works from the same typesetting as the trade publication, and so, while the binding may be nicer, you're not getting all that much for your extra money.

There is, though, a huge market for limiteds. The limited is usually sold out before its actual publication date, often doubling in value the moment the last copy is sold. An edition of between three and five hundred copies is standard. With limited editions, the lower the number on your copy, the better. Copy 5 of five hundred will always be worth fractionally more than copy 499. And if you're lucky enough to get one of the lettered copies—the newest trend, produced largely for the writer's own use—then you're sitting on a gold mine. Remember, primacy is always of value.

Of course, the value of a limited edition depends on the demand for the author. There are authors who produce limited editions only because their publisher is catering to their vanity; then there are other authors who do limited editions because they want to make beautiful editions of their works available.

Obviously the more unusual the edition, the more value it will add to your collection. Read notices in the catalogs carefully: with large trade publishers, limiteds are often just copies of the trade edition with a limitation page, a signature, and a slipcase added. Compare that to a handmade small press book with marbled endpapers, bound in leather. John Updike's many limited editions are all a joy to hold and behold: he requires that publishers take special care in binding, paper, and even type selection. He personally approves every detail in order to make the book a work of art, and with as many Updike limited editions as there are—up to two or three a year—you wonder how he finds time to write new books.

Limited editions are really prominent in the horror and science fiction fields, where they are a subcategory of collecting. In some ways, it is easier to deal in limiteds than in trade editions, since so few of the authors in these genres are published in hardcover. One of the prime purveyors of limited editions is Stephen King. He's done more limited editions than most people have done books. There's the limited edition of *Firestarter* with an asbestos cover; *Eyes of the Dragon* on handmade paper; the famous Donald M. Grant volumes of *The Dark Tower* series, and his near-fabled *The Plant*. *The Plant* is a series of three booklets done as King's Christmas cards over three years. Although an entire novel was planned, after three installments King realized he was only rewriting *Little Shop of Horrors* and abandoned the project. However, enough copies were circulated—many with notes in King's hand to other famous writers—that these booklets were the talk of the collectible world for months. Everybody had heard of them, but almost no one had actually seen a copy.

Finally, it's time for a note about "collector's editions," or the semilimited editions of presses like Franklin and Easton. These publishers put out fairly nice editions, usually bound in leather, frequently signed by the author. However, no one outside the companies is exactly sure how "limited" these editions are— estimates are usually in the several thousand copy range. These are nice books; they sell them new for about $35, and 99 percent of them will still be worth $35 ten or fifteen years from now. They're nice on the shelf, they're good to read, but they're not real collectible books.

Sometimes the Limited Editions Club gets lumped into the same category by beginners, but that's a mistake. LEC is closer to a fine press with rather large print runs: great typography, some really good illustrators (including Matisse and Picasso, in years past), and fairly carefully made books. There are collectors out there who buy only LEC books, which can get very, very pricy.

BOOK CLUB EDITIONS

Book club editions exist somewhere in a twilight zone between publisher's hardbacks and paperbacks. A book club book is almost always a hardback edition, and so it has more permanency and is more pleasing to the touch than a paperback, but it is also *different* from the publisher's edition, made with cheaper, often different-sized paper, and so it is closer physically to a paperback.

For the collector and the dealer, the fiction book club edition is the bane of existence. Remember that the most important thing in collecting is the primacy of the edition; obviously, book club editions, which are often not even run off the same press as the publisher's edition (book clubs maintain their own printing presses, which is one of their ways of keeping down costs), don't make it in the line of succession. There are a few exceptions, which I'll mention later, but book club books aren't collected, for the simple reason that they're book club books. They do not have the publisher's touch.

So how do you identify a book club edition? Don't worry, it's not the nightmare that identifying first editions is.

First of all, a book club book simply feels wrong. After you've handled enough books, you'll likely know a book club edition the instant you touch it. It's lighter, it's looser, it's rougher. Yes, there are a few trade publishers who could use a little upgrade in quality control, and a few whose books are barely distinguishable physically from those of a book club, but even on those, there's a difference to the heft, to the texture. Experience will teach you this.

Because book clubs must lower costs to offer you the volumes at 20 or 30 percent off publishers' prices, the clubs must cut corners on production. Using their own presses, book clubs are free to use cheaper paper and bindings. Paper stock is rougher, and while most publishers now use acid-free paper on first editions, book clubs never do, so ultimately the paper will degrade and crumble. Book club dust jackets don't have the sheen and shine of the publisher version. All this use of lesser materials also means the book doesn't have the same heft, the same feel as the "real" edition.

If after the heft test you're still unsure, open the book and look for a price on the dust jacket. Some publishers don't put prices on the jackets—notably art houses, where the books can change prices rapidly—but most do. Lack of a price on the flap is a good indication. And on the flap, some book clubs make it real easy for you: there on the bottom, in neat type, it reads "Book Club Edition." (It's important to note that this does not mean the same as a printing slug that says something along the lines of "A Selection of the Book of the Month Club®." Publishers sell books to the clubs months before publication; they'll use slugs like this to show that a book has wide appeal, so wide that the book clubs snapped it up. A line like this appears frequently on true trade first editions, and is often a source of confusion for beginning collectors.)

The next step in the book club test is to pull the dust jacket off and look at the outside bottom right corner of the back cover of the book. Many book clubs put a blind stamp here, a little square or round indentation that identifies the book club. This used to be a lot more foolproof than it is now, since many clubs have ceased stamping their books, but it is always the acid test: if there's a stamp, it's a club.

While you've got the jacket off, you can also check the boards. Book clubs don't spend their money on the bindings, and you'll see a considerable difference in the quality of material here. You're not going to find quarter-cloth bindings on book club editions. Nor will you find embossing. While book clubs will print author and title on the spine, most of them won't bother with niceties on the boards that trade publishers like to do, such as embossing the author's name.

Next, open the book to the copyright page. If you know the publisher was originally Random House, and you know Random House reveals a first by a number line that descends only to 2, you can look on the copyright page of the book club and see that this is missing. Book clubs don't need to worry about identifying editions, because they don't do editions, and so number lines or tag lines are very often missing. Of course, this doesn't help in the case of a book originally from a house that shows first edition by showing nothing; nor does it help if the book club is simply using publisher plates.

Finally, if all else fails, check the size of the book. Since the book clubs are working off their own presses, the size of book club books tends to be uniform, while a trade publisher can go any size it wants. Book clubs tend to make their books smaller than the trade publishers do. Book club binderies are also often limited in how many pages they can comfortably handle—the cheaper bindings used can't stand up to a thousand-page book—and so for those authors who get seriously wordy, a book club is likely to break the book into two volumes. This happens frequently to James A. Michener; nearly all of his books in club editions have been changed to two volumes, whereas the publisher put out a single, hefty doorstop.

Okay, now for the exceptions. To complicate matters, occasionally publishers will sell off excess copies of their trade edition to a book club. This usually happens when early demand does not meet expectations, and the publisher figures to get more money selling the books to the club than it would by *re-maindering* them (selling them at or below cost). This means that there are a very few books in the market where the book club edition is actually a first. Paul Theroux's *The Great Railway Bazaar* shows up in book club firsts, which are worth considerably less than the real item that came straight from the publisher. At best, they are worth half to a third as much.

To make matters more complicated, there are a couple of books where the book club edition is the *true* first edition. Peter

Matthiessen's *Under the Mountain Wall* was sold to two different book clubs by the publisher before the official publication
date. These books would have disappeared into insignificance,
except that the original publisher had made a mistake printing
them: the photographs, which Matthiessen had insisted be-
longed at the end of the book, were placed in the middle. Not
only did this goof up the page numbering, it infuriated Matthiessen. The mispaginated books, with a new contents page
tipped in (which does state "BOOK CLUB EDITION"), are the actual
first editions, finding their way into collectors' hands via book
clubs. The second issue of the first edition has the photographs
correctly placed at the end. While this doesn't make a huge
difference pricewise—over the past few years it's leveled out to
around a 40 percent difference—knowing the difference between the two is vital.

A lot of genre books have their first (and only) hardcover
publication via book clubs. The Mystery Book Club and the
Science Fiction Book Club both do hardcovers of books that
are otherwise only available in publisher paperbacks. These
hardcovers are rarely collected.

Finally, in the twenties and thirties, a few book clubs simply
bought publisher stock and sent the books out with no alterations at all. It's virtually impossible to identify which volumes
passed through club hands; and although it may matter to a
purist, because the books are real publisher editions, few people will ever be absolutely sure one way or another. It's not
something to spend time worrying about.

POINTS

These little differences, about where the photographs should
be, wrong lines printed in the book, etc., are known as *points*.
With modern technology, they are not as common on most recently produced books, but for books published earlier in the

century, when human error was still more common than computer error, points are an important field of study, one you can't
afford to neglect. If you didn't know the point on the Matthiessen book noted above, you could set yourself up for a very expensive mistake.

When book collectors get together, it isn't long before the
conversation turns to points. What's the code number? Does
your first have tan cloth or brown cloth? Is there a blurb from
Author X on the dust jacket?

The easiest way to start learning points is the obvious one:
pay close attention to the better price guides, which rarely fail
to list the major points. Never just look at the price; look at the
entire entry.

However, this may not always help. There are books where
no one is quite sure of the order of the points. Paul Theroux's
first novel, *Waldo*, was released with two different colored dust
jackets, one with red printing, one with white. No one seems
to know which came first, or if they do, they're not talking.

When there is no clear order in the points, then both issues
have equal status. If you've got a first *Waldo*, it doesn't matter
what color the jacket is. In fact, the discrepancy can actually
be a boon, because a true completist is going to want both, and
that gives you an extra chance to sell the book.

When there is an order, as with the first edition itself, earlier
is always better. On Charles Frazier's *Cold Mountain*, there's a
typo on page 25, line 16: the true first reads "she can go about
looking like a man-woman"; the second state has the corrected
"mad woman."

Graham Greene's *Travels with My Aunt* has its point on the
rear flap, where the blurb from Evelyn Waugh does not include
a quote from *Time* magazine.

The only way to learn priority on many books is to check for
the number of ads, or what other books are mentioned on the
jacket flap. The first issue of *Gone With the Wind* has the novel
listed in the second column on the back flap among the pub-

lisher's other offerings; the second issue has the book listed first. There's a better than 200 percent difference in the value of the first and second issues.

Because points are so vital, it's time to introduce one of the main themes of this book: to deal successfully, it is important to specialize to a large extent. You're never going to learn the full field of points—every single detail differing in every single book. In the comfort of a used bookshop, maybe the owner has time to run back to check twenty reference books and a half dozen specialized bibliographies to research a point (although probably not). But when you're standing in the store, looking at the book, and you're not sure, you're on your own. If you've specialized, you've got a better chance of coming up with the right answer. This is not to say you should never go out of your field; but in your field, go for depth. Learn everything you can. If you're a science fiction fan, a modern lit fan, a devotee of travels and voyages, there are specialized bibliographies (more on this in chapter 12) you can use to track down and discover new points. If you're interested in children's books, study those authors, and pay attention to every detail of the book in your hand. Do you know the date coding for *Where the Wild Things Are*? Knowing that bought me a vacation in Europe.

Also, to learn your field, look for books that popular, successful authors have written blurbs for. By plugging someone else's book, particularly a new writer, the author is indicating that she thinks this book is similar to her own great work.

CONDITION

We've looked at the details of the edition; now it's time to look at the details of *condition*. You can own a copy of the rarest book in the world, and if the boards are off, the hinges sprung, if there's writing and foxing on the pages and heavy water damage along the edges, all you've got is a lump of worthless paper.

This cannot be emphasized enough: *for a modern first edition book to be collectible, there is nothing that affects the price as much as condition.* Even the rarest first, if trashed, is just trash, not a collectible book.

When I've given prices in this book, it has been for volumes in *Very Fine* condition, the top of the line (some dealers don't use the Very Fine category; *Fine* is as high as they go). Every grade down in condition from there is a quantum leap down in price.

DUST JACKET

It is the condition of the dust jacket that determines the largest percentage of the book's price—some dealers estimate as much as 80 percent—and so this is where you should start grading. This, too, cannot be emphasized enough: *with very few exceptions, a wonderful book lacking the dust jacket it was issued with is just a reading copy.* Collectors want prime dust jackets. That's what they see first, that's what's displayed on the shelf, so the dust jacket should be treated like cash money. Any extent you go to to protect a dust jacket is worth the effort (see chapter 10 for the care of dust jackets).

So if you're grading a book, look at the jacket first, and then move on to the book itself. When you start looking at catalogs, you'll see most dealers will give one grade for the book itself, another for the dust jacket. The whole package is important, but the dust jacket has priority. Again, without exception for books produced in the last twenty-five years, there is nothing more important to the book's value than the dust jacket.

One quick caveat, though: some highly collectible books were issued without dust jackets. Most limited editions come sans dust wrapper. Watch for them. They're usually obvious, but looking for them can make it worth your while to pull an unjacketed book or two off the shelves while you're browsing.

GRADING CONDITION

Grades are given in descending order: *Very Fine, Fine, Near Fine, Very Good, Good, Poor.* Grading can be largely a matter of personal opinion—it's entirely possible to give a book to five dealers and get at least three different grades—but there are certain guidelines that are generally accepted.

Very Fine: A Very Fine book is a book in perfect condition. There is virtually no sign that this book has ever been read. The dust jacket is as bright and shiny as it was the day it came off the press, with no sign of rubbing, bumping, chips, dents, dings, or creases. The book itself is still tight—ideally, there should still be that new book creak when you open the covers— and it does not fall open to any particular page or section. (It's hard to find a book like this; most people open their books quite wide to read, actually cracking the integrity of the spine just as it cracks the spine of a paperback, and that can drop the condition from Very Fine to Very Good right there.) The corners should still be sharp, the headboard unmushed. Obviously, there should be no ownership marks of any kind on the book.

Fine: Fine is a very small step down. A tiny bump or two is allowed. The book may obviously have been read, but very carefully. The dust jacket may have lost some of its sheen, but it is still intact, with no tears or chips in it. (Very commonly, you'll see a book described as having some particular flaw—say, a small tear in the jacket—and "else fine." This means that the book is as I'm describing here, with one problem. On a hard-to-find volume, this won't affect the price much; on something more common, it can have severe results. But the truth is, on many books, the best you can hope for is an "else fine" copy.) Remember that some dealers consider Fine to be the highest grade.

Very Good: Very Good is a book that is physically intact, dust jacket on and reasonably unmarred, but a book in which some basic flaws are evident. These are the most common books on anyone's shelf, simply because about all it takes to downgrade from Fine to Very Good is one slightly careless reader. While in a Fine book the flaws are hints, by Very Good they're pretty easy to spot. The book may fall open to a particular section or page; there could be a small ownership mark, and maybe a bent corner or two on the pages. On the dust jacket, expect rubbing, a tear or two, and maybe even a couple of chips. It may be sun-faded.

One of the most common causes for downgrading a dust jacket to Very Good is price clipping, where someone has taken a pair of scissors and removed the book's original price. This means the jacket is no longer intact, and so it can't really be fairly judged any better than Very Good.

Very Good is also usually top of the line for a book that has been remaindered. You will see descriptions of remaindered books (books put on nonreturnable sale by publishers for the best price possible) where they're described as "else fine," but truthfully, a remainder mark is a mark of death to the Fine category. It is an alteration of the original book. Now this may not mean a lot to many people, and how much it means can alter with how the remainder mark was put on the book. But for our purposes of grading, consider remaindered books as Very Good at best, so you also need to watch out for copies that have been bleached or sanded (more on this later) to get rid of the remainder mark. Also, just note here, don't confuse a remainder mark—usually a black mark—with an edge stain, which covers the entire edge of the book and is part of the publisher's original design. With stains, think of cheap gilt edges; with rem marks, think vandalism.

An older book might be *foxed*—this is a chemical reaction that leaves spots on the pages like muddly animal tracks. If it's not too severe, a foxed book can still easily be in the Very Good category.

Good: By the time you've moved down to Good, you've

moved out of the range of most serious collectors. There are, of course, books that are rarely, if ever, found in condition better than Good: a Fine Kerouac or Fitzgerald is as rare as a meteor strike. In these cases, Good can be just fine. But for the standard fare, Good is only good for reading. We're out of the collectible market now, and into the reading-copy arena. In fact, once you know what a Good book looks like, it's kind of hard to figure out why they're called Good. A closer description might be not quite a disaster, but heading downhill fast.

A Good dust jacket is going to have serious problems. Large chips, tears, and price clipping are to be expected. There can be tape marks where someone has tried to repair the jacket. Stains and serious fading would not be out of line in this condition.

The book itself may be stained. The hinges of the book are likely torn or nearly torn, revealing the binding cloth beneath. The book may also be written in quite extensively.

The binding in this state may be *rolled*, where the book is no longer square. It may also be *shaken*, which means the binding is slanted or loose. This is often a function of the torn hinges mentioned above.

Still, despite all these problems, a Good copy is largely intact. The dust jacket is the original dust jacket, not one married to the volume later on. There are no pages missing, the flyleaf is whole. A Good book is still a full copy of the volume.

Good only appears in catalogs when there's little or no other alternative. Most serious collectors will have a couple of Good copies on their shelves while they wait to upgrade; once they have upgraded, they might keep the Good copy for reading, so as to ease the chances of wear and tear on the new, better copy. For a book scout, a book in Good condition is only worth buying if it is very cheap, and if a Very Fine edition of the book is worth serious money. If Very Fine sells for $200, Good *might* sell for $20 to $30. (You can use Good for trade fodder quite effectively, though; more about this in chapter 5.)

Poor: The final condition before the recycling bin is Poor. The only buyers you'll find for these are buyers who either can't find the book in any other condition whatsoever, or those who want a reading copy they can take to the beach.

If any part of the book is worse than what was described as Good, you've got Poor. Maybe the binding is coming apart, and there is a huge chunk torn out of the dust jacket. Water might have seeped into the book, bleeding the top edge decoration onto the pages. Perhaps the former owner took notes on the pages, highlighting them or scribbling annotations in the margins (of course, when Herman Melville's copy of *Paradise Lost* came onto the market, complete with endless annotations in Melville's hand, no one thought of the book as being in a Poor state). In short, this is an unattractive copy, and it's virtually worthless.

Library Markings: There is one other thing that makes a book worthless: library markings. These may be a stamp with the library's name on it, the glue from a return-card pocket, or stickers on the dust jacket. Ex–library books make excellent reading copies, but they are too flawed to be collected. Many secondhand bookstores won't accept ex–library books at all, even as reading copies; they're afraid it will encourage people to steal from the library and sell to them.

There is one very occasional thing a library copy can do for you, though. Libraries tend to wrap dust jackets in glassine and then tape the glassine down and put library stamps all over everything, killing the book; however, thanks to the glassine, you can find perfect dust jackets on trash books. I'll have more to say about the ethics of moving a dust jacket from one book to another later, but here's the truth: 80 percent of the value of a modern first is in the jacket, and if you can find a lovely library-saved jacket, you do have something.

RARITY AND PRICING

There is no set formula for how prices change with condition, and that's because of the third main point of this chapter: the rule of condition simply cannot be applied to every book. There are too many variables, and some books are just too rare for a person to ever hope to find in a Fine state.

In *Collected Books: The Guide to Values*, one of the most widely used price guides, Allen and Patricia Ahearn lay out their prices like this: from the 1970s and up, Very Fine is perfect; from the end of World War II until 1969, price clipping and perhaps a small, closed tear in the dust jacket would be permissible in the Very Fine category. They'll allow chips on the jacket of a book produced between 1920 and 1945. From 1920 until 1969, their estimate is that the lack of a dust jacket lowers the price by 75 percent on a fiction title, 20 percent on a nonfiction title. Although the first dust jackets were produced as long ago as the 1830s, for their pricing system, the Ahearns do not require a dust jacket on a book printed before 1920. Of course, if you're lucky enough to find one, you're in bonanza territory. For example, it's estimated that there are fewer than two dozen remaining copies of Edgar Rice Burroughs's first novel, *Tarzan of the Apes*, in the dust jacket. The Ahearns give the price as $3,000 without the jacket, and $50,000 with the jacket—although, truthfully, if a jacketed copy were to come on the market, there's no telling what it would really go for; they're that rare. The oldest dust jacket I've ever seen was from 1902; it was pristine, oddly enough, and I was almost afraid to touch it.

Even within the Ahearns' excellent framework for dust jackets, and what I've outlined about condition, there are exceptions to be made. Children's books, especially, are difficult to find in Very Fine state; often, they're hard to find in any condition much better than Good. That puts more leeway in the pricing of a volume. An excellent copy of an early Oz or Pooh book is going to be astronomical; but even poor copies can run upwards of a hundred dollars.

There are also those authors whose books you simply don't find in great shape very often, because they're the kind of writer whose books readers love to carry around with them, love to loan out to friends, love to read and reread. Jack Kerouac is a prime example. Getting a Fine dust jacket on a Kerouac is a major find, worth every penny it costs. Most of F. Scott Fitzgerald's books were so badly produced that the jackets have crumbled to dust over the years.

Believe it or not, there are also people who think dust jackets just get in the way, and so they toss them. Actually, this is what they were originally designed for: to let you get the book home in good shape. If you look at it objectively, the dust jacket is nothing more than an advertisement, and some people don't want shelves full of advertisements. This is probably a leading cause of death for collectible jackets.

Sometimes the jacket was simply badly designed by the publisher, and the hopes of finding a Fine copy diminish thanks to the art department. On Tony Hillerman's first novel, *The Blessing Way*, it seems as though the jacket was designed to fade into invisibility. Anne Rice's *Interview with the Vampire*, with its foil wrapper, was destined for heavy scratching from day one.

Very occasionally, you come across a situation where what you expect—a bad jacket on a good book—is reversed. For whatever reason—say, a library copy as described above—you find a pristine jacket on a copy of a book that is trashed. This most frequently happens when you find a copy where a previous owner tried to take care of the book and wrapped it in a protective wrapper, but then taped the wrapper to the book. The tape leaves marks, the book itself goes down several grades, but you still have a beautiful dust jacket.

Obviously, if the price is right, these are worth picking up.

You have a couple of options once you own the book: you can hold out, find a good copy without a dust jacket, and do a shuffle (see elsewhere in this book for a consideration of the morality of this), or you can try to sell the book as is, where, sooner or later, someone else will do the shuffle. In these cases, the book will not sell for 80 percent of pristine price—all you've really got to sell is the jacket—but if you find the right collector, you can work some very sweet deals. Good jackets can be very hard to find.

PAPERBACK ORIGINALS

While most of the market (and most of this book) concentrates only on hardback books, there are avid paperback collectors out there, and their number is growing, as hardbacks become more and more expensive.

Considering the shape of the retail book market now, where paperbacks make up the great majority of all books published, it's surprising to think that it wasn't all that long ago when there were no paperbacks: as we know them, they made their appearance in the late 1930s (there were earlier incarnations of paperbacks in the early 1800s and again after the Civil War). Even then, there was resistance to them. It wasn't until the fifties and sixties that they became easy to find in bookstores—prior to that, paperbacks had their own channels of distribution. Cody's Books, in the San Francisco Bay area, was one of the first stores in the nation to concentrate on paperback books.

Paperbacks were never meant to last. They were printed on cheap paper (even cheaper during the war), bound with cheap glue and cheap covers. They were meant to be read once or twice and tossed away.

However, because paperbacks are cheaper for a publisher to produce, and cheaper for a customer to buy, taking a flyer on an unknown writer, many, many now famous writers got their start in paperback originals—books that were never done as hardbacks. Therefore, the completist collector of, say, Lawrence Block or John D. MacDonald is going to have to have some paperback originals on the shelf. Kurt Vonnegut's *Sirens of Titan* is a very expensive little paperback, as is *Junky*, the first book by William Burroughs.

It's not only the classic authors, either. There are literally hundreds of authors today, well known as hardback writers, who got their start in paperback originals. This is especially true with genre books—mystery, science fiction, horror— where there is a large audience that reads constantly, buying too many books to be able to afford hardbacks for everything. Many writers now break into paperback originals, and then, if their sales figures justify it, a publisher will pick them up for hardbacks. Others seem to slide in the opposite direction. Stephen Womack won an Edgar Award for best paperback original for his first book, *Dead Folk's Blues*; the book was then picked up and reprinted as a hardback in England. Since then, though, all of his books have only come out in paperback, with no hardback edition.

Another perk for the paperback collector is the beauty of the cover design on many of them—especially on science fiction novels from the fifties and sixties, there is simply marvelous art to be found, as paperback publishers sought to make their books stand out on the racks. There are people who collect paperbacks strictly for the art, and will go to great lengths to find another title with a Virgil Finlay design, or that of some other favored artist, and there is a growing legion of pulp paperback collectors, out looking for the most lurid covers they can find from the fifties: just imagine what a good artist can do with titles (yes, these are real books) like *The Fatal Caress*, *Deadlier than the Male*, *French Girls Are Vicious*, and *Cry Hard, Cry Fast*.

All this means that if you want to enter the book market on a lower cost scale, it is possible to do so by dealing in paperbacks. The market for them is smaller, but it is out there, and it's full of possibilities. You'll find most hardback dealers will hardly glance at paperbacks—maybe give the shelves a quick scan to see if one of Richard Bachman's books got missed (Bachman is a pseudonym for Stephen King), and that's about it.

When you're buying paperbacks, the same general points hold true as for hardbacks. The better the condition of the copy, the better off you are. Cracked spines are the death of a book. Since most paperbacks are made with fairly brittle glue and paper, it can be nearly impossible to find a 1950s paperback without a cracked spine, unless the book has never been read. Also watch for the cover (paperback covers are called *wraps* or *wrappers*) coming loose from the book—this can often be repaired with the careful use of rubber cement—and folds or cracks in the book's paper.

To preserve paperbacks, use comics bags (see chapter 10), and keep the handling to a minimum. A good hardback book can last for centuries. Paperbacks are dying before your eyes as simple exposure to air eats away the acidic papers and glues.

THE LEARNING CURVE

How do you find out what the desirability of a certain edition in a certain condition is? The more books you handle, the more you're going to learn. I spent much of my early career working in the busiest used bookshops I could find, handling as many as twenty thousand previously unseen books a week. Under those conditions, every day was a treasure hunt, and every day brought new information that I was able to turn into money elsewhere.

But you don't need to work in a used bookshop. You just need to love books and like being around them; and you need to enjoy the company of serious book people. Spend as much time as you can in bookstores talking with dealers. Absolutely nothing replaces experience. The more time you spend around books and book people, the better off you will be. Handle as many books as you can, ask questions, look things up. Learn those points, learn which books are common and which are rare, and what state you're likely to find them in.

A warning here, which I'll develop in greater length in chapter 7: you are not going to learn books by staring at Web sites on the Internet. You need to handle books to learn books. The Net is a useful tool, but it will never, never, never teach you books. You cannot learn about books without touching books. Plain and simple.

REGIONAL CONSIDERATIONS

Early on in my career, I came across a signed August Derleth book. Not one of his Arkham House masterpieces, but one of his good, solid books on the Midwest. It was tremendously exciting at the time. Signed! August Derleth! The man who introduced H. P. Lovecraft to the world! Well, it turns out that, at least where I lived then, August Derleth's signature is as common as dirt. I handled another fifty in the next few months. But I did once sell a signed Derleth for a fair $75; then I saw it a month or so later in another dealer's shop for $250. He'd never get that for it; he just hadn't yet learned how common Derleth was in our neighborhood.

So in addition to the exceptions of conditions, there are also regional variations that can affect pricing and demand. John Updike is more heavily collected in the East than in the West, so you've not only got a better chance of finding an excellent copy of *Rabbit, Run* in the East, you've also got a better chance of finding someone interested in a less than perfect copy should one come your way. Likewise Wallace Stegner or Dee Brown are going to do better in the West.

Regional differences are a two-sided coin, of course. If an

author is at a premium in one particular area, the serious collector knows a Very Fine copy is going to turn up. However, less than perfect copies—Fine and Very Good—may be all many people can afford. Dealers know this and price accordingly, keeping the book on the edge of affordability, but rather more expensive than the book would be priced outside of its region.

Which brings up another point. Any time you're out of your home region, raid every bookstore on your route for authors that are hot back home or anywhere else along your route. This can pay off quickly; there just aren't that many people in Florida looking for Nelson Nye's westerns. I've made a lot of money by traveling back East and buying books on the West.

The Internet is changing this some, of course. Suddenly, you have equal access to books all over the country, and regional variations on listed books, on the books people think of as worthwhile, are smoothing out and leveling. However, inside shops, regionalism still rules: you can't price something for the Internet on an open-shelf store, you have to price for your local market. If you put it at that price on the Net, it may go quickly, but on shelves, there are still bargains to be found by exploiting regionalism. And the more obscurely regionalistic you can get, the better off you are: what are the odds of a dealer in New Jersey understanding the cachet of the Superstition Mountains in Arizona?

There's another thing to watch for, not exactly a category, but a categorical mistake that can help you determine a book's value. Given the large number of new authors each year, there is virtually no way the average used bookshop owner can keep track of what's hot and what's not. They'll pick up the McCarthys and the Burkes, but they'll miss the Van Giesons, the Rick Basses, the Jances.

However, in nearly every used bookshop there is a category of pricing that could be defined as "I don't know what this is, but just in case it's worth something, I'm going to jack the price to twenty bucks." This happens all the time with modern fiction, and if you've got twenty dollars cash or twenty dollars' worth of trade, these books can be incredible bargains. They can also be grossly overpriced mistakes. I've found $200 books marked at $20. I've also found a lot more utterly worthless books marked at $20, sitting right next to a $200 book. And I've found a lot of $20 books marked at $20, as the law of averages works itself out. So when you see that $20 tag on a used book, it may be that the shopkeeper thinks this book is worth something, but isn't sure what it might be. If you're keeping up on your information gathering, that may be an opportunity for you.

There are going to be times when you have no idea at all what a book is worth; this is particularly true if you start to move outside your own field. When this happens, you've got two choices: pass it by, or take a deep breath and hope your guesstimate is right. If you pass it by, you risk finding out later that the book was a treasure, worth a fortune. If you grab it, you run the risk of finding out it was a worthless piece of trash. Go with your instincts, and hope it balances out in the end. I've found it usually does.

Chapter Four

❧

BOOK SCOUTING

E very year, more than fifty thousand new books are published. Up to the recent arrival of the chain megastore, historically that's about twice the number of titles stocked in an average bookstore. So where do the rest of the books go? Where do old, used books go? The answer is simple: books end up just about everywhere. I've found rare books for sale in drugstores, in truck stops, and in the sale bins of some grocery stores.

To be a good book scout, you have to keep your eyes open at all times. Anything can be anywhere. Never drive past a place that might have books for sale. Although this chapter offers an overview of the main places to scout, remember this is only the tip of the iceberg: you never know when you'll find a copy of a vintage Elizabeth Bowen book for a quarter in a bin at the local hospital, or when you'll discover a previously unknown cache of rare books at the local PTA sale.

Garage and Estate Sales

It's the dream of every book scout: you go to a garage sale and hear the magic words: "I don't know what they are. They were my grandfather's. You can have them for a dollar a book." And when you open the boxes, you find pristine first editions of Hemingway, Faulkner, and Fitzgerald.

Sound farfetched? Maybe so, maybe not.

A couple of years ago, a friend was at a garage sale and spotted a collection of Herman Melville books. He opened them up and discovered that every single one of them was a first edition. Their rarity made up for their poor condition—a couple of the books were starting to fall apart—but with a find as valuable as this, repairs are feasible (see chapter 10 for details). So my friend was all too happy to pay $500 for the set of books. Then he took them across town to a specialty dealer and made an immediate $14,500 in profit.

Not a bad day's work.

As another example, somebody once bought a copy of *Tamerlane* by "A Bostonian" for fifteen dollars at a garage sale. That happens to be the first book by a man better known as Edgar Allan Poe, and the lucky garage saler sold it off for around $175,000. There's no telling what one might go for if it should show up on today's market.

In yet another example, a ninety-one-year-old man was selling his collection of books. As he had worked in the publishing industry his whole life, he'd accumulated several thousand volumes, all inscribed, from the top writers of this century, from John Steinbeck on. The value of his collection was perhaps a half million dollars. He knew what he had, and he knew how much they were worth, but it didn't matter to the book dealers who lined up for a crack at the collection. Every piece was in mint condition, and every piece was signed. Even if you paid a high price, you might double your money.

The point is, garage sales and estate sales are where you can expect to find the high and low end of the rare book business.

GARAGE SALES

Most full-time book scouts won't bother with garage sales, unless they're checking them for other reasons—maybe to buy bookshelves. Even then, there's not much hope of a major score. They do turn up, but you'll meet with a lot more success if you're willing to look for nothing more exciting than semi-valuable books for trading (which, as I'll explain in chapter 5, can also be pretty exciting).

There are a couple of readily evident problems with garage sales, the luck of the man who found the Melville books notwithstanding.

First, people running garage sales are getting rid of what they don't want. The odds are low that their cast-offs will be your dream, simply because the average person doesn't treat books carefully. Remember, condition equals value, and the chances of finding a Fine condition book on a table in someone's yard in the middle of a garage sale, where neighbors, bargain hunters, and assorted animals are running around without supervision, are minimal. Also, most serious book people (a very small percentage of those having garage sales) have a pretty good idea of the value of what they own, and will either price it accordingly, or, more likely, take it to a specialty dealer. Conversely, nonserious book people very often overvalue their books to a ludicrous degree. They see a book from the 1920s and think, "It's old, so it must be expensive."

The main problem with garage sales is simply that they're too hit-and-miss. In even a small town you can waste your entire weekend running from neighborhood to neighborhood, digging for gold. What you're most likely to find, though, are a lot of old *National Geographic* magazines, *Reader's Digest* books, and book club editions. Really, garage sales are best only if you're interested in that kind of thing to begin with. Of course, they can be a lot of fun: you can get the whole history of a book, a dish, or a toy. But as a professional scout, give them a look once in a while and hope, but don't hope too much.

ESTATE SALES

Estate sales, on the other hand, are considerably different from garage sales. Here, the surviving relatives are selling, often to the highest bidder, sometimes just by tagging individual items and opening the house, the estates of their loved ones. Or perhaps a lawyer or an auction company is handling everything. For the book scout, an auctioned estate sale can work considerably better than an open house, if only because auctions usually don't attract as many people. Estate sales are usually announced in the classified section of a newspaper, usually with viewing dates and auction dates. However, a lot of times "estate sales" are nothing more than glorified garage sales, not auctions.

True estate auctions are where you'll find some of the best material. The fact that the entire contents of a house are being sold off means that things are probably in better condition than if they were tossed out on a garage sale table. At a viewing, you're often able to see the books on the shelves where they've been sitting for years.

When you go in and say you're interested in the books at an estate auction or sale, the people running the sale are probably not going to let you pick and choose. You may be able to do this if there are some acknowledged high-line items that the seller is hoping to cut a deal on, but more likely, you'll have to put in a bid on the entire book collection. This is not necessarily a bad thing. Maybe there are a couple of lovely books and a lot of reading copies. Figure your price—something less than a dollar a book on hardback reading copies—and bid accordingly. You'll be able to use the reading copies as trade material in stores (more about that in chapter 5), and meanwhile, you've caught the lovely books in the deal.

I was once called in to make a bid on books from an estate sale. The books had been haphazardly boxed, and the boxes piled ceiling-high in the storeroom of a lawyer's office. I was given fifteen minutes to open as many boxes as I could and make an offer on the entire lot. I offered $500, and that was good enough. When I took the books back to the shop and examined them closely, I found a complete run of William Faulkner first editions hidden among the paperbacks. It was a good day for me. But even if the Faulkners hadn't been there, it still would have been a good day, because I'd organized my bid according to what I thought I could get out of the books strictly in trade credit when I took them to a different shop and tried to trade them for other material. My bid included allowance for my profit even if every book in those boxes was nothing more than a semiuseful paperback that I'd only be able to use in trade.

When making a bid for a book or a collection, remember the Rule of Three mentioned in chapter 1: a book must be worth three times what you paid for it if you're going to turn it around for an immediate profit. With an estate sale, that three times could be in trade credit, it could be a cash value (as you'll soon see, those two values are very, very different), but you must figure it in, or you're wasting both your time and money. If there are items you think you can let sit for a few years while they increase in price, fine, change the formula accordingly. But if you want to turn things around immediately, you need a 300 percent increase.

Also when you make your bid, you have to figure in the fact that a certain percentage of the books are going to be utterly worthless, not even useful for trade. Their bindings will be shot, pages will be missing, or the books will be heavily marked up.

You'll have to make this assessment as you view the books. This is easy if the books are still sitting on the shelves, but much more difficult if they've been boxed up. When I had the boxes in the lawyer's office, I was risking the fact that the ten boxes I had time to look in were representative of the twenty or thirty boxes I did not have time for, and I was right. The boxes I looked in contained good books, in good shape.

Personal book collections are usually treated the same. If some of the books were well taken care of, the chances are good the whole collection is the same (although be suspicious of someone rigging the viewing; open boxes at random, not just a select few offered by the seller). If, on the other hand, you find a lot of books in poor condition in several of the boxes, it may not be worth your time to look in too many more boxes or shelves.

There are a few sale categories vaguely related to the garage sale and the estate sale. Storage facilities often sell off collections of articles when someone fails to pay the monthly rent. You can find some amazing stuff at these, but it's not for the faint of heart. You're not likely to get only the books; most facilities require you to buy the entire lot, so you'll also end up with furniture, old clothes, and a lot of junk. Usually, the quantity and quality of the books aren't enough to make it worth the trouble.

Flea markets and swap meets can be profitable, but they fall into the garage sale category: very hit-and-miss. If you enjoy browsing swap meets, fine. But be prepared for a mobile garage sale, with an extra dose of madness thrown in.

ANTIQUE STORES

The antique store entices more people into the idea of buying and selling books than any other place. Inside there are these wonderful, musty, dusty volumes half remembered from your childhood, tucked in among valuable furniture and crockery. There's an old *Tarzan*! And next to it a copy of *Mary Poppins* from 1940! And an entire run of Thornton W. Burgess's books, including *Old Mother West Wind*, his first children's book. Around those wonderful items from the past—the Hepplewhite chair, the Shaker cabinet—surely these books must be equally valuable and exciting.

But the truth is, they almost never are.

There are exceptions, of course, but the true hard-core book scout doesn't spend a lot of time in antique stores for several reasons. First is the simple matter that antique stores make their stock and trade in old items. That's the definition of antique. And when you walk into an antique store, there is the automatic, subconscious association that *old is good*. But all too often, old is just old.

Books in most antique stores are old, and often quite beautiful: tooled leather bindings covering gilt-edged volumes full of color plates. However, they tend to be simply old books, and when you open them, problems immediately become evident: hinges wearing, pages loose, every leaf heavily foxed. Because the antique dealer is not a book dealer, these things may not mean as much to them. The antique dealers, too, are in the "old is good" mind-set. They see a book from the turn of the century or the heart of the Depression, and immediately pop a $20 price tag on it, no matter that the book's structural integrity is gone and thus the book is essentially worthless. The age prevents them from noticing that even if the book were in perfect condition, it's nothing but a forgettable book from a forgettable author.

You also have to keep in mind that, as the antique mall has evolved, "old" seems to mean, more and more, the 1960s. It's an odd world, practically self-contained, in the antique malls. You do find the occasional treasure there, but it's rare, because even more than age, antique stores make their money on nostalgia, on selling your childhood back to you. The antique store owners know that the unsophisticated buyer is going to go in, see a copy of a book he loved as a child, and buy it, regardless of the price.

And that's not a bad thing. If that's what you want, antique stores may be the best place to look, because of how they get their books: usually from buying out an estate, selling off whatever might actually be valuable to a rare book dealer, and then keeping the rest to sell. So the odd book that you loved as a child, or that you remember on your grandmother's shelf, is actually more likely to show up in an antique store than in a bookshop. However, it's also probably utterly worthless from a financial standpoint.

Again and again I've had people come to me for appraisals of books they've bought at antique stores for forty or fifty dollars. Often they are beautiful books, lovely old copies of *East of the Sun and West of the Moon* or *The Jungle Book*, but again and again I have to tell them the price is sentimental, and they're holding a five- or six-dollar book. What they have bought is not a collectible book, but a piece of their own past.

But an antique store can be a great place for *ephemera* (for more details on ephemera, see chapter 9). If you want picture postcards of your favorite writer, magazine articles about books that came out in the 1920s, advertising signs, posters, all these little disposable items that grow up around books and then disappear, the antique store may be one of your best bets. Are you a fan of *The Wizard of Oz*? Think of the posters, toys, games, puzzles, and more that have been made with Dorothy's face over the years, the magazine articles published on the film and the girl and the munchkins. The possibilities are endless, and all related to the central joy of collecting and dealing. A good collection of ephemera, sold as a lot with the book that spawned it, is a valuable thing on the collector's market, if only because of how long it can take to put together such a collection.

So don't hesitate to stop in and browse an antique store. But don't expect any great bargains.

OTHER IRREGULAR SOURCES

A couple of other places are worth checking periodically. Make regular stops at the Salvation Army or any of the other charity organizations in your area.

Charity stores can swing wildly on prices. Sometimes, they get the idea that all of their old books are worth a fortune. Sometimes they're more right than they think, but that's a determination better left to a professional. Other times, they seem to have so many books they're giving them away. Look for thrifts that sell books for under two bucks. The best thrift score I know of? A friend found James Lee Burke's *Half of Paradise* for a buck. Sold it for a grand.

If you're doing the thrift store rounds, though, be prepared to sift through mountains of dreck.

The same holds true with library sales. In my city, the local library holds a massive book sale in the town's biggest auditorium once a year. Up to fifteen thousand people show up in a buying frenzy. But only the first dozen or two through the door get a good look at things before the crowd becomes too thick and all the good items get swooped up.

Another problem with library sales is that library books are never collectible. A "Discard" stamp, the glue markings of a torn-out due-date pocket, a library stamp, even a pasted-down dust jacket so common to library copies, immediately ruins the value of a book. This can be particularly frustrating when most of a book's small first printing was swept up by libraries—Thomas Pynchon's *Gravity's Rainbow* is a good example—but library copies are never collected, so pass them by.

Of course, not all books at library sales are library books, and you can find bargains among the stock donated to the library by individuals. A friend found a Japanese copy of the Mailer bio of Marilyn Monroe: the jacket was different from the U.S. edition, and there were significant layout changes, which made the book very valuable to Marilyn collectors. Me and my crew can expect to clear a couple thousand dollars for each hour spent at a good library sale. But it's hard work, and there's a lot of pushing and shoving involved. Go early and prepared for battle.

The irregular market for books is practically unlimited, and it's a long shot at best. You could easily strike it rich or you could easily waste a lot of time. Mostly, this market is for people who enjoy going to these places anyway.

If you're going to be a professional, a very large part of your business is going to have to come from other professionals.

THE BOOK FAIR

Caught somewhere between the garage sale and the bookstore, the book fair is a reasonably new event that's catching on all over the country as books become the hot new collectible. Held in convention centers, high school auditoriums, and library multipurpose rooms, fairs are designed to bring in the maximum number of people to pay the admission fee, and the maximum number of dealers to come in, set up tables, and offer their wares to the public.

Most fairs charge about a $5 admission fee. However, by the time the doors are opened, the best deals have already been done, and for most of the dealers the remainder of the fair is used for getting publicity, making contacts, and trying to sell some of the midline stuff that has been sitting around their shops or homes for too long.

Hours before the book fair actually opens, the dealers start dealing with each other. It's not at all unusual for a single book to pass through the hands of four or five dealers before the doors open, increasing in price each time it moves. For example, Dealer A has a copy of Edward Abbey's *Desert Solitaire*, a good piece of Southwestern Americana that lists for around $750 in good shape. This copy is also signed and dated in the year of publication (which may mean nothing; Abbey liked the idea that such dates raised the value of his books, and often dated his inscriptions in the publication year even if he was signing a decade after the book first hit stores). Regardless of the date, the signature raises the value of the book markedly, especially now that Abbey is dead. But Dealer A is a Northeasterner, and his market isn't going to go for Abbey's radical desert environmentalism. So he offloads the book to Dealer B for $400. Dealer B, who does some work in the Southwest, but who prefers the Pacific Northwest, was really only interested in the signature. He runs into Dealer C, who specializes in the desert Southwest and who has a list of five customers looking for the book. Dealer B makes himself a quick hundred bucks by selling the book to Dealer C. By the time the doors of the fair open, Dealer C has the Abbey volume sitting on his table at a neat, if overpriced, $800. And if he doesn't sell it here, he knows he can sell it the minute he gets home for $750, and still do just fine.

So obviously, the trick is to get in before the doors open. Most fairs make this easy to do. While they charge the public $5 to get in, there's usually an advanced viewing available to select dealers for $20 or more. This is always worth the price, because this is when the best deals are available. Be prepared to wheel and deal.

As can be seen by the Abbey example above, regionalism can play a major part in the price of a book. *Desert Solitaire* isn't going to sell for the premium in Albany that it will in Albuquerque, and maybe the Internet—but not your local shops and contacts—are overloaded with copies, all similar, all priced too high. So if you have some out-of-your-region writers on your shelves, a fair can be a good time to sell them. Big fairs bring in dealers from all over the country. Find the specialists who are interested in the same kind of book you are; and then find the specialists who aren't at all interested in what you are. By buying from the latter and selling to the former, you can do a brisk trade.

If you go into a book fair as a customer, things will look a little different. Dealers will be sitting behind tables piled with neat, shiny books in protective jackets. A good dealer will have a mix of high-line and midline works, trying to appeal to the broadest spectrum of customer.

You will not likely find a lot of underpriced books at a book fair. However, you can still do a considerable amount of wheeling and dealing at a fair. Never consider a price to be fixed; when you find a piece you like, ask the dealer what he likes. Maybe you have it on your own shelf, and you can work out a further deal.

And when in doubt, flash cash. Especially at a slow show—and with the proliferation of book fairs in recent years, there are occasionally very slow shows—dealers just need to make back costs. Even a small table at a small fair is costing the dealer upwards of $500, and they need to make some sales. The hours before close can be a great time for making deals.

Finally, consider book fairs a great chance for education. You get to see a lot of books in a very short time, and you get to see a wider range of books, usually, than from just the dealers around your hometown. When you go to a fair, plan to spend the day there. Look at everything you can.

NETWORKING

The other main value of the book fair for a professional is to network. Find out who is selling what and what they're paying for it. I've previously mentioned the importance of some specialization; now's your chance to find out who else specializes and *how* they specialize. Get names; get business cards (don't hesitate to make a few notes on the back); stop and talk to the dealers who have stock that interests you.

If you don't get into the advanced viewing of a book fair, don't worry: there's just as much money to be made afterward. Work the connections, build your network. Then, when you find a first edition of *Shakespeare's Bawdy*, a work on the huge number of dirty jokes in the plays of the Bard, you know exactly the dealer who is going to want that. If you find a signed Tenzing Norgay Sherpa (who was with Sir Edmund Hillary on the first Everest ascent), you know a dealer who specializes in fine works on adventures and voyages. Connections can be even more important than knowledge, and almost as important as luck. Book fairs are a great chance to get hooked into the system.

THE NEW BOOKSTORE

It's easier to spend twenty dollars to make twenty dollars than it is to spend two dollars to make three. If you're willing to spend more to get the exceptional book, you'll make more money when you resell it. But this is a psychological hurdle for many scouts. They look at it from a percentage basis: this five-dollar book is worth ten bucks, so that's a 100 percent gain. Then they miss the book they can buy for $150 and sell for $200. (This does not break the Rule of Three: if you can sell it to a dealer for $200, that dealer is going to price it at $400–600; more later about how you can sell it yourself for $600, and remember that at the higher end, the Rule of Three can work on a sliding scale.)

Thanks to this unintended stinginess, a lot of scouts miss one of the prime picking territories: the new bookstore. If you had been on top of things, if you'd been reading *Publishers Weekly* or the *New York Times Book Review*, you might have known that Amy Tan's first book, *The Joy Luck Club*, was going to explode in value. By the time the tiny first edition made its way into used bookstores, it was already priced beyond most people's means. The same with Cormac McCarthy: in just over a year, his *All the Pretty Horses* went from $20 on the shelves of the new stores to over $200 in specialist catalogs. I know quite a few children's book specialists with nice, shiny copies of *Harry Potter* firsts sitting on their shelves.

The new bookstore is going to be one of your best friends. Find a good, independent store (although it's getting harder and harder to do, stay away from the mall stores and the chains, with their cookie-cutter personalities and corporate buyers too far away to read regional trends) and get to know the people there. An independent bookstore cares about what it's doing; nobody's in there for the money, because there really is no money in running an independent.

If you're on good terms with the owner or the buyer, they can help pass on tips of what's looking like it'll be hot. When I worked in a new store, we had ten copies of the first edition of Tom Clancy's *The Hunt for Red October*. We all knew the book was going to take off, and we encouraged favorite customers to pick up a copy. Those who listened to us now have a $900 book. Same with Umberto Eco's *The Name of the Rose*, a masterpiece of semiotics and detection. It was an unlikely bestseller, a mystery set in a medieval monastery, the plot revolving around a lost book of Aristotle—but booksellers, who avidly read whatever they can get their hands on, knew it was going to fly from the day it came out. (An interesting point: on the paperbacks of *The Name of the Rose*, after the first printing, most of the Latin passages were removed. This means nothing, valuewise, but it offers an interesting insight into marketing techniques.)

So take the time to get to know the people in a favorite shop. A good employee of a new bookstore is on top of all the current trends and knows what you should be looking for. Better yet, most new shops don't particularly care about resale value.

There is a slight snobbery involved, but most people at new shops aren't interested in dealing, investing, or buying used, secondhand, or rare books. They get what they want when it first comes out. So they're not competing with you; they're in a different mind-set.

Often, in smaller new stores where stock turnover isn't so high, you can pick up incredible bargains, first editions that sold out quickly and increased in price, but are still here because they don't match the interest of the clientele. When *Smilla's Sense of Snow*, an obscure Scandinavian novel that somehow made it to the *Times* best-seller list early in 1994, was selling for sixty and seventy dollars in first edition in specialty stores, I knew of a new shop with four copies at list price. The buyer for the store had spotted that it was a good book, and had bought multiples; but it was simply wrong for this particular store, and the copies didn't sell.

But I got mine.

In another store, I found the first poetry book of a famous poet. Late one night many years ago, this poet had told me, when he was very drunk, he broke into the warehouse where copies of the book were stored, and he burned most of them. He wanted to create a collectible, and he succeeded. Somehow, a surviving copy found its way to a store I frequented; the store did not believe in returning poetry books, and so there it sat for years until I found it. Had I not known the story, it might still be sitting there.

Another area where the new bookstore can be a wonderful help for your business is advance reading copies. ARCs are hot items on the collectible market. As discussed in chapter 2, ARCs are paperbacks made for promotional purposes, printed, bound, and distributed months before the hardback first hits bookstore shelves. An ARC of a hot book can sell for double what the trade edition goes for, and yet most new booksellers treat ARCs as something to be read once and then discarded. This is partly due to the fact that they see so many of the things, as publisher's rep after publisher's rep drops his thick advance paperbacks on their desks. The other reason is that in the new book business, paperbacks are nothing to get excited over.

Yet there is also something wonderfully special about holding an advance copy. Here is a book in a state only a step or two removed from the author's original typescript, the first way it faced the public, in a state that almost no one, except for a privileged few, ever saw.

And the easiest way to get one is to make friends with a new book dealer. I have a small network of friends working in new bookshops who are happy to pass off the advance copies to me.

After you're on good terms with the owner of your local bookshop, after you've established yourself as a regular, thoughtful, and good customer, look into what she does with her advance copies. Odds are, they sit around on a shelf in the back room for a while before they're tossed. The shop's garbage is money in your pocket.

THE REMAINDER TABLE

Another area in the new shop (and many used shops) that can be invaluable is their remainder table. Remainders are publisher overstocks: the publisher prints more books than it can sell at full retail, and so then sells the books out at bargain prices, often for as little as 20 percent of their original cost.

One of the great joys of a remainder table is that books appear there when it's becoming clear they're going to be highly prized and collectible. In a single day, a friend and I each spent a mere twenty bucks on remainders and picked up nearly five hundred dollars' worth of books. There were stacks of the first edition of Michael Connelly's *Black Echo*, a pile of Tony Hillerman's *Skinwalkers*, firsts and seconds mixed in together of Robert R. McCammon's *Boy's Life*, a novel which won not only the Bram Stoker Award for best horror novel of the year, but also the World Fantasy Award for best fantasy novel. That crossover appeal meant that each copy of the first we picked up out of the remainder pile could immediately be sold for forty to fifty dollars. The other day I got eight signed Walter Mosleys off a remainder table.

A bookseller wiser than me once commented that successful dealing is as much a matter of storage as it is of brains. When you see deals like this, grab as many copies as you can. Sooner or later, you'll be out, wishing you had a few more. I could use a couple of those copies of *Black Echo* back now—and at one point, I had bought a dozen.

A side note on remainders: you can also shop for them in the comfort of your own home. Check the ads in popular magazines for "Publisher's Overstock" or "Huge Book Sale." They're talking remainders. But when you buy from a mail-order catalog, you don't have the luxury of checking every copy for edition or condition; it's a "pay your money and take your chances" kind of deal. If you want a reading copy, or you know you can use any edition as trade fodder later for a profit, the catalogs are great; if you want an investment copy, don't buy until you've seen the copyright page and the dust jacket.

Bookshops get new remainders regularly. Ask when the new shipments are coming in. The best time of year is Christmas, when remainder tables are stuffed with the previous year's hot books. Get the new remainders as quickly as possible: remainder tables are notorious book killers, producing jacket tears, rolled spines, bumped corners, and worse.

There is one other hazard inherent in remainders: the dreaded remainder mark. Because the publishers are selling off these books for a very low price, they want to be sure that the books don't come back to them as returns at full price. To identify remainders, most publishers mark the book on either the top or the bottom edge. The mark may be a simple black slash with a Magic Marker, or a fancier stamp from the publishing house. Remainder marks detract from the value of the book; how much is a subject of debate, but it's quite safe to assume the mark knocks 20 percent or more off the full value of a mint copy. Still, there are many books where remainder firsts are the only ones appearing on the market; they are still collectible, simply not *as* collectible. And many publishers don't mark remainders, so you have a very good chance of finding a clean copy.

PUBLISHERS' CATALOGS

What else can your local new-book dealer do for you? Check their file of publishers' catalogs to see what's coming out. Many novels, even from important writers, have very small first editions. If you don't have your order in ahead of time you're not going to get a first. Publishers' representatives knew that the *Harry Potter* books were going to be bigger than pet rocks. In under two years, the first edition of the first book went from $15 to $2,500, and it's still climbing. Insiders knew this was going to happen, and snapped them up.

Catalogs are also great for finding out what's happening in the limited edition production field. A serious collector of limited editions has a hard road ahead, and we'll go into that in more detail later. Just keep in mind that one of the best places to find new limited editions is in publishers' catalogs. And the way you get to see publishers' catalogs is to make friends with a new-book dealer.

A lot of book scouts pass over the new bookstore. They can't bring themselves to pay full list price for a book. But they're missing a valuable resource. Don't make the same mistake yourself.

Remember, by the time some books make it to the used bookshop, they've already doubled in price—despite a downgrade in condition from having been handled. Get them while they're hot and shiny on the new bookstore shelves, and you'll never be sorry.

THE USED BOOKSHOP

We all have this vision of the perfect used bookstore: it seems to come out of a Dickens story, or maybe the film version of *The Old Curiosity Shop*. The shop would smell of pipe smoke, and be stuffed with books in every available nook and cranny. More books would be piled on the floor or lying about in boxes. Mixed with the pipe smoke is the smell of aging paper and glue, leather bindings rubbed smooth by generations of hands. Near the front of the shop is an antique cash register, and behind the register, a clerk as eccentric as the store itself, asking if you'd noticed the latest additions, a stack of books full of botanical illustrations from late in the last century, inscribed by John Gould, one of history's premier nature writers.

But the days of the single-proprietor, know-it-all bookseller are nearly over. Such stores do still exist—if you know of one, treasure it—but the used bookstore is moving into a new era, one of clean, well-lighted shelves, immaculate order, and prices higher than in new bookstores, at least on some of their books.

And that's your opportunity.

As stores get larger, two things happen: the overall quality of the stock tends to decrease, and the number of quality items that slip through cracks in the system increases. After all, if a store is processing two thousand books a day, they don't have time to check each and every title for collectibility. While they're going to get the Rockwell Kent first editions, or the beautiful Limited Editions Club books and mark them sky-high, they're likely to miss the Harry Crews novel worth $200. While the highly collectible book market is becoming extremely specialized, the book market overall, especially used bookstores, is becoming more generalized. When you enter a used bookstore, try to find out what the owner does and does not know.

One of my favorite shops, a lovely store with dark oak book-cases, with each book neatly wrapped in a Brodart protective jacket, is always accurate on modern literature. You'll never find a mispriced Pynchon or Updike or Bukowski. But the owner doesn't much care for horror or science fiction, and so he doesn't much care about the prices on books in those genres. He'll sell off a British first of William Gibson's *Mona Lisa Over-drive*, signed, for half its true worth; Cordwainer Smith (not to be confused with Cordwainer Bird, who is really Harlan Elli-son) is a throwaway item to him.

Before you ever make your first purchase in a store, you should walk through it, check the shelves thoroughly, and find out what the shop's interests are. Doing this well and carefully is the boundary line between success and failure as a book scout. You have to know what to take where, and what to buy where. Rule one in looking in a used bookstore: *find the hits and misses*.

In one store where I worked, technical items were missed. Nobody had the time, the energy, or the inclination. The more profitable modern firsts were stacking up. And so while you could never squeeze a Don Marquis by the staff, nine times out of ten they'd miss an early science book—say a copy of *Psycho-pathia Sexualis*—that was worth every bit as much or more. During all my time in that store, my main function was catch-ing what had been missed by the rest of the staff (which was not to say I caught everything; nobody can do that).

And that should be your main goal when you scout used bookshops: catching what got missed. Because not only will you find the bargains if you know where to look for the bar-gains, you'll get your money and more back out of a book if you know where to sell it.

Ultimately this is what a book scout spends much time do-ing: taking books from people who aren't really interested in them, and selling them to people who are.

In order to do that with maximum efficiency, you need to learn how a used bookshop works.

THE USED BOOKSTORE SHUFFLE

What happens when a book first reaches the counter of a used bookstore?

Let's say you've come in with five books: an early Ludlum, an early Le Carré—both later printings—a good general book on gardening, a home improvement piece, and the special piece, a first edition of Neil Simon's play *The Odd Couple*. You know you've got two okay books, two nothings that are only good for, hopefully, trading up, and one fine piece worth some major money.

The clerk takes a look at the books, assesses condition and desirability, checks it against what she knows the store is or is not looking for, and makes an offer. Seems simple, right?

But in the minute or two the clerk is looking at the books, there is a whole marketing scheme going through her mind, and understanding that can make the difference between success and failure for a scout.

What are the store's standard terms? The clerk has to compare the usual deal with the desirability of your books. Say the standard offer is one-half the shop's selling price in trade, one-half of that in cash (by the way, this is not a great deal; if you're after cash, you should be thinking about taking the Simon elsewhere); she's got to decide if your books are worth strictly formula rates, or if there's something special there that she really wants on her shelves and is willing to pay more for. Obviously there's nothing special about the two nonfiction books you brought in. Those are going to get you strictly standard rates. The Ludlum and Le Carré have a little room for movement, but not much; only their first four or five books are of particular interest, because after that they were popular and collected, and first editions were huge. Besides, these are later editions. The Simon is your leverage piece; it's worth an easy $250 in Fine shape. (Although it's not a sure seller; a lot of dealers may shave the price a bit just to get it moving off the shelf. Remember that everything is relative.)

The Simon is also your test piece. You know what it's worth; does the buyer? Depending on the store's training procedures and the natural inclinations and experience of the buyer, maybe, maybe not. Very often, not. If she comes across with an offer of $20 in trade for the Simon book you can either (a) look for another buyer in the same store or (b) head for the door. I've seen a lot of people walk out of stores all across the country when they realized they knew a lot more about the books in their hands than the clerk did.

Of course they knew more; the books were theirs.

Every used bookshop buyer has very different abilities. In a small store you'll likely only have to scope out the abilities of maybe two or three people. In a larger store, like the Strand in New York or Powell's in Portland, you'll be dealing with huge staffs working at all kinds of levels of efficiency. Either way, the rule holds true: know who you're dealing with. Take the time to find out who knows what; it's the only way you're going to get the best deal. Ask who handles rare or collectible books. Find out their interests. I've worked in shops where the rare books "specialist" was really only interested in a specific, narrow genre, and if you brought in something fantastic outside of that, he'd pass it by. And this in a general-stock store.

AFTER YOU GO

Depending on the size of the used bookshop, any one of a number of things could happen to the books you've just dropped off.

A small shop, staffed by one or two people, will put the books into a processing pile, and within the next day or two your old books will be side by side with the shop's stock. There's not much lag here, and in a small shop, inventory can turn over quickly (yet another reason to make friends with the clerks who can put aside books that might interest you).

A large shop, one with four or five buyers (or more) and a larger floor space, handles matters differently. The book buyers pass the books on to the processing staff. There, the books are assessed, compared with what's already on the floor, and priced. Some of these huge stores may have four or five people working on nothing but pricing, and *that's your opportunity.* Your chance for bargains actually increases, because they each have their weaknesses, and because there will be less consistency to the floor prices. One puts five dollars on good nonfiction, another ten. Sometimes that little gap is all you need to pounce. If you know there's someone putting good, serious history at five bucks a book here, and that across town they eat up history and put a premium on it, you're in trade fodder territory. You might have to outlay a little more than you would on standard items, but when you take them in across town, they'll appreciate the quality and give you a better deal on what you're looking for there.

Look for the holes. Look for the margin inside which you have room to move.

After the book is priced—rightly or wrongly—it's passed on to the stocking department. In a small store, this means the guy at the counter puts his pencil down and moves to the shelves. In a larger store, stocking gets done in slack hours; some of the very largest stores have people who do nothing but put books on shelves forty hours a week. Get to know these people. In the pecking order, they're nothing more than shelf-gnomes, but as far as information goes, they can be gold mines. Find out their routines: maybe they do the sections that interest you on a particular day. That means you can be there, ready and waiting, as soon as new stock comes out.

The processing time in a small store can be a matter of seconds; in a big store, where books work their way through five or six different people, it can take as much as a month before the book hits the floor.

Does every book that comes into the store end up on the sales floor? Not necessarily. In one large store where I worked, I sent four or five boxes of unsalable books—each one bought by our counter people—to charity organizations every day.

If you're running a lower-end scouting business, this junk can actually profit you. If there's a big store nearby, find out what's happening to the books they don't think they can sell. You might be able to pick them up for pennies—or even free, if you're willing to haul them away. What doesn't sell in a bookstore is not necessarily unsalable; it could fly out in a garage sale or a flea market. If that's the clientele you're aiming toward, check it out.

But don't bring the discards back around to the front door of another shop—because the sad thing is, it's very often the dealers and scouts who are bringing in the worst books, and the shops will never forgive them for it.

Once you know the system, you can slide some things past it to your benefit; on the other hand, if you get a reputation in the store as always bringing in garbage and always trying to hawk a deal on the primo items, you'll quickly find that the shop is not cooperating with you the way it once was. You'll find the buyers turning down more and more of the books you bring in, even books that are perfectly acceptable. They're remembering the time you burned them last week, and you're paying for it now. Store policy dictates that they be nice to you, or at least polite, but they have a lot of leeway. Remember, they're setting the prices that you're getting at the counter. Suddenly those book club Victoria Holt novels you've always been able to unload on them before for a couple bucks are "overstocked." Suddenly they're not interested in Grosset & Dunlap books anymore. (For more on what you should be bringing in, see chapter 5.)

What has happened is that you've offended them. They're working for a business, out to make money. So are you. You have to find the middle ground where both you and the dealer are profiting. And when you find that middle ground, you'll start to find that the shop is giving you special treatment. You'll become a resource to them, not a drag.

One way you can enhance this relationship is to share your knowledge when scouting. Do you see a book marked as a first edition that's really a second state? Tell them. They'll appreciate your help and professionalism. Is there a piece you're not interested in, but you know is seriously underpriced? Tell them. I've helped shop owners put another 30 or 40 percent on a book. It was out of my area, and even if I had thought I could turn it around quickly, the loss of that one sale to me meant nothing compared to the goodwill I'd get when somebody else walked in and bought the book off the shelves. The next time I come in, the owners will be smiling and happy to see me.

This is a basic rule of the book business: everything that goes around comes around. The book world is a very, very small one, and reputations spread fast. When shop staffs get together, they tell rude stories about customers, even ones they like. Everybody knows everybody. Treat the shop people fairly, and they'll treat you fairly. Don't take advantage. Work the system to your benefit, which is really quite a different proposal entirely. Ignore this stuff, and the rest of this book is a waste of time.

SCOUTING USED BOOKSTORES

To be a successful book scout or collector, you'll need to be in the right place at the right time. Knowing how books are processed through a used bookstore should help you find out when the right time is: are books put out all day? Is new material stocked first thing in the morning, or after-hours? Find out the patterns, if any. Even a small store run by a single proprietor is likely to have patterns. Learn them, make friends, and stop in often.

Obviously, you can't make friends with everyone in all of the bookstores in your area, especially if you live in a big city. So you must learn *how* to be in the right place at the right time.

A store I frequent specializes in limited editions. They've got shelf after shelf of nice, leather-bound or slipcased books, all signed and numbered by the authors. These books are displayed in four huge cases, and they are the first thing you see when you walk in the door. The mere fact that the books are signed bumps them up to premium prices. This store is one of my favorite places to look for autographed books. Not for these limiteds—I don't like limiteds myself. But because the people who work there spend so much time poring over the limiteds, they short the time that should be spent researching the other books. In fact, they often don't even turn to the title page. These people, who specialize in autographed material, commonly miss autographed trade editions. They don't flip the pages.

This is where getting to know the strengths and weaknesses of a used bookshop pays off. I'd never buy a limited from these people; they know them all, they're right on top of the trade. On the other hand, I've found quite a few signed regular editions that have slipped by them, especially in the horror/science fiction area, which is already underpriced by 30 percent.

I go there a lot.

Now compare this with another shop, across town. This one believes that all first editions are valuable; they look at the guide prices and then add at least 20 percent to that. If the book isn't in the guides, the mere fact that it's a first edition, out-of-print book makes it a minimum of twenty bucks, even if it's a diet book or a popular novel that made the rounds of the remainder table for years because the publisher seriously overprinted the edition. This shop spends so much time overpricing their books that they look to attract only one kind of customer: the uninformed, those who think that high price and quality go hand in hand. Two trips to this store were enough as a customer. One trip to find out what it was like, another to confirm that the first trip's impressions were correct.

But I'll certainly go back a third time to sell them something I can't unload anywhere else.

That's how you succeed.

Get a notebook, and head up each page with the name of a bookstore in your region. If you live in a small town and have only one or two bookshops, expand your horizons on monthly trips into the nearest big city. To successfully scout, you'll need a base of at least a dozen shops. The first thing you need to do is narrow down the stores you're going to put on your regular route. In a small town, maybe you can hit everybody. In a big city, though, you're going to have to find out who meets your interests.

CHECK SUBJECTS

Go into the first store on your list and start looking around at which sections are strong. Is there a huge science fiction section? Or does the store lean toward modern literature? Say they're entirely enthusiastic about modern lit and love to put Updike and Ann Beattie and Amy Clampitt on the shelves. But where does their knowledge of the last thirty or forty years end? Do they catch the early chapbooks of Jayne Anne Phillips? Ellen Gilchrist's books of short stories? Ivan Doig? Eudora Welty? Make notes of this in your notebook: which writers are amply covered, which writers seem to be lacking. Are children's books your field? Look for A. A. Milne, Michael Bond, Beatrix Potter, Heath Robinson, Arthur Rackham.

With your notebook in hand, go through the store slowly and make notes of which sections are strong and which are weak. One good, easy indicator of a shop's interests is simply the condition of the bookshelves: if the owner is deeply into modern lit, you might find the mystery shelves with books leaning over or a thin coating of dust, while the literature shelves are neatly kept. Children's sections are not usually a good indicator, because they're always a mess, but you can look to see if the better books have been separated and put up higher, out of reach of enthusiastic young fingers.

CHECKING PRICES

What else can you look for? Prices, of course. By now you should have a good idea of what certain writers are going for in your area, or at least an idea of what the guide prices are on your favorite writers (remember guide prices and shelf prices are not always in the same ballpark).

Prices on the writers who are considered the Giants of Literature are not helpful indicators. If a bookstore has a first edition of F. Scott Fitzgerald's *Tales of the Jazz Age*, it's going to cost plenty. Shops don't miss that kind of item very often. So don't worry about the Fitzgeralds, the Hemingways, or even the Stephen Kings and Sue Graftons. The bargains here are few and far between. Where you make your money is on the next level of writer, and those are the ones to start checking prices on.

Suppose there's a first edition of Sue Grafton's *"A" Is for Alibi* for $1,200. Maybe a little high, but fair enough. Now, run down the shelves a little. Check the Amanda Cross prices. Check the Elizabeth Peters prices; see what Dorothy Gilman's Mrs. Pollifax books are selling for. These will help you gauge how interested the shop is in these writers. If you see a copy of James Crumley's *The Wrong Case* in Fine shape for $30, grab it and put some gold stars in your notebook beside the name of this store. That's a $500-plus book, and this shop is going to be a place where the money rolls in for you. Put it on your regular circuit. On the other hand, if modern lit is your main interest and Paul Gallico is selling for $200, you're not going to find too many great bargains here.

But don't file the store away yet if everything is overpriced. We'll have a use for it later, when it's time to turn our finds into cash.

Again I must stress the usefulness of getting to know the people behind the counter in the shops. Bookstore staff may drop plenty of clues about where their interests lie and where they don't. I do a lot of dealing in early horror/dark fantasy, and you would not believe the number of dealers who will flatly state that they're not interested in that kind of material. And yet the nature of a used bookshop requires that they deal in it, just because it comes over their transom and they're trying to keep a good general stock to draw in maximum customer traffic.

Which means they sell it, but they don't sell it well. They don't spend the time researching it to determine accurately the full price of a Fine item. They don't care if the author has won three Bram Stoker Awards.

But I care. And I buy the books from them. And they're happy to have my business.

And then I turn the books around in a store that does care, and I make money off them. Or if it's something I've been looking for, I keep it, and it gives me immense satisfaction while I'm reading it or when I glance across the room and see it there on the shelf and think I paid only a fraction of its value to own it.

It'll take you a half hour or an hour to get the full measure of a store. Pull books off the shelf and check prices and condition. Not just the rare item that you might be looking for, but see also how they treat run-of-the-mill books, too. Because what you're hoping is that they'll think the book you want is just another run-of-the-mill book, and treat it the same way they treat that book club edition of Tom Clancy over there.

While you're doing this, talk to the owner or staff as much

as possible. Don't make a pest of yourself—these people have work to do—but find out whatever you can about the shop, even if all you're finding out is that they're way too busy to talk to you. Or that business is so slack they're willing to talk your ear off.

Under subheadings in your notebook, one for each section that you're interested in or know something about, take down the writers that the shop seems to concentrate on; make a note of anyone conspicuous who is missing. Used bookshops are not entirely dependent upon their customers for stock; a good store will search out important books they're low on, or offer a premium for it at the counter. No shop wants to get caught without the new, hot book.

Now look at the store's prices for a standard assortment of writers: the people you'll find in the same section in other stores. If you're in mystery, note the prices for Grafton, Hillerman, Leonard, Parker, and a half dozen more. If you're in more mainstream fiction, look for writers like W. Somerset Maugham, Graham Greene, Katherine Mansfield, John Galsworthy, and Booth Tarkington. For the moderns, maybe the Johns—Irving, Updike, Grisham—and one or two on the up-and-coming list, like Bebe Moore Campbell or Julia Alvarez. Always check the edition of each volume. You never know when you'll hit the jackpot with a good first.

Your notebook, with main authors, comparative prices, and notes on general standards of the store, will serve as an important tool when you start trying to put together your route. You need to know who prices high, who prices low, who treasures the same things you do, and who couldn't care less. Later, you'll want the notebook to keep track of what you buy and sell with each store, tracking your income and making notes of particular deals (this is to supplement, not replace, the bookkeeping system we'll talk about in chapter 11).

The notebook is also a good place to record things that come up in conversations you have with people in the store: clues to what they want, what they need. Don't just come in blind with a stack of books and hope. Working in used bookshops, I've seen hundreds of people bring in thousands of books for trade or cash without ever having been in the store before. Almost always, they go away disappointed, because they didn't bother to see what the store wanted first.

The more you know about a shop's business, the more valuable you'll be to that shop—and the more valuable they'll be to you.

Remember the store you went into that had lots of books you liked but they were too expensive? Go back and take another, more detailed look around, this time as a seller not a buyer. Note prices, and pay special attention to the condition of the books. Find out what the gradient is, how the pricer is measuring his stock. Are a few bucks marked off for a tear in the dust jacket, or is that a 20 percent deduction? Are the corners on the prices clipped? Any trace of remainder markings (black pen lines across the bottom of the book, or a stamp mark on the bottom edge)? Are those markings figured into the price? Or are all the prices simply in line with the "Fine" measures in the guides, regardless of the book's true state?

How is the dealer caring for the books? Are the dust jackets carefully wrapped in protective wrappers like those used in libraries (the Brodart company is the best-known brand), or some other archival material? Pull a jacket off, see if there's tape on the back of the protector. Tape is one of the worst things that can happen to a book, and no matter how good a store looks, heavily taped jacket wrappers can indicate that these people either don't know as much as they think they do, or that they simply don't care.

What you're doing on this visit is looking at the place as a market for your books when you bring them in to sell. You want your books to fit into the mood and definition of the store and be something the owner desires. If he's big on the early pulp writers, take him early pulp writers. Search out those unusual Robert E. Howard editions, especially the Conan stuff. Look for Lester del Rey's first books. Go to a library and check back issues of old pulp magazines (if you're lucky enough to have such a wonderful library nearby) to introduce yourself to some new writers. Not only is this a great way to find the B-level writers who are often missed, but you may find yourself making new friends among writers you never would have discovered any other way, no matter how interested you are yourself in the field.

Another example: if you love poetry, read all the regular magazines, go to local readings, and check the new poetry books in every store you go into, you're still only seeing about 5 percent of what's out there. There are the literary magazines, the little magazines and small presses, where the bulk of poets work, and although these are published in truckloads, few ever make it to the local newsstand. If you don't do your homework, if you're not up on current action (or, in the case of pulp writers, the old action) in a field, you're going to miss out on the next Robert Frost or T. S. Eliot. Or Beckian Fritz Goldberg. ("Who?" you ask. If you're a poetry lover, you'd better find out now while her first books can still be found, because she's going to be the next big thing—and she just published her first limited, fine edition.)

In other words, getting good at this is going to take a lot of work and a lot of knowledge. But what work it is! Reading and going into every bookstore you see! It's the kind of job most people dream of.

By now you should have a pretty good definition of which stores cater to your interests. In your notebook, break down the stores into two categories: *Buy* and *Sell*. Very simple: *buy at the stores that don't like what you do; sell at the stores that love what you do.*

Of course these categories are fluid, and if you expect to develop a good relationship with a dealer you'd better not just be selling him things; you'd better be buying, too.

At my shop, I have a customer who will buy virtually every

modern mystery first I can dig up. He spends a few hundred dollars a month with me, talks to me to find out what else I've seen, and listens if I point him to new authors. Every now and then, I give him a bargain not to be believed, just because I know it will make him happy and keep him coming back.

When this starts happening to you, you're doing your job well.

CONTACTS AND WANT LISTS

Once you're recognized by dealers as a professional yourself, you'll find that the networking in the book world is amazing. Serious book people like nothing more than getting together and talking about books. Because of this, many of the best books never reach the sales floor.

Go back to our scenario in the used bookshop. The books have been processed as outlined, but this time one is held out of the deal, say, a first edition of Ford Madox Ford's *The Good Soldier*, one of the most perfect books of the twentieth century. Now, here where I live, there are at least a dozen dealers who know that I'm looking for a Fine copy of that book. They know me, they know my standards, they have my number on file. If a copy comes up, I'll be the first to know because I'm in the network.

Letting shops know what you're after is important more for the items you collect than for the ones you deal in. Conversely, finding out what stores are looking for can make them one of your best sources of income. In some states, particularly New York and California, scouts work for one primary store, offering up their finds and being assured a fair price, as well as getting a cut in price when they want to take something back out.

One of your strongest tools should be the want list. Actually, two want lists: one for you and one for the shop where you do most of your business.

Your want list is the books you're out to get, maybe because you want them for yourself, or maybe because you have a client who wants them.

The shop's want list is, in effect, your shopping order. These are the books the store has told you they want, so the sales are guaranteed.

Your want list is a methodical, careful consideration of the books you are ready to buy. It is *not* books you only want to see. If you put a book on a want list and circulate it among dealers, you'd better be ready to lay out cash.

One thing dealers hate above all else is a want list that says "Anything by . . ." The people circulating those probably already have nearly everything by that author. They're just hoping for the odd item. An undiscovered Wodehouse. John Berryman's "Dream Song 14" in a separate edition (something I didn't know existed until I saw it listed in a catalog; it had been missed by Berryman's bibliographer—more about bibliographies in chapter 12). They don't really want "anything;" they want a specific thing that they're not sure exists. A bookseller's nightmare. And a promise that the list is going to be discarded.

Your list should be as specific as possible. Include the exact titles, authors, and publication dates. List the points, if you know them. Do you want the British or the American edition? Was the first issue in the red dust jacket or the gray one? It can make all the difference in the world to the serious collector. An example of this is Stephen W. Hawking's *A Brief History of Time*. The book came out in a white dust jacket, and then was immediately recalled. Those copies can be worth five or six times what the standard, blue-jacket first edition sells for. So if you want only the white-jacket first, the first edition in its first state, say so. You wouldn't believe how many request forms I've shuffled in the shop that don't list an author, have notations like "the title has something to do with . . ." because, amazingly, the person who has filled out the request is not even sure what the book is about. We actually had someone turn down a filled request because the book was a British edition. "No," she said, "I want a copy in English."

Know what you want, communicate it clearly, and be prepared to wait (understanding world language groupings doesn't hurt, either).

Now, one way to make a dealer happy and more interested in finding your books is to bring in the books she wants. So get her want list.

This one you carry with you always. And again, specificity is the key. If you have a good relationship with a dealer and she asks you to keep an eye out for a first of Bruce Chatwin's *The Viceroy of Ouidah*, find out how much she's willing to pay. Find out if she has a ready customer—and if so, what the customer's standards are—or if she's just looking to fill a gap in the stock. *These are sure sales.* Or as near to sure sales as this business gets. Take advantage of every opportunity that presents itself.

Having a regular deal can take a lot of the fear and frustration out of book scouting. Keep this in mind when you're going through your regular round of stores. Treat the dealers fairly, and you'll find they reward you richly.

Chapter Five

❧

THE ART OF BOOK TRADING

W | hat you're about to read is strictly insider information. I've worked both ends of the used-book business— as both scout and dealer—for years, and one thing I've consistently found is that dealers don't know how scouts work, and scouts really don't understand how dealers work. There's no communication between the two groups; a mutually antagonistic relationship is at work. The dealers are sure the scouts are trying to rip them off, and the scouts are sure the dealers are stealing them blind and trying to starve them by never offering a fair price, either for stock brought in or for items taken out.

Although many scouts graduate to being dealers, it seems once the transition is made, earlier lessons are lost. It's sort of like vowing, at the ripe old age of nine, that you'll never treat your own children as badly as your parents are treating you now; then, when you finally have kids, you proceed to treat them the same way. So at best, the basic relationship between dealers and scouts—even among those who've been dealing with each other for years—remains a kind of friendly antagonism at best. But the truth is, dealers and scouts need each other, just like they both need collectors and readers to sell their books.

On the other hand, despite this mutual need, scouts and dealers are not going to share any information—where they find the great books, contacts they've made—with each other. They're certainly not going to share the kind of information that lets them do their jobs well. They'll talk your ears off about points and condition, but just try and find out how much someone really paid for a book, and you'll find out how quickly they can clam up.

Neither dealer nor scout is likely to share any insider information with you, either, because that's just adding to the competition. If you make friends quickly and easily, or if your specialty is so far out of line from theirs as to pose no threat, you won't have any problem picking up information on *what* to look for, but nobody is going to tell you *how* to look. And both scout and dealer will defend their trading secrets to the death.

So what you're about to read is top secret information: How to trade. How to shoot straight for the middle of the bell curve with the great majority of your purchases, and still find yourself with wonderful books that belong way up in the narrow end of the scale. This is what the dealers and the scouts don't want you to know.

So far we've mostly talked about how to spot things that the dealers have missed. But now we're going to move to the other side of the book business, one just as profitable and useful to your dealing and collecting in the long run, but not nearly as glamorous. Now we're going to talk about how you can get what you want even if somebody else—in this case the dealer—has spotted it first.

The ugly (for the scout) truth is, although there are always bargains out there waiting to be found in the stacks, dealers aren't dumb. For every Steinbeck first found mismarked at five bucks and tossed on a sale table, there are a thousand more properly marked, sitting in a special case behind the cash register.

Another truth is that for every Fine Steinbeck in a glass case, there are a million or two reading copies of half a million or so different book titles on the shelves. Now what is the dealer depending on more for his daily bread? The one Fine book, or the endless sea of reading copies that most people want for simple entertainment? These are the customers who keep shops in business. The $300 sales are just gravy. Meat is a $3.95 paperback. Meat is a $10 hardback on a good, solid subject.

A simple example: In 1993, first edition copies of John Grisham's first novel, *A Time to Kill*, sold for $2,000. Scouts everywhere were scouring shelves looking for this particular book from the publisher Wynwood—the only Wynwood book anybody had ever heard of. Each copy of the book jumped a hundred dollars or so every time it changed hands, and a very few people made a lot of money.

Meanwhile, 27 million Grisham books were sold that year—a publishing record—and with used copies at three or four bucks each, dealers were able to pay their bills a little more easily.

To be a good book scout and to give shops material they're going to want and be able to use—material they're going to give you money for—you need to think not only of the prime material that brings tears of joy to the shopkeeper's bibliophilic heart, but also of the kind of material that's going to pay his light bill. Because while every store in the country would love to have a copy of the first edition of Dickens's *A Christmas Carol* (shelf price starting around $4,500) to display and draw attention, they also know that it's probably not going to sell quickly. To balance that drain of the two grand or so they spent to put the Dickens on display, they need to sell a lot of $10 books.

In other words, while you're looking for the Wynwood first, if you find a really cheap paperback of the same title at a sale somewhere, you're doing yourself a favor if you pick it up. This is prime trade bait, an opportunity missed by many scouts. A lot of little trades can lead to some very expensive books, as long as you keep trading up. And since not all that many people are out there doing it, it's surprisingly easy.

So instead of walking out of a bookstore empty-handed just because there wasn't a first edition of Lindsey Davis's first novel, *Silver Pigs*, on the shelf for $10, put some effort into making lots of little scores. You'll discover that they can add up to more than the big score. I know a casual scout who makes his car payment off twenty- and thirty-dollar books. He just has a knack for picking them up for a buck or two and knowing where to sell them off.

And even if you're not able to find that copy of the first Perry Mason book, *The Case of the Velvet Claws*, mismarked for three bucks, you just might be able to get one anyway. With enough Grisham paperbacks, with enough $10 books on good, solid subjects, you can trade for the Perry Mason.

To put it simply, you can often hit the big score by concentrating on the little ones.

This is where the real scouts separate themselves from the dilettantes: in understanding how to trade up from almost nothing to something. And, just as importantly, in understanding how to do it without taking advantage of anyone.

By the end of this chapter, you'll not only have a good idea of how to be a successful scout, working trades with confidence and always to your benefit, but if you've been reading carefully and have a reasonable book background, you should be able to go into a used bookstore and take over their trade counter for the day, cutting the deals needed with confidence. It's only by knowing how things work on both ends that you're going to get anywhere.

For the rest of this chapter, forget the dreams of finding a mispriced copy of *Farewell, My Lovely*. Think about taking in boxes of good, solid stock, and walking out happily with a fairly priced copy of Charles Go Finney's *The Circus of Dr. Lao* that you paid for with nothing but some time and a few good books you weren't interested in anyway.

Now we're going to go after those expensive books selling at fair market value, the books you simply must have to fill holes in your collection. And we're going to go after them by laying out as little cash as possible, which means first we've got to clean up a few mistakes you've probably already made.

The Joy of Mistakes

By now you should have some idea of what to look for and how to look for it, so far as the big score goes, and hopefully a good idea of how to work with dealers and bookshops. If you went shopping between the last paragraph and now, you should have a couple paperbacks by hot authors, picked up for a dime or so at a garage sale (although there are some collectible paperbacks that can cost big bucks, if it's for trade, never pay more than about a quarter for pocket-sized—what the industry calls "mass market"—paperbacks; if you do, you'll never get your money's worth, unless they turn out to be early Jim Thompsons, or the work of some other major author whose first books never saw hardback publication).

If you're like most novice book scouts, you should also have a few hardback mistakes on your shelf. Perhaps an author who wasn't as popular as you'd believed. Maybe you mistook a book club edition for a trade book. Don't let these mistakes discourage you. They happen to everyone, and you will make buying mistakes time and time again, no matter how long you've been buying books. There's a marvelous scene in John Dunning's *Booked to Die* in which the detective-hero enters the house of a dead book scout: the house is littered with books that seemed good at the time of purchase, but which the scout—somebody who made his sole living off books—couldn't get rid of as quickly as he'd thought.

Mistakes are an inevitable part of the game, but don't worry too much about them, because most mistakes can be corrected.

So hang on to the paperbacks, keep the reading copies, don't toss that book club edition. Don't despair over money lost. You're going to use those seemingly worthless, common, and distinctly not collectible books for trading.

This is where the game really is: trading nothing—your mistakes on your bargain-bin buys—for something as exciting as a beautiful first edition.

PART ONE: PRE-TRADE

If somebody had enough faith in it to publish a book once, odds are somebody else out there somewhere will still want to buy it. All you have to do is find that person. The beauty of the used-book trade is that there is a market for almost anything.

Keep in mind that I say *almost* anything. You're never going to be able to get rid of books that are falling apart, books that are heavily water damaged, book club fiction editions with no dust jackets, or Reader's Digest Condensed books.

However, there is a market for most other books, no matter how lost they may look at the beginning. Perhaps the books look like lost causes to you because you're thinking of them from the perspective of a collector. Fans look at things rather differently, and they may be happy to take that old Judith Krantz novel you somehow ended up with. The shop is happy to pick it up cheaply, the customer is happy to find something to read cheaply, and you've got trade credit to use for something you really want. And that's what makes the used-book world go round: trade credit.

Best of all, in the trade world, the scout is dealing from a position of strength.

What you've got going for you in this trading process are three key points: First of all, by now you know the local market, and you know who's interested in what. Second, you've got time. This is not a get-rich-quick scheme. This isn't even a get-middle-class-really-slowly scheme. Third and finally, you've probably got a lot of books. The good trader knows that the more she offers up over time, the more the shops will take. The more that gets taken, the more trade credit she builds up. And with enough trade credit in your hand, you can buy the world.

It's important for you to realize that if you start trying to shovel garbage off to the local stores, you're going to find yourself shut out quickly. There are scouts I've dealt with who frequently bring such trash in to my store that my criteria for them are considerably stricter than they would be for someone who makes an effort to conform to my market. They bring in books missing pages or stained by water, or self-published vanity titles that even the author's mother didn't read. Somewhere among the flotsam and jetsam there may be a worthwhile title, but is it worth my effort to find it? These scouts have made a bad name for themselves that will be difficult to overcome.

Don't fall into that trap yourself: never do a trade without knowing who you're trading with—what's their market, what's their niche, what are their interests? While it's okay to try to pass off some marginal books, never do a trade without a fair percentage of good books that the shop is going to be genuinely glad to have. Some may call it salting the mine, but I call it doing business correctly. Put the shop in a good mood and you'll get a better deal, and at the same time you'll be able to pass a few of the more marginal items off on them. If I have a box of great stuff come in for trade, I'm usually more than willing to take a few lesser items to keep the customer happy and to urge him to come back with more great books in the future.

Think like a dealer when you're trading, and your deals will go better. The dealer's main concerns are first, salability—how quickly can he sell this particular book, and for how much?—and second, keeping customers happy. If he rejects all of these books, he's never going to see this person again, so what can he do to get him back? It can be a tightrope act if he's looking at a box of junk books. It can be a divine pleasure if he has a box of excellent stock material that will fly off the shelves. When that happens, when you're offering a box of fine, new fiction that fits right into the store's self-image, good serious history, and an Abrams art book or two, the dealer will be more generous, a lot more encouraging. Surely someone with one good box of books to trade has more, right? Let's make that person very happy.

As a scout trying to trade, you want to be that happy person. In order to be that happy person, all you have to do is make the shop happy: give them what they want. Do that, and you'll find they'll also gladly take in a few things you don't want off your hands.

PART TWO: CHOOSING TRADE STOCK

Any used bookstore worth its salt sends away 80 to 90 percent of the books that come in the door. These books have all the problems I've already described—dirt, poor condition, bad editions—but the most common reason for rejecting books is that the scout or seller is completely out of touch with the current market. They bring in a title that was hot five years ago and expect the shop to jump for it. "Hey, this book sold a million copies!" they squeak. But the shop has been looking at half of those million copies for years, and the book probably stopped moving quite some time ago. Diet and exercise books are prime examples of this: they move in fads and once the fad is over, you can't give the books away. Twiggy's beauty secrets? Get serious.

The same holds true for a lot of fiction categories. If lawyer novels are hot this year, riding on Grisham's coattails, you can bet they're going to slack off into a glut someday soon, just as serial killer novels did within two years of *The Silence of the Lambs*. Romance novels, mentioned nowhere else in this book, date more quickly than any other category, but current titles are usually welcome. Still, you'd be surprised how many would-be traders bring in bags of romance titles ten years old. Romance fans may buy every title Barbara Cartland ever wrote, but they really don't care much about Dora McCullick.

In short, you need to think current. Or timeless. Anything else is just junk as far as trades go.

There's little difference, except in degree, between the high-line items a dealer wants and the low-level. If they love to sell expensive, collectible mysteries, odds are they like mystery paperbacks as well. If they get top dollar for a first Borges, they're going to like reading copies of modern lit as well. You've been in the shops now. You know.

Dealing in reading copies works the same way as dealing in higher-priced items. Buy where the books are undervalued and sell where they're prized—building trade credit works the same way. Buy mysteries from the lit dealer, buy lit from the mystery dealer.

The serious trader has another market for buying that the serious collector really doesn't. If you start performing trades regularly, it's time to check out the irregular market I mentioned in chapter 4—garage sales, estate sales, library sales, etc.—that I earlier said could be bypassed by the collector.

There is a different mentality between buying collectibles and buying trades. Shoot straight for the middle of the bell curve when you're after trade material.

The ultimate idea is to have as much trade credit as possible

*in as many locations as possible; this way, you never pay cash
when you see what you're really after, no matter where it is. You
also keep a large number of books moving around, constantly
doing yourself benefit.* You are always working on adding to
your credit balance, which translates to cash in the bank in the
long run.

Where I live, there are three bookstores where I spend a lot
of time. One is a giant store that tries to appeal to the widest
possible audience. They have something for everybody there,
but they pay low, and there isn't a whole lot to interest the high-
end buyer. One of the other shops shoots straight for the
middle-of-the-road market, picking up on tourists passing
through and the general book lover who just wants good things
to read. The last shop reaches a highbrow, literary kind of market.

Between those three stores, I can sell virtually any *acceptable*
book.

So what's an acceptable book?

Almost anything published in the last two years, for starters.
The current year is even better.

Nonfiction is almost always better than fiction (with the exception of textbooks; stay away from those). For collectors, fiction is where it's at; for bookshops, nonfiction is the backbone
of the business. Again, you want to offer newer titles, on per-
tinent subjects. Nothing dies faster than a trend.

A tip when scouting for current books: look for authors that
a particular shop is overburdened with. While working in one
store, I got twenty copies of P. D. James's *Devices and Desires*
in a three-week period. They were too good to turn away since
the book was only a few weeks off the best-seller list, but there
were just too many of them, and I ended up selling them off
for a few dollars each. Scouts picked them up, took them across
town, and doubled their money. Okay, it's only a two- or three-
dollar profit, but this is how you start to build your business
and collection, and work toward the books you're really after.

So current topics are good for trading stock. What else is good?

Actually, it's a lot easier to discuss what isn't good for trading than what is; but remember, everything is dependent upon the market in your area. Still, to make life a little easier, here's what generally *doesn't* sell.

While nonfiction certainly outsells fiction, buying it can be a little risky for the inexperienced buyer or trader, because there are a lot of books that look good, but really aren't. Shops are overburdened with them. Stay away from Time-Life series, unless you know of a specific market for them. Everybody and their dog owns a set or two of these, and nobody seems to want them secondhand. Despite being of reasonable quality, they date quickly and are quickly superseded by new information. About the only exceptions are the Old West series and the Flight series, which have devoted audiences. In some areas, the New Age/mysticism series can also be good.

There is probably not a used bookstore in the entire country looking for a book published by Reader's Digest—any book published by them, even the nice big picture ones. The only possible exception might be one or two of the home improvement books they did. Nobody, nowhere, wants a Reader's Digest Condensed edition.

Sadly, National Geographic books also fall into this category. Everybody already owns them. They're good books, great for school libraries and families with kids, and they always look like a better buy than they are. Stores get buried under them.

Picture Books. Along the same line are picture books, those big, expensive, scenic things of Nantucket or the English coast or the Florida Everglades. These sell as souvenirs to travelers or would-be travelers for about $30–$50 new. A year or two after the vacation, the traveler loses interest and tries to unload the book. Unfortunately, they've already been beaten to the punch by two hundred other ex-travelers. Very little sits on the shelves of a used store as long as these things do, and dealers are rightly very wary.

Reprint Books. Falling into the same hole are reprint books. These are very nice editions of once hot books that are now past their prime. Octopus, Bonanza, Oxmor, and Crescent are a few of the publishers specializing in this kind of book. You often see them with their prices marked "Originally Published at $XX" and then a cheap sale sticker on them. While the books are nice and fill a definite niche, most dealers are overburdened with them. Some books from these houses are original books, though, and can be worthwhile. They do a lot of animal picture books, which can be a boon in the right market, and a lot of military picture books. If you know the right dealers, these books can be a great bargain, because of their hot subject matter—if you can pick them up cheaply enough. Puppy and kitty books go over big with kids who might otherwise be bored in a bookstore, and military people tend to be fanatical about finding pictures and stats on weaponry. First be sure you have a market, though; otherwise you might find yourself with more puppy pictures than you know what to do with.

There is one exception to the reprint house guidelines: Dover, which publishes only reprints. They take classic books that are now in the public domain, and publish cheap, durable editions. These are always good for trade.

Art Books. Art books are another borderline category. Norman Rockwell? Forget it, except around Christmas. Then there might be some hope. Again, everybody who wants such a book already owns one. The same with other general reprint art books. What do sell are serious titles with a lot of high-quality illustrations and a dense text to go with them, and those artists for whom there is always a market—primarily the major Impressionists. Ethnic art—African, Asian, South American—is always a good trade, since not much of that turns up.

Sports Books. Sports books are very iffy, unless they're bios of hugely popular players, preferably autobiographies. Baseball sells, but basketball, football, and tennis titles tend to sit on shelves forever. Good golf can fly out the door, but only golfers seem to know what's really good and what isn't. Kids' "how to play" books are good, if the haircuts in the illustrations are reasonably current. Hiking books are good for between five and ten years, but any sports book with statistics in it dates after two years. Forget the Olympics, unless it's something from at least twenty years ago.

Biographies and Autobiographies. The entire category of biographies and autobiographies outside of sports figures is also an iffy prospect. Star bios date faster than milk left outside, and shops are usually glutted with them. The obvious exceptions are the timeless stars: Monroe, Dietrich, Garland. Any book on Marilyn Monroe is a prime trade item.

Politicians are in the very doubtful category, especially long-dead politicians. Most stores could tell you horror stories of how many books they see on the Kennedy assassination—and not only books, but magazines, newspapers, and every other bit of ephemera that every single person in the world saved, hoping it would be valuable some day. It's usually not.

Politicians do move in cycles, though. After Nixon's death, a lot of books on the star of the seventies started to move again. Prior to it, you couldn't have given away *RN*, his autobiography, but after his death, it couldn't be found no matter what the price. So watch for comebacks, scandals, and falls from grace.

Travel. Travel guides date more quickly than any other type of book. Stay away from these unless they're the current issue. Travel literature can have a strong following in some regions, but you need to know the market well before starting to deal here. Cousin Ernie's trip to China isn't going to excite anyone, but there's always a market for Redmond O'Hanlon, Peregrine Hodson, Geoffrey Moorhouse, and a few others.

History. History is one of the strongest nonfiction markets in nearly every store. The Civil War, World War II, and the Vietnam War (although here you have to watch out, because certain titles dominated the market for years, and now there's a glut of them; check your area shops) move the best. The other wars—Revolutionary, World War I, and the Korean War—not only don't have as much written about them, they don't have nearly the market, although quality items will always sell for good prices.

In foreign history, the Middle Ages tend to sell the best. Asia sells more than the Middle East, and the Middle East well outsells Africa. South America comes and goes in popularity, and except for Robert Hughes's *The Fatal Shore*, it's virtually impossible to find anything at all readable on Australia. The Arctic and Antarctic always have markets, as do certain moments in history: the *Bounty* mutiny or Lewis and Clark, for example. And, of course, anything at all specific to your area. Area-specific dealers and scouts are some of the most prosperous.

Although history seems like something that shouldn't date— it's already over, isn't it? the truth is, it dates quickly. New information, new interpretations come in place of the old works. The standard works of the twenties and thirties don't even move off library shelves, unless some historian of historiography gets curious.

Cookbooks. Always trade with serious cookbooks. Again, stay away from heavily advertised series, and look for the more arcane titles. Famous chefs have their day, which seems to come and go pretty quickly. You'd have a hard time giving away a Galloping Gourmet book, and even Jeff Smith can be overstocked at times. It's better to pick up bread books, baking books, books of sweets and delicacies with names you can't pronounce. There isn't a general-stock used bookstore in the country that isn't happy to get good cookbooks. One thing to watch out for: comb bindings. Unless the book's title is printed on the plastic comb, these are difficult or impossible to display. Many great cookbooks are passed up because they'd disappear on store shelves. Make sure the books you buy have visible spines, and you'll have a much easier time selling them. *In any* *category, books without titles printed on their spines are a very tough sell.* Cookbooks are the category where the greatest number of these spineless wonders are published. Microwave books, even with spines, can be a hard sell, since it seems that although everyone owns a microwave, nobody much cares for how food tastes coming out of one.

Health. Related to cooking are the health books, but while good cookbooks are always welcome, you'll find health and diet books are among the hardest sells in the used market. Absolutely nothing dates faster than a health book, and the trends come and go with such blinding speed they're impossible to follow. Unless you have a serious personal interest in the field and can stay on top of it, it's best to stay away from health, be it diet, exercise, or nutrition.

Self-Help. Psychology books are one of the hottest categories in many stores. For the foreseeable future, recovery books are probably the surest sale. It doesn't seem to matter much what the book purports to help you recover from. Classic titles in the psych field sell year after year after year—there will always be a good market for the works of Freud, Jung, Erickson, and their ilk. With psych books, often the more technical, the better. Psychiatrists read a lot, and they have the money to do so.

On the more popular side, M. Scott Peck's *The Road Less Traveled* has been on the best-seller list since the early eighties. *I'm O.K., You're O.K.* still sells. However, it's easy for a store to get overstocked on this sort of perennial. The men's movement, once worth a shelf in most stores, is as far gone as the dodo.

Buying psych can be risky unless you recognize the names of the main gurus. As with all categories, the classics are always a safe bet.

Religion. The same holds true for the New Age and religion categories. You need to have a good understanding of who's who. Crystal books trade well, as do books on witchcraft, druidism, and ritual. Dream interpretation tends to do better than past-life memories. Sri Aurobindo outsells Babaji. Yogananda outsells them both. In most stores, Eastern religion and philosophy well outsell European. If you're buying Christian religious titles, stay away from books published by Zondervan, Harvest House, and their ilk. These titles sell well in religious bookstores, but general trade bookstores tend to skip them. Better is theology interpretation and church history. Titles that present philosophies instead of espousing them, in other words.

Science. Good science and nature sell consistently. There are the classics—Darwin, Einstein, etc.—and the moderns such as Stephen W. Hawking and Douglas R. Hofstadter. Chaos theory sells well, as do philosophical interpretations of the implications of particle physics. Thanks to Edward O. Wilson, who won the Pulitzer for writing a thirty-pound book about ants, there has been a resurgence in good nature books, specific to certain animals. On the other hand, "save the world" books have hit a slump and aren't really moving anymore. Forget books on environmentalism.

Mass-market Paperbacks. Paperbacks—mass-market, or pocket, books—are another category entirely, one pretty much all to themselves. (Larger paperbacks are called *trade paperbacks*, and they're taking an increasing share of the market.) Fiction or nonfiction, the only mass-market paperbacks dealers are going to be happy to see are things that have been on the best-seller list in the past year, and classics. This is not a problem for you, because best-seller means just that, and the books are everywhere, ripe for the picking. Get good-condition copies—there's no reason to settle for less on a book with a million or so copies out—and stay away from any book whose spine is cracked. A good paperback should not fall open to any particular page, and you should never be able to see the glue of the binding from the inside of the book. All the pages have to be intact. If the binding itself is coming off an otherwise good copy (which does happen), Elmer's Glue will fix it up fine. Dab some along the spine, then keep it tight for a day or two by wrapping the whole book and cover in rubber bands. After it dries, the book is as good as new. Any noticeable flaw in the binding of a paperback means it's a dead book, and that's just dead weight you'll have to haul back out of the shops with you when you go to trade. Before you ever buy a paperback, pick the book up and flip through the pages. Virtually every flaw can be detected with a good flip. I've actually got a fair-sized callus on my thumb from flipping paperbacks, checking condition. It's the only way to be sure you're not wasting your money.

Paperback categories work the same as the hardback categories; you're simply dealing with lesser values. But you're also often dealing with books that are easier to get. There are some used bookshops that don't deal much in paperbacks—these tend to be the higher-priced stores leaning more toward the collector's market than the reader's market—but good paperbacks are still the backbone of the book industry. It's not at all hard to find someone willing to shell out trade credit for a nice, shiny paperback.

When you buy good books and avoid bad, three things are happening that are going to help your career as a scout and collector. First, you're building your reputation in the industry. In my shop, I have one scout who never brings in a title we've already got. He's in every week, and while someone is inspecting his trade, he's in the shelves, checking to see what we might need. He caters to us specifically. He brings in good literature, the occasional special item, and we never have to send him back out with more than one or two of the books he's brought in. He's been doing this for years, and we give him very special treatment because we want him to keep coming back. This is the same kind of treatment you want, and to get it you need the same kind of awareness. It'll also help when you've got specific requests that the local dealers are, hopefully, looking out for. They're going to be a lot more helpful to you if you're helpful to them. Stores take care of the people who take care of the store.

It's astounding how many people simply show up at a shop they've never been in before, hoping to sell their books off, assuming a bookstore is interested in everything that can be called a book. Sorry, but we have a business to run here. A little homework and research would save everyone a lot of trouble.

So once again, the point: the nicer you are, the nicer the dealer is going to be. Learn what the store wants and cater to it. It sounds a lot more obvious than experience teaches me it really is.

The second thing you're doing by trading with quality is building your trade credits. Every good book you bring in gives you more credit and gets you closer to the book you're really after.

There is also an intangible asset building here, one that nothing else can replace: you are handling more and more books. There is no better education in the book world than to handle a lot of books. Reading about them, finding out what's hot in the magazines, and talking to dealers, will only take you so far. You've got to put your hands on the product. The more books you get your hands on, the better you know books—any scout worth his salt can spot a book club edition from twenty paces. Likewise, the more you deal this way, the better you get to know the local markets, and, as a little bonus, the better chance you've got of hitting that big score while you're working the stacks looking for other material you can use. The best book job I ever had was handling stock for a huge but mediocre bookstore. A couple thousand titles a day went through my hands. I got to the point where I could tell almost to the week how quickly a book would sell, as well as the reasons for its success and failure. Working there also introduced me to the ins and outs of books and categories that I never would have looked at on my own. People who used to work for this company will get together and moan and groan about how awful it was, and how much we hated the place; and then, when we've calmed down, every single one of us admits that we learned more about books there than we ever could have anywhere else. You learn best when you handle the most books.

The Final Category. One final note when you're looking at books, hoping to sell or trade them. Ask yourself honestly: if I were interested in this subject, would I be interested in this book? If the answer is no, you can bet a store is going to have the same answer. It's a simple question that can save your back a lot of effort carrying deadweight books around.

BUILDING INVENTORY

Okay, now, where is all this trade coming from? I've told you what kind of books to look for (and perhaps more importantly, what not to look for), but I haven't told you how to actually acquire them.

Think snowball effect.

The funny thing is, the more books you trade, the more books you end up owning. Anybody seriously trying the methods I outline had better plan on building a few bookcases, because if you don't, you're going to have stacks and boxes all around the house soon. Not just of books you're collecting, either, but of hundreds, possibly thousands of books waiting for the right moment to be traded off. As you get further into the business, the deals and possibilities expand.

First you need some start-up stock: those books that are just taking up space can be used for better acquisitions. That novel you read once but have never looked at again? Get rid of it. Those art books you picked up while taking a class in college? Now's the time to put them to good use. Be as merciful or as merciless as you wish, but if you're like most bibliophiles, you can find quite a few books that you can honestly do without. That should get you off to a good start. If not, then the next place to turn is to the flea markets, garage sales, and the Salvation Army, as described in chapter 4.

Earlier, I said these were not good places for the serious book collector. They're not. But we're not shopping or collecting now, we're trading, and we're looking for acceptable fodder to trade. For this purpose, these places are a gold mine. For a quarter or fifty cents a book, you can pick up pieces that you can then turn around and trade to the dealers for at least triple, and often a lot more. One Saturday morning of running the local thrift stores should give you enough books and—if you're careful—quite a bit of change left over from a twenty-dollar bill—to get the first hundred-dollar deal you'll swing.

Clean your grandmother's attic; head to the flea market. It's time to start serious trading, and the less capital you tie up to begin with, the more you end up with in the end. The more acceptable books you can find cheap, the more your bottom line is going to be. Just remember the rules of what's desirable and acceptable—otherwise you might find yourself shut out of shops before you ever really get started.

PREPARING YOUR STOCK

Before you head to the dealers, you need to prepare your stock of books. Remember: clean books are good; very clean books are even better. I've had people bring in boxes of books for trade that have been floating in cat hair—in fact, in the middle of one trade, a friend and I pulled a cat's ear out of a box of books. I've talked to shops where they've found live scorpions, black widow spiders, and other assorted wildlife in boxes. And I've even sent people out of my stores because their books were simply too filthy.

So, to make your deal look more appealing, clean the books (see chapter 10), and arrange them neatly in the boxes. Do not carry your books around in trash bags. You want your stuff to look like garbage before anybody even sees what you've got?

To the dealer, it's unbelievably annoying to get a box into which the books have just been thrown haphazardly. It's a clear indication that there's nothing in the box worth the time it'll take to look at. If there once was something worthwhile, it's probably gotten damaged in transit.

If you have marginal books—and you probably do—spread them out over the boxes you're taking in. Don't put all the iffy stuff in one place, because then the buyer may not want to look at the other boxes.

If you have good hardback books that are still marginal, say classic but slightly outdated nonfiction, or fiction authors who are past their heyday and may or may not be worth their shelf space in the average shop, there is a very simple trick that almost always works to ensure that the dealer takes the book: put a protective jacket on it. This costs a little, but it often impresses the buyer. A wrapped book takes on a special aura, whether it is a special book or not. I've actually known scouts who have taken second editions of books from publishers where edition identification is tricky, wrapped them in jackets, and then hand-penciled in "1st Edition" and a high price. And I've known shops that have fallen for this morally appalling act, largely because an inexperienced buyer was drawn in by the shine of the wrapper.

A pretty book is a desirable book. Do what you can to make your trade prettier. Look over chapter 10 on cleaning and caring for books, and take a couple of minutes to spruce up your trade material. It's time well spent, because every shop knows the shiny book sells first. It's a never-fail axiom of the book industry. Don't always think, *"What can I sell this dealer?"* but also think, *"What can I supply to this dealer that he can sell quickly to his customers?"* If you're a customer in a store and see two identical items, don't you always pick the cleaner one, the one in better shape? Haven't you found yourself taking the second magazine in a stack, figuring the first has gotten bunged up from browsers? Everybody is like that. Book dealers know it, so give them clean stock they can sell fast. We're all in business here.

One more point often missed by book scouts: store personnel hate being hovered over while they evaluate your books. If you've got something special, point it out and then move on to browse the shelves. While it's good to start with a little conversation, once the buyer starts examining your trade, give him room. If you stand there and watch what he's doing, you might lose 10 or 20 percent, whether it's deliberate on the buyer's part or not. And if you've brought garbage and you stand over the buyer, trying to talk him into taking the books, you'll annoy him for sure, and most likely you'll be hauling those heavy boxes back out the door.

If you see something in your trade that the buyer passed on that you honestly believe the store could use, comment casually on it. Give the trader a valid reason why he wants to buy that book from you; nobody knows everything, and I've bought some great books and learned about some new subjects from people who knew their books better than I did.

That's the psychological warfare part of the trading game. Now it's time to move on to the actual battlefield.

PART THREE: IN THE STORE

Okay. Desirable books neatly packed in a clean box, maybe one or two of them wrapped in a protective jacket just for show (don't get too showy, or they start wondering what kind of nut wraps everything), it's time to go book shopping for real. Only this time, we're going to try not to spend any cash money. We're going to try to get everything on trade.

Remember, trade credit is always worth more than cash when you're dealing inside stores. The store will give you more for your books in trade than they will in cash, which lets you take better books back out (and hopefully trade them off somewhere else for even more), and trade also helps keep the money value in your business. We'll work on cash values later, at the end of the trade.

What I've tried to teach you so far is the craft of book scouting, the nuts and bolts. Now it's time for a little art.

There are two ways to work trades, and you'll need to do them both. The first is to simply build trade credit. You buy a book you know you can sell higher, take it to the store, and accept trade credit instead of cash. That way, when you see something you want, you're never paying cash. The second way is more focused: trading with a specific object in mind.

Both approaches require the same skills; in fact, working the second way is a lot easier if you've been working the first way for a while.

The longer you've been doing this, the easier it will be to swing a deal where you need to move nine hundred dollars' worth of books; if you've been doing this for a while, you've probably already got that kind of credit available.

Now, this does not mean you should dump enormous amounts of stock on a shop at one time, simply to get it over and done with. From the store's point of view, they'd rather see you come in with five or six little piles over the course of several weeks, than one huge pile that ties them up for several hours. If you bring in a huge box of stuff, they'll start looking for a reason to send most of it home with you. The store might be intimidated by the amount of cash or space a huge deal requires. It is easier for them to absorb a smaller quantity. You will get a better deal and better treatment if you trade in small lots. Thirty to fifty books is an ideal trade size.

WHEELING AND DEALING

Now you're ready to wheel and deal. Suppose you're at the counter, and you have $20 in trade, and you want a $23 book. How important is that percentage of difference?

find books cheaply. As you are dealing, keep in mind the Rule of Three: a book has to be worth three times what you paid for it (at retail) in order for you to make any money. If you paid $5 for it then the dealer must price the book at $15 on his shelf. If he only prices the book at ten dollars, you break even, because trade credit is usually half shelf price. If he prices the book at $15, you will get $7.50 from him in trade, a net gain of $2.50.

By the same token, if you now take one of ABC's books from its shelves for $7.50 worth of your credit, you'd better make sure that it's really worth closer to $25. The leaps required by the Rule of Three get both harder and easier (depending on what the local stores miss) as prices increase.

You have to be thinking of trading up at all times; otherwise, entropy is going to eat away your stock and you'll wind up with nothing.

At ABC, you drop off your history, take your trade credit, and then, having already pre-scouted the shelves, pick up some books that you know BCD Books is going to want. BCD specializes in mystery, and although ABC carries it, they don't really care about it, and so you've got some prime pickings here. Your fifty books that you walked in with have perhaps changed to a dozen or so books, but those books have increased greatly in value while you've picked over the shelves.

And so the process goes on. Trade in what's wanted, take out what isn't. Keep in mind the Rule of Three at all times, and remember that you can nearly always sweeten the pot with some good paperbacks or solid nonfiction.

However, once you've figured out the chain you're going to follow, don't narrow your focus too much. Okay, I'm taking mystery out of BCD, but since I'm looking to trade for modern lit by the end of this process, I'd be a fool not to look at their lit shelves. No telling what may turn up. The earlier in the chain you can find items for the end of the chain, the better your

The point is, you're taking out a book, so the shopkeeper is happy, because he knows a few dollars is nothing in trade. Especially if he sees you all the time, knows he's going to see you again, and knows you bring in good material. His profit margin is already assured. It's all the better assured if he keeps you, a valued customer, happy. So with just a wink and a nudge, you can possibly bump yourself a healthy percentage in trade values.

Not every dealer is going to go for this, of course. Some would rather lose a sale than budge an inch. But there are no fixed prices in most stores because of the trade margin for profit. A little flexibility is always better from the dealer's point of view than losing a sale over a couple of percentage points, especially with the trade margin so generous. If you're dealing with a particularly large or small store, then that potential margin becomes even greater, for the simple reason that, in the large store, the person you're talking to has no idea how much was originally paid for the book in question, and in the small store, the person you're talking to knows exactly how much was paid. Both of these work in your favor: in the big store, they're likely to swing some generous deals out of not knowing; in the small store, if the dealer knows he got the book in for practically nothing, the same deals are possible.

Knowing this has the same effect as sprucing up your books some before you bring them in; it's playing the margins, looking for that little bit extra. It doesn't necessarily mean the difference between failure and success, but it can mean quite a few extra dollars or nice books on your side of the deal in the long run.

One other place to look for an extra percentage point or two: many (but not all) stores code their books in some way, so they know how long a particular item has been on the shelf. Most shops use a one- or two-letter code placed near the price, indicating the year and the quarter the book first came in. This is vital information for the shop, because it helps them to spot mistakes and trends, and control buying. It also helps them decide when to put the book in a clearance sale.

Now, if there are two identical copies of a book you want on the shelf, and you know how to read the code, you can pick up the older one and say, "Gee, it looks like this has been on the shelf awhile, any chance of getting a buck or two knocked off?" Most of the time, the dealer, seeing the old book, will gladly come down, just to move it out before he has to junk it or price it at a quarter on the rack outside the front door.

How do you learn the codes? The easy way is to ask. They're not a trade secret. Bring up a book, point out the code, and ask what it means. If being direct doesn't work, trade in some books, then come back later, find your books on the shelf, and see how they're coded. Compare that to other books on the shelf. If yours have a C on them, and the ones nearby are all B's and it's April 3rd, there's a pretty safe bet that the first quarter of the year was B in the coding system. Find a Z—that should be last fall. The shops aren't trying cryptography here, they're simply keeping track of their stuff.

Of course, you can only push wheeling and dealing so far. Your success at it depends not only upon your own personality, but also on the personality and mood of the dealer. Don't push your luck. Put out gentle feelers, and see how it goes. You're in this for the long run, and there's plenty of time to work up connections with dealers that will help you push the margins a little further.

TRADING UP

Now, if you've been taking books in to favored stores on a regular basis, you should be running a credit balance in your favor, ready to go toward that fine piece when it shows up.

If I've been doing this for a while, I'm not faced with the task of dumping nine hundred in retail on a shop all at once to get what I want, but rather I've got a hundred or two or even more

already on file, and, most importantly, I've already been trading up.

Now it's time to trade up again, building on what has gone before. But this time you have a particular book that you want, one you need for your collection or you have a known customer for. This is where the fun begins.

For example, suppose XYZ Books has a first edition of W. Somerset Maugham's *Of Human Bondage* that you want. XYZ has a slightly low $450 price tag on it because the local market is soft. You have a lot of books, but no money. You also know someone in another town who's willing to pay as much as $600 for this particular book in excellent condition. XYZ's is truly lovely, bright and crisp. So what you are going to do here is buy a $450 book and make $150 profit without paying much money for it.

Let's say that after getting to know the local stores, you've got a list of five that are worth concentrating on. Start at the one with the fewest books you're interested in, but with the highest prices, which is ABC Books. They've got good history, great literature, and prices 20 percent higher than anywhere else in town. You've only ever bought one or two books here, because you keep hoping you can find the same book cheaper somewhere else.

This is a great place to start because, first of all, you won't be tempted to cut a deal right then and there without looking toward moving up. It's also a good place to start because if they price high, maybe they're going to buy high. Maybe not, but it's worth a try.

You go into the store with two boxes of books, fifty titles in all, heavy on the history. Remember, you should have already scouted out the store, and now you must try to make your offer fit with what they want. They want history, so give them history.

The history books you're offering have come from other sales, off your own shelves, from wherever you've been able to

potential profit. Know what your next step is, but don't be afraid to skip it if the chance arises.

This sounds complicated at first, but after a while, you're so used to the local market that it becomes second nature. In chapter 4, I told you to keep a notebook of the type of books each store wants. This is where that work pays off. If you have a network built and understand the local stores, you should be able to keep your trades on an upward spiral.

In my town, there is a specific store where I always start my trades. They make no effort to sell expensive titles (at least not so far as they know), and show no interest in learning what is expensive elsewhere, so there are some great deals here. On a good day, I can gather enough material to trade for almost anything I want anywhere else in town.

It's important when you're working on a series of trades like this one to have a plan. Work it out in advance. As much as possible, know exactly what books you're going to be trading for, and exactly what you're going to be taking in and out of each store in the chain. The better you have it planned out in advance, the better chance you have of getting what you want for minimal outlay.

Odds are, the first few times you try this, you're going to fail somewhere along the line, which is understandable. Don't worry about it. If you understand your own mistakes, it's a lot easier for you to find mistakes other people are making, and to profit from them. Keep records of each trade in your notebook (the only way you'll ever know just how much a particular deal ended up at real cost, the actual amount of money your trade material cost), and then if things fall apart, go back over the steps you've taken and see if you can figure out where the breakdown occurred. Did you trade with a cheap store too late in the cycle? Trading expensive books with a store that prides itself on being the cheapest in the city can kill the trading-up process. Did you take the wrong category of books to a store, and so lose out that way?

Work up to the huge deals. On your first tries, you might want to work up only a two- or three-store chain, trying to get a forty- or fifty-dollar book. Learn what you're doing before you get too ambitious.

So the chain builds. You have traded books in one, two, or ten shops if necessary. You've been building trade credit, and taking out books that you know the next store in the chain is going to want, or, where possible, books that will find their last home at the store with the Maugham.

Finally, you're ready to go after the Maugham. Because the store that has it specializes in modern literature, you should have been trading your way into prime modern lit.

Remember, you're going to need at least $900 (retail) worth of books to trade out for that Maugham for $450.

Which leads us to a slight digression: is it worth it, or is it better to take the money and run?

CASH OR TRADE

Before you take out that lovely *Of Human Bondage*, stop and ask the simple question: Could you have made more by taking cash for the books you traded up for? Have you shuffled around a ton of books when you could have gotten the same amount of money by cashing out earlier?

Remember, you have a sure buyer for the Maugham, lined up and ready to pay $600. If you get the book for $450 in trade, you're making $150 profit, in addition to any trade credit left in the stores you've been dealing with. To get that $150, you've shuffled probably more than a thousand dollars' worth of books.

But that's $150 cash above the trade value of what you've put in; it really has nothing at all to do with the amount of cash you've invested. If you've done this right, you should have spent less than $100 of your own money. You've been letting the books do the work and make the money. That means your true profit is around $500, not $150.

How much more profitable for the store is trade over cash? As an example, suppose the average customer brings in a book the shop is going to sell for $20. They give her $10 in trade for it, and she selects a nice $10 book to take home. She's happy, and the store is happy.

Why is the store happy? Think: how much did they pay for that $10 book the nice lady just took home? Five dollars, which may not actually have been $5, but a $5 book that they took in for $2.50 in trade. The profitability of a used bookstore depends upon this kind of reductio ad absurdum, where the amount that has actually been paid out gets smaller and smaller. It's the only way used bookstores can afford to pay their light bills.

But the question is, could you have gotten more money if you'd simply sold off the items you were trading for, instead of going for the Maugham book? Not a chance. You've moved, say, $1,000 worth of books. That's $500 in *trade*, the same as your true cash total on the Maugham deal, or, at best, $300 in cash. Likely, rather less.

Why less? Because if you own a used bookshop, you don't have a lot of cash to spare, and paying cash is not nearly as profitable as trading.

The cash policies of stores vary greatly. A high average might be roughly one-third of the resale value of the book. That is, if they're going to sell the book for ten dollars, they'll give you three in cash.

But that's high. Few shops are that generous. More likely, cash is one-half to one-third of the *trade* value. Which means for your $10 book, you might get between $1.50 and $2.50.

It gets worse. Because cash hurts, a lot of stores will not pay cash on every book that they would offer trade on.

Used bookshops hate to pay out cash for books for several simple reasons: first, that's an expenditure that has to be immediately covered by sales. Pay out cash, and immediately your cash flow is down. Second, the idea for the store is to get you, the customer, to leave more in the store than you take out (of course, your goal is to take out more than you bring in, but you do that by paying the store's price on items they didn't know were worth more; that way, everybody is making their money). They can't do that with cash. When you walk out with cash in your hand, they've lost business. There's a corollary to that, as well: if you're taking out trade, the store knows it has a customer, someone who will come back. If you take out cash, you're nothing more than a supplier, so there's no point in treating you as well as they would a customer, since customers are more valuable to the store than suppliers and, thankfully in this business, more numerous. Finally, the store can always get books on trade, which is a lot less risky and a lot more profitable than paying you cash to bring in your books.

Especially on paperbacks, the cash value could be so low as to make it not worth your trouble. Stores see mass-market paperbacks all the time, and it's not at all unusual for a store either to refuse to pay cash for them, or to offer only a dime or a quarter—garage-sale prices. If you've gotten any of your trade in paperbacks, you can very likely lose a lot of the value if it gets converted to cash.

So if I've been trading up a mix of paperbacks and better books, my cash value should be between $75 and $100. If I've been trading, and figure that I spent $50 to buy my trade stock, and another $20 on gas, I haven't done myself much good, have I? Compare that to the Maugham deal, and you see the wisdom of holding out for trade rather than cash.

TRADING VARIATIONS

Now, let's examine a variation on this theme, one that can lead to greater profits.

Maugham is a writer who's trading at close to peak value for the moment. Although he's a blue-chip stock in the book world, his books are not going to make any drastic moves on the market, because most who collect him have done so for some time. There's not a lot of new blood or money being pumped into the Maugham market, and that cuts down on the potential for your deal, despite the great man's reputation and quality. He's never going to go down in value, but don't go pricing Cadillacs hoping for a bull market. Your profit was assured because you were getting the novel either for yourself or for a known buyer, but now let's say you don't have a buyer. Could you make more money simply by choosing a different book to trade up for?

It's entirely possible. But it's a matter of timing.

Let's suppose, for the same money, you could get *"B" Is for Burglar*, Sue Grafton's second Kinsey Millhone novel. Her first book, *"A" Is for Alibi*, sells for upwards of a thousand dollars now, but you can pick up *"B"* for half that. Of course, these are first editions in Fine condition.

Which is the better buy? The Maugham, which is a timeless classic, for which there will always be a steady market, or the Grafton, which is riding the waves of the author's popularity?

Just like people who invest in the stock market, now you're going to have to indulge in a little market timing.

Strikes against the mystery novel: it's her second, which is never as good as the first; her character has started, in the more recent books, to undergo some strong personality changes, which could affect the market for the new books and have a kickback effect on the value of the older books; the prices, for something as recent as these books, are close to ludicrous. For the price of *"A" Is for Alibi*, you could buy a couple of Kiplings. Who's the world going to remember longer, Grafton or Kipling?

I'm not biased, but I've got to think Kipling. Okay, so maybe I am biased.

On the other hand, Kipling, like Maugham, is trading close to his peak right now. The market is stable. As with any other commodity, you've got to strike when the iron is hot.

Right now, mysteries are hot. And that fact means more than

any other problem with the Grafton book, because you're going to be able to sell it faster and easier than the Maugham or a Kipling. If you want to sit on it for a while and risk your sense of timing, the payoff can be even more considerable.

So let's say you pick up the Grafton book instead of the Maugham, and shop it around town a little. Dealers are offering you about $250 for it knowing that they can turn it around very quickly. The Maugham is going to sit on the shelves, and may get you offers of $150–$200. With a little wheeling and dealing, you can probably get the shop's offer on the Grafton up close to $300 for the book, double what the Maugham would have made you.

While it's always good to have those classic titles that will sit and draw prestige to the store, people are always willing to deal more when the money is closer.

Now, selling the Grafton to a dealer for $300 still brings you a lower profit than if you had a collector lined up, as I did in the Maugham example above. There, I made $500. But if I hadn't had the collector, I would have sold the Maugham to a dealer for, say, $175, and my end profit, after expenses, would have been maybe $100. On the Grafton, I've made $200. These are *cash* values. Trade profit depends on how well you worked the deal. Later in this book, I'll show you how to line up collectors and end buyers so that you're always getting full value from your books, instead of making money for dealers.

FINAL PROBLEMS

Time for a few last complications. Over and over I have stressed the importance of maintaining a good relationship with dealers. Now for the reason why, and it's not exactly one that makes good sense: they don't want you to trade up to the good stuff.

Part of it is simple prestige. A true book lover would rather have a $500 book sitting permanently on the shelf than have fifty $10 books fly out the door. Everybody has the $10 books. The $500 piece sets the store apart, giving it a special aura.

Part of it is a matter of offense. What gives you the right to come in here and walk out with a $500 book when all you've brought in is a bunch of stuff I could find anywhere else?

Or sometimes the dealer is irrationally attached to a piece. I once offered a dealer a copy of *Mortal Stakes*, a $200 book by Robert B. Parker, in trade for Agatha Christie's *A Murder Is Announced*, a $100 book. He wouldn't go for it. "I know this doesn't make sense," he said, "because I end up with a two-hundred-dollar book and that makes me a hundred dollars ahead, but I can't do it." To him the Christie was a more desirable piece. I'd argue, but it was his shop.

But that was then. This is now. He knows me now. He'd do it now. Not because he wanted to—he'd still rather have the more famous Christie than the Parker (if only because all bets are still off on whether or not Parker will ever regain his old form and so escalate or drop in price accordingly)—but because he's trying to keep me happy and he knows I'll be back.

All the dealing I've outlined in this chapter is, in a very real sense, taking advantage of the rules. The shop has to offer you trade, and the books on their shelves are up for grabs. Their only way around this is to establish explicit store policy of no trade on the hot stuff, or marking certain books "net." And sometimes even then the books are not really for sale, at least not that day. There are high-end stores that will never trade for anything, ever, and all deals have to be cash.

You can't get around any of this unless they know you. And not always then.

You will find many stores have a policy that keeps you from trading for the good stuff: they'll have different levels of trade, or they'll simply take only cash for some items. It's a way of protecting stock that the store has had to lay out more for. You've got a couple of possible ways around this: first, bring in such good trade that there's no way the shopkeep can resist (doubtful, but possible), or second, convert to cash there or elsewhere, and pay for the prize item. It makes your job harder, but not at all impossible.

This is why I've stressed the importance of bringing in the best stuff possible. The shopkeeper is going to be a lot less cranky about letting the prime book go if he's getting good, salable items in return, as opposed to midline stuff he sees a hundred times a day.

Your goal is to acquire the maximum number of fine books with the minimum cash outlay. Always make sure you have more trade than you need. Never figure on the big-ticket item and stop there, because you have to be ready for the impulse purchase when you stumble across a real find. It's using the same logic that decreed building up excess credit to begin with. This is how your collection is going to build, and this is how you're going to get great items to deal. If you have trade credit or tradable books left after a big score, use them. Sometimes you get a second chance, but you can't count on it. Plan for future trades every minute you're in the shop.

Chapter Six

SPOTTING TRENDS
AND PICKING
AUTHORS

Now we know that, given an equal opportunity to sell a piece, you may be better off going for a modern writer than a classic writer. That's how the Grafton brought in more money than the Maugham.

But why? People have been reading Maugham longer than Grafton has been alive. They'll probably still be reading him when her books are used for firewood. Why is she worth more money?

The question here is a deep and serious one, one vital to your success: what makes a writer valuable and desired? Why are some writers collected avidly, while others fall by the wayside, with or without a brief moment in the sun?

START WITH WHAT YOU LOVE

Do you have a favorite author, someone whose books you buy the instant they hit the bookstores? If the author has any measure of fame, and if you've been following this author for a few years, there's a reasonable chance you have several valuable first editions on your shelves. I bought my first Ann Beattie book because it looked interesting; it's still interesting, but now it's also fairly expensive. Some new writers' books can shoot up $100 or more within months of publication.

This kind of collection-building happens by sheer luck, but nevertheless it happens all the time: you see a book by an author you've never heard of, pick it up because it looks interesting, and you're hooked. If you're lucky, it was the author's first novel. A little less lucky, the second. If your curiosity had been piqued by Tom Clancy's first book, *The Hunt for Red October*, when it first came out, you'd have a seven- to nine-hundred-dollar book on your shelf now, depending on its condition. If you're a collector just now coming to Clancy, buying that first book is going to hurt. The sooner you know who you like, the better off you are.

The rest of this chapter is going to show you how to spot up-and-coming authors and how to anticipate trends in the market. Although, like gambling, much depends on luck, this information will at least lower the odds and increase your chances for success.

To begin, think about the writers you've been buying for years. Odds are, other people love these same writers too, and that may make them collectible; it may mean there's a viable market for them.

Remember that what you love is your strength, and one of the best routes to success for a book scout. You're already enthusiastic about the author or the genre; and because you've already got the background you need to be successful, it's a lot easier than trying to watch for trends.

So one simple answer to the question of what to look for is this: what you're interested in. What you'd buy anyway. The best—and most valuable—collections are built from the love of your subject.

Of course, collecting is an expensive passion. It costs me more than my monthly house payment, considerably more. I've seen people drop two and three thousand dollars in under an hour, picking up good stacks of modern firsts for their collections.

How do we pay for this? I've found one of the easiest ways to pay for my own collection is simply to buy two copies of everything. Sometimes three or four copies. I do buy carefully, picking multiples of books I think will increase, but then I have the books I love, and when I sell them I'm spreading them around to other people, hoping they will love them, too.

That said, in case that's not enough for you, I'll try to broaden the field a little.

TRENDS

Like all other fields, the book market moves in cycles. While, for example, John Galsworthy was the hottest writer around fifty years ago, you can find his books easily now for pennies on the dollar of what they used to sell for. F. Scott Fitzgerald, on the other hand, was much ignored in the decades after his death, and his books, grossly expensive now, could have been purchased cheap in the forties.

There is more short-term money in spotting trends than there is in buying classic writers, but there is also a lot more risk. Trends come and go, while the classic authors move slowly but steadily.

Which is one of the reasons why it's important, even in books you're planning to deal, to buy things you like. There's no telling when you'll get stuck with them. If you're a collector, forget about trends and values, and simply buy what you love. You can never go wrong doing that. Dealers have to look at things a bit differently.

What you must remember is that all hot books have their day, and that day almost invariably comes to an end, sooner or later. If you're buying a book for resale, not just for collecting, it's important that you constantly monitor the price guides and the catalogs and the Internet for fluctuations in value. Particularly with the hypermodern books published within the last decade, it's all too easy to hold on to a book too long, or to pay too much for something that's liable to drop. Speculators, not collectors, are absolutely running amok in the hypermodern arena. For example: thanks to the popularity of John Dunning's mystery *Booked to Die*, speculators were paying $150 and up for advance copies of Dunning's second novel in the series, *The Bookman's Wake*. But is that a good investment? If you're a Dunning collector, yes, you're getting a book you want. But is there a lasting interest? For the same price you can buy works by writers who are much more likely to still be read in the next century.

On the other hand, nothing jumps in price quite like a genre title—until it stops jumping.

And five years after *The Bookman's Wake* came out, you can probably pick up the ARC for an easy fifty bucks. A lot of people took a gamble and lost on that one. I saw people pay upwards of $800 for *The Bridges of Madison County* when the movie came out, sure they were buying a blue-chip; you'd be very lucky if you could sell one for $200 now. When the value drops and books start falling, everybody dumps their copies onto the market, and the bottom just keeps getting lower and lower.

If I were in for long-term appreciation, I would have skipped the Dunning completely and gotten a T. S. Eliot or a Gertrude Stein or a Graham Greene. I'd stick with the people who've been around for a while. There's not a whole lot of difference in the price. I got the Dunning because I wanted it. I also got my first of Eliot's *Four Quartets* because I wanted it. That saves me a lot of worry about whether I'll ever make a profit out of them. It's an elitist attitude, perhaps a luxurious attitude, but I try never to buy anything I won't be perfectly happy to be stuck with if the deals fall through.

Of course, thanks to careful planning and trend watching, the deals almost never do.

GENRE FICTION AND SPECIALIZATION

As I have said repeatedly, the best thing you can do for yourself is specialize. You don't have to specialize in a period, no matter what you collect, but you do need to specialize in a genre.

If you're a modern lit lover, it's a lot easier to keep track of a dozen or so up-and-coming authors than it is to keep track of every author of the six thousand or so novels that are published every year, in fields ranging from romance to science fiction. While other people will specialize in the same area—for instance, right now mysteries are probably the hottest field, and the arena is crowded with dealers—no one will ever know quite the same things you do. Right now, I can go into stores specializing in modern lit and almost surely pick up Jayne Anne Phillips, Ellen Gilchrist, Amy Hempel, or one of a dozen other women writers. Although these authors are working successfully in the modern lit field, they're not getting as much attention as T. Coraghessan Boyle, Tim O'Brien, or other comparable male writers. That doesn't mean there's not a market for them. Although there are fewer specialists in this area, there are dealers who handle these women writers, and I can make my money while buying and selling authors I love to read.

But modern women writers are not the trend. While there's money to be made, I can make a lot more by riding a trend. Because, as I said in chapter 4, booksellers, just like good book scouts, also specialize. If I take a copy of Jayne Anne Phillips's *The Secret Country*, a lovely limited edition, into a store that has never heard of her, I'm not going to get much value for my book. I've got to find a specialist.

But if I want to make more money, if I want to expand the number of titles I'm handling, I've also got to know who's not a specialist. That's where you start catching the latest trend, and that's why you've been keeping your notebook with the strengths and weaknesses of local dealers. General-title stores must keep up with the trends and adapt to them if they're to survive. If everyone is buying science fiction, most general stores will increase their stock of Isaac Asimov, Ray Bradbury, and Robert Silverberg.

But although the shops have to go where the money is, it may not be what they're interested in. And they may not really know what they're doing. Every used bookstore in the country has been expanding its mystery section over the past decade. If you specialize in mysteries, there is no time like the present to cash in. Okay, they know Agatha Christie, but do they know George C. Chesbro or Randy Wayne White? If you know your specialty and they don't quite, here's your opportunity.

This is one sure way to spot a trend and to capitalize on it: when you start seeing a subject everywhere, it's a safe bet that half the people displaying it don't know what they're doing.

Find what you're happy with, find what you love, and get ready to enjoy yourself. Sooner or later, your time will come.

LIVING IN THE GENRE WORLD

If I read mysteries, I don't have to have any Tony Hillerman books on my shelf to know which titles I can sell elsewhere. Or I may love modern lit, but not be particularly interested in Saul Bellow. Still, I'm not going to pass up a first of *Henderson the Rain King*. And the fact that I'm already in the mystery and lit section will make it easier to find these great authors, whatever genre I've chosen as my field.

I use the term *genre* advisedly, because genres are where the money is and where the trends go. Mainstream authors, those people you see in the supermarkets and chain bookshops with the huge displays by the window, are not terribly collectible. It's the subfields (modern literature and the "serious" writers are considered to be a subfield) that are collected most. The best-seller general fiction titles tend to be ignored by collectors; besides, there are usually so many firsts of Sidney Sheldon, Danielle Steel, Clive Cussler, and other perennial best-selling authors that, at least beyond their first or second book, their market value is nil. A few years back, *Firsts* magazine did a study of the collectibility of number one best-sellers, and found that, almost across the board, they stank.

Mystery, modern lit, science fiction, and children's books are the hottest genres. Poetry is very collectible, but the market is small, and since most printings of poetry books are very, very small, it can be a difficult field to collect. Horror has a strong following, but the number of findable authors is small; you have to look deeply into the specialist/small press market to get far. Romance is almost never collected, partly because of the marketing strategies of the publishers, the readers they aim at, and partly because very few of the titles are ever published in hardback. (In nonfiction, where it's not a matter of genre, but of subject, there are strong collectible markets for regional titles, cookbooks, travel—although primarily only works from early twentieth century and earlier—and art.)

Genres are actually a fairly late development in the book publishing industry. While in the nineteenth century there were certainly genre works being written—think of Edgar Allan Poe as the originator of both the horror tale as we know it and the detective story—they were simply lumped into the mainstream. They were "writings," and an author could move through whatever subject matter he or she felt comfortable with. Wilkie Collins wrote serious literature and lighthearted mysteries. Charles Dickens wrote novels of social commentary, as well as ghost stories. It was only in the years following World War I that genres became more clearly defined, with specialty publications like the old pulp magazines.

In the decades since, genre fiction has grown to where a hundred books with nearly identical covers compete frantically for your attention during the three weeks of shelf life they're allowed in the shops before the next onslaught of new books arrives. Many writers who seek to go outside the genres where they are established find huge resistance, both from readers as well as publishers.

Although this is unfortunate for authors who pour their heart and soul into their work, it is an opportunity for you. First printings, especially of first novels, are generally small, because publishers know bookshops won't devote much space (if any) to an unknown, and because of the economic uncertainty. Shelf space is at a premium in shops, and a bookseller is more likely to give the new Robert Ludlum a lot more space by displaying ten sure-selling copies of that than shelving a single copy of the first novel by an unknown.

Of course, next year when the unknown's second novel hits the best-seller list, the few people who were able to find copies of his first novel and who were wise enough to buy it are going to consider themselves very lucky. That was the case with Michael Connelly, whose first novel, *The Black Echo*, came and went despite critical acclaim. It was only with the second in the series, *Black Ice*, that his name became well known. This pattern repeats itself endlessly. First novels are difficult to choose, and even harder to find. And many people won't pick up a first novel in hardcover, because they simply don't know what they're in for. When you buy the new Katherine Kurtz, if you've read her others, you're pretty sure what you're getting yourself into. New writers are a risk, both emotionally—there you are with a book you want to love, but what if it turns out to be a dud?—and, from the dealer's point of view, financially.

However, from the dealer's point of view, there is also nothing more profitable than the first novel of an author who later makes it big. William Gibson's first novel, *Neuromancer*, created the cyberpunk genre in science fiction; it was originally published in paperback, and if you can find a copy in good shape, that's an easy $100. If you can find a copy of the later hardback edition, first printed in Britain, you're looking at upwards of $500. Your original investment, had you bought them new on the shelf, would have been about $4 for the paperback or $15 for the hardback (actually, just under £9).

So if you can get advance information (see chapter 12), find out who's up-and-coming, you're ahead of the game, because you'll know to head straight for these new literary lights. You can get your copies before anyone else has heard of them, and along the way you'll discover the joy of coming across new writers and supporting them at the beginning of their careers.

What makes a trend? Right now, perhaps nothing so much as a hit film. *The Silence of the Lambs* created a new market for serial killer books; the novel the film was based on had done well, but those sales did not compare to the way the book took off after the film. The same can be said about nature books, before and after *A River Runs Through It*. Norman Maclean wrote two books in his lifetime; that was the first, and if you can find a copy in the first edition, expect it to cost. And on his coattails rode other authors: no matter how good Gretel Ehrlich is, would her book *A Match to the Heart* have gotten nearly the attention it did had Maclean not paved the way?

Watch for cycles. Watch for books in new categories. Some writers have a strong enough vision that they are undefinable, and these writers tend to be especially collectible in their early works. Tom Clancy and William Gibson are two prime examples I've mentioned elsewhere. Both dealt with the effects of technology, but in rather different ways. Another writer who broke out of convention in the same way is Neil Stephenson, whose third solo novel, *Snow Crash* (he did a couple little nothings before, including a campus sex comedy novel), blended computer science with martial arts and pizza delivery. In a more classical vein, what makes Thomas Pynchon so collectible is that he did what no one else had ever done before: he made paranoia funny. He made you believe in alligators in the sewers. At the other end of the reality spectrum, Richard Brautigan made you believe that life was, ultimately, pretty darn funny. His novels were more like prose poems, truly original works, and Brautigan is highly collectible today.

Watch for what's new, for who's on the cutting edge, because even if you look at classic collectible books, you'll see that those authors, too, were pushing the envelope. That's what has made them worthwhile for so long: Hemingway's restrained prose; Steinbeck's social consciousness. T. S. Eliot reinvented poetry, as did Allen Ginsberg. That's why their books are still sought after, still read and discussed. These people knew how to write, and high quality is a rare and wonderful thing. Especially in a young novelist, in a first book. Read Kirstin Bakis's *Lives of the Monster Dogs*, gasp in wonder, and wait anxiously for her to write again. Quality is ultimately what works. *The Silence of the Lambs* created the serial killer trend because it was a really, really spooky book. The horror market boomed on the coattails of Stephen King's *The Shining*. These are all writers who did something different and marvelous.

While you want to find the cutting-edge authors, if you're buying trends, it's equally important to see who's trying to follow. No one has managed to be collectible in the techno-thriller arena except Clancy. This despite the production of enough titles in the genre to sink a battleship. Nobody was able to do anything different with the genre. You can only make an M-16 just so sexy. On the other hand, Bruce Sterling (whose cyberpunk novel, *Outfield Kid* actually predates *Neuromancer*, but he gets none of the credit for inventing the genre that Gibson does) rides comfortably on Gibson's reputation in science fiction's cyberpunk subgenre, and tramped a few new trails of his own along the way, and so is highly collected. Same with Neil Stephenson. Many of the Beat authors are collectible simply because of the writer's association with Ginsberg or Kerouac; while many of them cut new trails—Gregory Corso is a fine example—many others simply stayed along for the ride. In other words, watch for the trailblazers, keep an eye on prime secondary writers, and ignore the sheep. Again, to use the Beats as an example, close to forty years since the publication of Ginsberg's *Howl*, there are more sheep following the Beats than there are cropping grass in New Zealand. Just sit in on any university poetry class to find out how true this is. And so while the sheep imitators imitate, other poets—Sharon Olds, Carolyn Forche, Rita Dove, Adrienne Rich, and dozens more—cut their own path. If you're knowledgeable about your genre, it will be easy to sort out who falls into which category.

How else can you find who's at the edge, who's starting the trends? Carl Hiaasen started the Florida mystery craze; by the mid-1990s, it seemed like half the mysteries being published were set in Florida. But how many of them were good? Few. Very few.

Which brings up another point: you're not going to be any good at this if you don't read what you deal. Learning names isn't going to cut it, because how else would you know that, say, James Hall, although his stories move along pretty well, is never going to be really collectible? He's making a fine living on the Florida mystery craze, but there isn't that flair of originality that makes an author sought after. Certainly nothing as original as Hiaasen feeding tourists to alligators in his first novel. Hall may come into his own later, but the odds are against it.

Then there are authors who are made into trends by outside forces. When *Granta* magazine named its twenty top young authors, their stock boomed. Prices for their books doubled overnight, and a whole new category of collecting—the *Granta* list completist—was born.

The point is, read every book you have time to read. The average person reads about seven books a year, but a bookseller once told me that if you read a hundred books a year, you're addicted; if you read two hundred a year, you're a dealer. There's no other way to keep up. If you don't read, how can you expect to know what's happening?

THE RISE OF THE HYPERMODERN, THE PEAK OF THE CLASSIC

It's common for people to think older books are, by nature, more expensive than newer books. But they're not; they're simply older. In fact, for the most part, newer books are considerably more expensive than the classics, as they are driven up in price by a speculator's market. For the price of Minette Walters's first novel, you could buy half a dozen Graham Greenes. For what people are paying for Cormac McCarthy's signature on a copy of *The Crossing*, published in 1994, you could buy two first editions of D. H. Lawrence's *Sons and Lovers*, which has been on the short list of classics since it first appeared in 1913.

This remarkable rise in price of the hypermoderns offers both the most profitable and the riskiest area for both dealers and collectors. The reputation of a hypermodern writer hinges on very little work—often a single book—and while his or her stock can soar through the roof, it can also, without warning, plummet through the cellar.

The classic authors are already established. This means several things: first, that the market for them is already stable. If you're looking to finance your collecting by picking up underpriced writers and selling them higher, you're going to be pretty much out of luck with the classics. They tick along slowly, gain-ing 5 or 10 percent a year. Everybody knows who they are, and it's a safe bet that anytime a Robert Frost book of poetry goes through a used bookstore, someone on the staff checks to see if it's a first edition. Mistakes do happen, oversights do occur with the classics, but they're few and far between. On the other hand, because of the ever-shifting market for the hypermoderns, mistakes are common, oversights a daily occurrence.

The next thing about the classics is that, because the market for them is already established, the prices are a lot steadier than in the volatile hypermodern market. This stability is a boon for the collector. It's usually safe to wait a year or so to buy, looking for a better copy, knowing nothing dramatic is going to happen to the price. But such stability is a bust for the dealer. The prices are not going anywhere. You've got almost no hope of making the Rule of Three on a cash deal with a classic. If you're picking it up in trade, okay. But the classic bought for $500 today is likely to be worth no more than $550 a year from today. Barring a complete reinterpretation of an author's career, which is rare, the classics are steady and stable. On the other hand, it's really quite easy to pick up a hypermodern for a few dollars and turn it around for a few hundred.

So consider classics to be the blue-chip stocks of the book market, and hypermoderns the risky penny stocks. A stockbroker will tell you that you never lose money in the long run if you stick to blue chips. There may be some fluctuations, but if you stay in ten years, twenty years, you are guaranteed a healthy return. That's what classics are like in the book world. For the happy collector watching her beloved volumes increase in value every year, this is a wonderful fact; for the dealer who has a car payment looming, there may not be time to wait. The dealer has to take the risk. When it pays off, it can pay off big. And the initial investment is so low, you don't get stuck with much if your gamble fails.

So if you're looking for a quick turnaround, or to trade up

to a classic without moving truckloads of books, you're going to need to move into the hypermoderns.

This doesn't mean you have to leave your genre, even if every writer you really like is dead. All you have to do is look for other writers moving along the same lines, but still blazing new trails. If Raymond Chandler is a classic, Stephen Greenleaf is a hypermodern following in Chandler's footsteps. So is Michael Stone. So is Michael Connelly. So, in a really interesting and violent way, is Dennis Lehane, the mystery genre's best hope for rebirth. None of them are imitating Chandler; each is original in his own way, cutting out different pieces of territory. But it's a pretty safe bet that if you like Chandler's *The Lady in the Lake*, you'll like Greenleaf's *Book Case*. You never have to get away from the kind of books you love, the kind of books you'll be happy to have on your shelves. If you like Graham Greene's novels set in distant countries, you're going to love Pico Iyer or Alec Garland.

And so suddenly the classic collector finds a new world opening up, while the scout finds a new market.

This gives us one more possibility to consider in the scenario we used in the last chapter: instead of Sue Grafton, who is an established hypermodern, what if you went out on a limb and picked up *North of the Border*, Judith Van Gieson's first novel, or *Track of the Cat*, Nevada Barr's first mystery? What about Ben Elton's *Popcorn*?

If you've been watching the trends closely, you should know if these writers are holding their value. Hypermoderns tend to trade ridiculously high for a short while, and then sink to a more reasonable level. Don DeLillo, one of the best writers working, ticked along in a fairly stable price range until the buzz on his novel *Underworld* said that it was going to win the serious awards for the year. When it didn't, prices sank.

To make it work, you have to know where the writer is headed. You have to have current market information, and you have to have a feel for where the next trend in your genre is coming from, and how the writer in question will fit into it.

Time and experience are going to be your teachers here. If you're looking to build a collection, then these points are moot. Buy and trade for what you love. If you're looking to maximize profit, go where the profit is: for the sure sales. If you're looking for a little more excitement, a little more risk, then keep up on the hypermoderns. Find and ride the trends. Just be ready to bail out at a moment's notice.

Chapter Seven

～

BRAVE NEW WORLD: BOOKS AND THE INTERNET

B ookselling has changed more in the past five years than it did in the four hundred years before that; from all indications, the next five years are going to bring even more change. The perfect technology of the printed book is meeting the ever-evolving technology of the Internet.

When two booksellers get together, they're going to have at least three opinions on the Internet. But to boil it down, here's the deal: any bookseller you talk to is going to tell you that the Internet is the worst thing that ever happened to used bookselling. Then they're going to tell you that they can't live without it and that it's increasing their bottom line by leaps and bounds. For the art of the book, it's not so good; for the commerce of the book, it's a magic genie popping out of its bottle.

However, here's your warning: someone working only on the computer will never, ever become a good dealer in books. Books are a tactile thing: they must be touched to be appreciated and examined. We'll get into more detail on this later, but for now, suffice it to say that any time you spend working books on the computer should at least be doubled, if not tripled or quadrupled, with time spent in shops, with time spent handling books.

This chapter is going to look at the Internet and its effect on the book market from a number of angles. But to sum it up quickly, here's the gist: the Internet is the best friend you will ever have when it comes to selling a book; it is, however, the worst enemy you will ever meet when it comes to buying with a plan to resell.

THE ENDLESS STACKS

If you've got access to the Internet, right now, you have access to more books than you can even begin to imagine. If there is a title you've been looking for in every store you've gone into over the past twenty years and never found, odds are there are a dozen copies up for grabs on the Net. Just ABE, only one of the main book search engines, lists over *20 million* books for sale. For the collector, this is a boon not to be believed. Holes in collections that had seemed impossible to fill can now be taken care of with a few mouse clicks.

With a few more twitches of the mouse, you'll find riches that you never dreamed of: magazine articles, reviews, chat rooms about your favorite authors. You can spend weeks discussing points of Stephen King books with a collector on the other side of the country; you can find library collections that you never imagined (Arizona State University has William Burroughs's papers—how did they end up there?); you can find fans in other countries, or you can just browse the author's own

Web site and find out what's going on. You can e-mail your favorite author, and you'll likely get a response. It's amazing. The Internet allows a level of accessibility and contact that the world has never before known. In a lot of ways, this new age of the computer and international access is what book lovers have dreamed of for centuries: the ability to get your hands on anything, anything at all.

BUYING

So if you're a collector, the Internet is paradise. You can find just about anything.

If you're a dealer, there are a couple of problems, but the good still outweighs them by far.

What's the book you've been looking for all your life? It may only take about five minutes to find a copy now.

There are truly rare books in the book world. *Tamerlane*, Edgar Allan Poe's first book, is as scarce as hen teeth. Signed Vladimir Nabokovs come up once in a career.

Other books are fairly scarce. A good definition for these are books a dealer will see once every five years or so. Pick your own highspot of literature; chances are, it's a truly scarce book.

One thing the Internet has done is to make scarce books nearly commonplace, and rare books actually findable.

GETTING STARTED

You probably already know how to buy books on-line, but if not, here's the drill: log on to one of the used book sites—ABE (ABEbooks.com) or Bibliofind (Bibliofind.com), for starters. A screen will pop up with a search field. Type in what you want to find, and hey, presto, you're probably going to find it. In fact, odds are you're going to find a lot of copies of the book you're looking for.

Now pick the copy you like, click on the dealer name or on the "purchase" icon, fill out another form with your shipping address, e-mail information, and so on, and you're done. In a day or so the dealer will let you know if the book is still available or not, and if so, you can arrange payment.

Yeah, it's that simple. No tricks to it at all.

And there are only a couple of minor subtleties. When I'm buying from people on-line, I prefer to buy from people I know. As I've said elsewhere, the book world is a very, very small place. We all know each other, at least by reputation. On-line, your only guarantee is reputation already established. This doesn't mean you shouldn't try somebody new. It means that, when you're looking for your books on-line, buy from dealers who are working at a professional level, who lay out their policies clearly, and describe the books well. It takes time to set up a good business on-line, and that time spent shows in the final product.

Always make sure the dealer you buy from has a fair return policy. You should always be able to send the book back for a full refund if it is incorrectly described, or if there's some other problem with it.

If there's a book that's immensely cheaper than any other copies out there, find out why—after you've already jumped to reserve it. Could be there is an undescribed flaw. You will not find a lot of smoking deals on the Internet when you buy. For reasons I'll explain later, the advent of the book search engines has been a great leveler—and even more frequently raiser—of prices.

There is one hope of getting a deal: if there are particular books you're after, the search services let you file them as *permanent wants*. Then, if somebody lists the book on-line, you get an e-mail message that says it's available. You can grab it right away.

Most dealers have their hot books flagged this way. It's their only hope to stay ahead of the competition. If you're looking for, say, a first of the first Harry Potter book, you're going to encounter a lot of other people out there looking, too. And a lot of them have their wants already registered at the search service.

Putting up your wants also gives you a crack at deals. If somebody lists a book at half the going price, the people who already have it up as a want are going to be the ones who get it. It's not likely to last past the first day it's listed. More than once I've had multiple responses within hours of putting a book up for sale on-line—people with want lists getting advance notice. They're the ones who get the books.

That's about all there is to buying on-line. Thousands of people are out there waiting to sell you books, both new and used. A lot of the bigger used bookstores, like Powell's, have their own Web sites (Powell's.com), and you can spend a lot of time looking around, picking which sites you like to work with best.

Bookfinder.com is one site that takes in several other sites, giving you comparison prices from around the Web on used books. I spend most of my time on the larger sites, making occasional forays into lesser-known territory. At any given minute, a dozen people are out there trying to build new book sites, and only time will tell what will survive and thrive. Predicting the Internet's future is a fool's game, and I'd rather spend my time reading. Just keep your eye out for new developments.

SELLING

In the old days (say, the mid-1990s), when you wanted to sell your collection of books at a professional level, you produced a catalog, gathered a mailing list, sent the catalog out to your prospective customers, and waited by the phone. It's a massively inefficient way of doing business. Half the customers will hardly look at the catalog; another portion won't have any disposable cash that month; and the shelf-life of a catalog is, at best, a couple weeks. If the orders aren't in three weeks after you've mailed the catalog out, they're not coming.

The Internet makes the traditional catalog seem as extinct as the dinosaur.

Think of the larger search engines on the Net—ABE, Bibliofind, Alibris (Alibris.com)—as huge catalogs with endless shelf lives. If you've got books for sale, keeping your listings current takes a fraction of the work that producing a print catalog does. You still have to do all the same work of accurately describing, pricing, caring for the books; what you don't have to worry about is somebody tossing your carefully made listing aside in a week or two weeks. On-line, there are endless numbers of customers, and sooner or later somebody is going to come along who wants the book you have.

This new method of bookselling is truly marvelous. You no longer have to go through the slow pain of building a mailing list; you no longer have to pay your kids a couple bucks an hour to staple the catalogs together for you after you've dragged the loose sheets home from the local photocopy place. (Then, of course, sometime after the kids have stapled together six hundred copies or so, you find a mistake and everybody has to start all over again.)

The Internet is a never ending, never expiring catalog that's as easy as pie to update and correct.

The other lovely thing going on here is that it's much easier to get to the point of regularly dealing books. If you've got good stock, you end up selling enough books that the whole idea of a catalog becomes moot. Over the past year, we have planned out several catalogs; however, before we can gather enough material to do a specialty catalog, half the books we were planning to include in the catalog have sold off the Internet. The fact that the books are selling quickly, rather than waiting on the shelf to be cataloged, means that we have more money more quickly to buy more books with, which we can then turn around and sell. Money saved on the Internet as opposed to catalogs has let me buy books that I might otherwise have had to pass on.

And yet, like most things on the Internet, this is both good and bad. Dealer catalogs remain one of the best places to learn new things; once you have a few years' worth, they also make lovely reference material. That's going by the wayside as more and more dealers are making their sales on the Web.

How many books can you hope to sell on the Internet? A recent article in the *ABAA Newsletter* suggested that average numbers for dealers right now are running one sale per day per one thousand to three thousand books listed. In other words, list a hundred, hope for one sale every two weeks to a month. This doesn't sound like much, but it is a huge amount of books. The average used bookstore has maybe fifty thousand titles; if they've been ambitious enough to list them all, they're getting thirty sales off the Web each day. At, say, an average of $20 per book, that's $600—a fair chunk of rent.

I don't know anybody who has listed the entire store. There must be some people out there who put twenty or thirty thousand titles on-line, but they don't seem to move in the same circles I do. Most of the people I know working the Net have a couple thousand books listed. It's a good number. It's manageable—fits in the garage or in a really big spare room—and it's a fair average for a specialty dealer. There's no way you could run an open shop with such a thin stock, but you can run a very nice business from your home with it.

This is where the Internet truly shines. People who may want to have a store someday have a good outlet for books, a source for income, while they're out scouring for more books. People who don't want the hassle of an open shop have a good, consistent outlet for their books. Best of all, the Internet is an outlet that potentially reaches millions of people—quite a number, compared to the four or five hundred catalogs most dealers used to send out.

GETTING STARTED

The first thing you need to do is pick one of the search engines to list your books. These are huge conglomerates of dealers that band together to get their books out in front of the public.

Right now, as I mentioned earlier, the two largest search services are the Advanced Book Exchange (ABE) and Bibliofind. A somewhat distant third is Alibris, although, at least for the time being, they have the listings of the Antiquarian Booksellers Association of America, which gives them added cachet. There are more sites out there being developed all the time; watch for ads in the book magazines, and try your browser to see who you come up with.

You do not have to be a computer genius to work one of these systems. They have all been made as simple as simple can be. The services all work much the same: for a fee—around $20 a month—you can upload descriptions of your books onto the service. A customer comes along, finds your book, and contacts you by phone or e-mail. It's quick, it's easy, and there are very few drawbacks.

On the straight advantages side, you have access to customers all over the world. I've had orders from four continents for my books, and obviously, these are people who would never in a million years find their way into my shop. Nor would I be likely to find them if I were mailing out my catalogs.

The services also allow you to take credit cards via their own accounts. They'll take the payment and transfer it to you. Because getting fixed up to take plastic with your local bank is a serious hassle, this is a wonderful advantage to the search engines. It also allows the customer easier ordering. A lot of people will zap off credit card numbers much more readily than they'll go through the trouble of writing a check.

DESCRIBING YOUR BOOKS

There's no difference between describing a book to list on-line and describing it for a catalog. You've probably already seen enough listings to have an idea of how it all works, but there are subtleties, and better ways of doing things.

Let's take a sample listing:

> O'Donnell, Peter. *Modesty Blaise*, Doubleday, 1965. SIGNED BY AUTHOR. First American edition of the first Modesty novel. Spine slightly rolled, else fine in fine dust wrapper with slightly bumped corners.

This information would be followed by the price. Here, the price would have to be adjusted down quite a bit because of the rolled spine and the bumps. However, although the condition isn't great, the book is a fairly hard find, and the signature probably sets it apart enough to make it desirable.

The book description listing is an excellent place to list any information about the book that would entice buyers. Here, I've mentioned that this is the first Modesty novel, which also makes it the hardest one to get. If it were unusual in any other way, this would be the place to mention that. If the book rarely turns up in an unfaded dust jacket, and yours is still bright and pristine, brag about it (just try to find a copy of Isabel Allende's *The House of the Spirits* or Leslie Marmon Silko's *Ceremonies* where the jacket spine is still bright). If you've seen a dozen copies of the book and every one has been trashed, brag that this volume rarely shows up in such good shape. In other words, think advertising. Book descriptions are, in their simplest form, advertising. Advertising is why I've put "SIGNED BY AUTHOR" all in capital letters. It catches the eye, and it draws in people who may not otherwise go for the book. In advertising, design is important. Many dealers underline the signed notation (which doesn't always show up on search engines, whereas all capital letters does—just don't get carried away with them), but I think all caps stands out more and immediately draws the eye right to it.

This brings up the subject of keywords. Search engines let you look for books by edition (first) and whether or not the book is signed. This means that in your description, it's imperative that you list these things if they apply to your book. However, remember that computers are intrinsically stupid, and they do not think the way a person does. To a computer, only "signed" is signed. A person might list the book as "inscribed" or "with a handwritten note by the author," for example, but the search engine will not pick these up, because they don't have the word "signed" in the description. For the same reason, writing out "first edition" is safer than just putting "first" or "1st ed." Make it easy for the computer when you're describing your books.

Also be careful of misleading descriptions. Again, computers are stupid. If you write "signed by Aunt Mary to her nephew Tim," on a Hemingway first, that's going to show up on the search engine as a signed copy, just because you used the word "signed." If you ask the engines for a "first," they'll give you any listing that has the word "first" anywhere in it, whether it relates to the edition or not. More on this later.

Finally, in the sample description above, note that the book has gotten one grade, the dust jacket another. If the dust jacket and book condition match, this isn't necessary (although extra information is never a bad thing), and many dealers simply say "fine in DJ," about which you can assume the book comes in a Fine dust jacket. But any flaws at all have to be noted, and if the book itself is flawless in a slightly flawed jacket, you're safer going to a second notation. You do not want to surprise the buyer when she opens the package in the comfort of her home.

HANDLING RESPONSES

Once you have your books listed, you'll probably be surprised at how fast the first responses come in, assuming you've got reasonable books at reasonable prices. Respond quickly when customers respond to you. Keep a copy of your listings by your phone and computer if you don't think you can remember all the books and prices you have listed on-line, and mark off what's sold as soon as you sell it. That way there will be no confusion when a call comes in. If you've got the possibility of other people answering your phone or checking your e-mail, teach them how to react.

Get the books listed, keep your fingers crossed, and start looking for more books.

FEAR OF MAIL

The final step is sending the books out once they're sold. Once you've gotten payment in hand from the customer (only ship ahead of payment if you've been dealing with the customer awhile), pack the books tightly and carefully. The best dealers I've dealt with wrap their books in acid-free tissue paper—never, never in newsprint, which can smudge on the books—as well as in bubble pack, before fitting the package into an appropriate box. Make sure the book can't move, shake, or rattle in the box. You can use the post office, UPS, FedEx, or whatever shipping company you want, but no matter what, make sure you've gotten the registration numbers to make it easier to track when something goes amiss. And sooner or later, something will. Just hope it isn't when you're sending the signed first of *The Great Gatsby*.

If you don't know how to pack and ship, you've got no business selling books. The number of customers who send books back due to improper shipping is staggering. Think about it from their side: they're looking forward to getting their book, and when they do, it's been eaten by mailing machines.

SOME SELLING TIPS

The only possible drawback to selling on the Internet is the availability of material. And this can, actually, be a big enough drawback as to make it not worth your while to even list your books. Remember, books that are scarce in shops are common on the Net.

Say you have a great collection of 1930s mysteries that you want to put up for sale. In your neighborhood, it's likely that nobody has ever seen these books before, and you can sell them with ease. Once you get into the global marketplace, though, you're competing with booksellers all over the world, and your special books may not be that special anymore.

Take a reasonably unusual title, something you only see locally once or twice a year, and then run it on the search engines. Odds are, you'll find a hundred copies of it listed for sale. This means that in order to get really good sales on the Internet, you're going to have to do one of two things: be cheaper than anybody else, or concentrate on less common books.

Cheaper is not a bad option, assuming you've been buying well. I'll have more to say on Internet prices in a bit here, but for the most part, the middle of the market, the great fat part of the bell curve, has been bloated beyond belief and priced out of range on the Internet.

Don't be afraid to follow your instincts. If you think you can sell the book a bit cheaper and move it out, go ahead and do so. You make a lot more money by selling books for a reasonable price than you do by jacking prices up as high as you can and waiting around hoping someone will bite.

The second part of the Internet equation is that unusual is potentially better. There are a huge number of people out there selling the same hundred authors. Any visit to a book fair will demonstrate this to you. And all of these people have their books listed on-line.

It's hard to make any real generalizations, but I've had better luck with more unusual stuff. I can sell off a book about Taiwan before the Guomindang invasion long before I can sell off a reasonably priced copy of Charles Bukowski's *Women*.

When you're selling on the Net, be aware of the competition; whatever you can do to set yourself apart is, in the long run, going to do you some favors.

Here's a quick example of the dynamics at work: I was looking for a copy of Paul Bowles's *Let It Come Down*. The cheapest copy I could find on the net was $125; I bought a copy for $45 from a dealer who sent me a mail quote.

Think about it for a second: even with a classic writer like Paul Bowles, what's the demand for his books? I don't honestly believe there are fifty people out there looking for copies of *Let It Come Down* who can support that high price tag.

In other words, by following the crowd, you can easily be pricing yourself right out of a sale.

Even dealers with the more esoteric items are following the herd, bumping prices up to unheard-of levels: a year ago, the classic *All About Tea* was a $700 set; now it's $1,200, if you can find it.

So what do you do? Here's where you have to make the decision between owning a book for a long time, trying to get top dollar for it, or just moving it out and making your profit. My own attitude is to never be sorry if you make what you want out of a book, no matter what everyone else is selling it for; but your own experiences may teach you otherwise.

THE DOWNSIDE OF THE INTERNET

The book search engines are often treated as great big price guides by both buyers and sellers. This does not really work to anybody's advantage.

I mentioned earlier; now let's look at the scenario in a little more detail: You have a book in your hand, and you check what it's going for in ABE or Bibliofind and mark it accordingly. This is all well and good. However, thanks to the global scale of the Internet, the next person who gets the book is going to look up what the thing is going for elsewhere, and do the exact same thing. Or worse yet, he'll think, well, my copy is better than that, and add 10 percent to the price.

Okay, fine, so what's the problem? A buyer is willing to pay the extra 10 percent or she's not.

But part two of this is that a huge portion of any dealer's sales are to other dealers. As traditional dealer-to-dealer discounts have almost disappeared on the Net, he's paying full buck for the copy he buys from you. Once he gets it, he then marks it up so he can pay his own rent, maybe eat something besides macaroni and cheese. The next time he goes to sell the book, he's going to list it on-line with this profit margin already figured in—and yet another person is going to look up, find, and price her book according to this new, higher price.

This is the rachet effect I mentioned before. Prices are getting higher and higher, sometimes by small increments, sometimes by large.

Another reason for increasing prices is the fact that the Net has all but eliminated the wholesaler. A few years ago, if you found a book that was worthwhile but not in your field, you'd wholesale it out to a dealer who could use it. Now, because the Net gives you access to stadiums full of customers, why not just try to sell it off yourself and make full price on it? But from there, if a dealer buys it, he's got his markup to consider. And the books get a little more expensive.

THE VERDICT

If you've got good stock, you will sell more books faster on the Internet than any traditional dealer ever dreamed of. It is a huge sales machine, and there is no way to overstate this. The Internet has opened up the entire world to your books, and it's brought your stock to more people than would find you in a hundred years of advertising your traditional catalogs.

You face only one real difficulty when you're selling your books, and that's the overwhelming amount of books out there being sold. The market has increased, but so has the competition. Make sure you have good books at good prices.

On the buying side, for now, I don't think the Net is the place to go for most dealers. Dealers use the Net as a tool, of course, and buy a few harder-to-find items there, but a good dealer still spends more time working shops, catalogs, connections, and is always on the lookout for where the books are.

But all of this will probably change. As the midline books get more and more common, there will be nothing to justify the high prices. Books that were once scarce locally, remember, are common as dirt nationwide. Like my example with Paul Bowles earlier, are there really adequate numbers of buyers to support some of these higher prices? I doubt it. In the long run—and it's impossible to say yet how long that run's going to be—good books will go up, so-so books will go down. But for now, watch out.

A final thought about collecting on the Internet: I've used on-line dealers to fill a few holes in my own collections and will continue to do so. But I will never let on-line buying replace going to the stores. The fun of building a collection is the hunt. Find your own balance here. It's easy, at first, to spend so much time on-line that you forget the stores are out there. So why fight traffic? Because of that old beauty, serendipity. Anything can be anywhere. It's the hunt that's the fun part, not necessarily the capture.

ON-LINE AUCTIONS

A companion to the book-only search engines are the on-line auctions from eBay, Sotheby's, and the like. Virtually all of the auctions do books only as a small portion of their business, and I don't know any dealers who have a lot of good to say about these things.

With the book search engines, you're buying from people who are at least serious enough about their books to shell out $20 a month or so to the service to try and sell them. Even this tiny filter has been removed from the auction sites, the world's largest garage sales.

But this doesn't mean they can be ignored.

If you've got something truly odd, an auction might be the best way to go with it. But it has to be fairly unusual, or quite highly desirable in the wider world to really make much of a ripple among the billion or so items listed for sale at the auction sites.

For the buyer, the auctions can provide the surprising deal. These are closer to the garage sale than the store: because there are few professionals, the occasional really underpriced item flies out. I know people who've gotten great bargains on the Internet auction sites.

My advice on Internet auctions is to take a look. Go to e-Bay, or the Sotheby's site, and see what's for sale. Pick one thing to look for, something very specific, and see what you can turn up with it. Like the search engines, the auction sites are made to be easy. You're not going to have any trouble navigating on them.

The question becomes one of time: the material may be out there, but do you have that kind of time to sit and look for it? Can you wait a week or so to find out if you're actually going to get it?

Auctions do work for some people. I'm not going to recommend them, though. Your time is better spent elsewhere, if you're seriously looking for books. Think of these as hobby sites, maybe. Check in every now and then and see if you can come up with Rhett and Scarlett salt and pepper shakers to package with a *Gone With the Wind* collection.

THE INTERNET AND YOUR BOOK EDUCATION: A FINAL CAVEAT

Not long ago, someone in my shop did a search for a book for a customer. The customer wanted it, we found it on the Net, contacted the dealer, sent off our check, and waited for the book to show up.

When it finally arrived, it turned out that the book had been completely misdescribed. Not only was it not a first edition, it was a book club edition! When we called to find out just what was going on here, the ersatz dealer replied, "Book club edition? What's that? How can you tell?"

With the Internet, anybody, absolutely anybody can put books up for sale. The problem is, not all of them know what they're doing. In fact, the percentage of knowedgeable dealers seems to be getting smaller and smaller as the number of books listed becomes larger and larger. The Internet is not only the world's biggest store, it's also the world's biggest garage sale, with half the wired population trying to clean out their old possessions.

The world of the Internet is still, in many ways, its own world, and I think, ultimately, that one of the main drawbacks of the Internet is that it is endlessly self-referential. The outside world seems no longer to exist once you've got your face glued to the screen.

For a bookseller, this is the kiss of death.

In the shops now, we're seeing younger booksellers who have

grown up using the Net; it never occurs to them that what happens there is not necessarily real. Just because you can find a book listed for $400 on the Web doesn't mean you can sell the book for that.

These are the things you learn by handling books, and by talking to people out in the real world who handle books. You remember books by touching them, feeling their weight in your hand. Books are objects that live in touch, smell, and sight. The only way to learn about them is to get up close. And the more books you can get up close to, the better off you are. Even the days when you go out scouting and find practically nothing are not wasted, because you saw more books, you added a bit to your store of knowledge. Sooner or later, this is going to pay off, and pay off big.

For those who rely solely on the Web, there is little or no serendipity. You learn books by handling huge numbers of them, whether they're books you'll ever sell or not. And you tend to find the best books when you're looking for something entirely different. This is not going to happen on the Web: first, because you're not actually touching books; and second, because what you find is what you're looking for. The possibility of happy accident is almost eliminated in the Boolean search engines.

AND A FINAL HAPPY NOISE

Okay, you've probably gotten the idea that I have reservations about the Internet. True, I do. But I also recognize the fact that it has made selling my books easier than anything else I have ever done. It has also allowed me to buy books that I had given up on ever finding. It lets me keep my customers happy—they come in and ask for a book, and odds are I can get them one pretty quickly by buying it on the Net—and keeping them happy keeps me happy, allowing me to make my car payment.

The Internet is changing everything in the book world, in ways that we can't even imagine yet. There will come a day in the not-too-distant future where it will be possible to actually see the books on-line, to flip through them. Any day now, that Dick Tracy idea of the videophone will be as common as the TV, and then you can get on the Net and have the dealer show you the book page by page. I'm really looking forward to all this. Every day brings changes and new possibilites.

The Internet is a lovely tool that allows you to do things book buyers and sellers have never before been able to do. It's only going to get more miraculous.

But just remember that nothing ever replaces the feel of a book in your hand.

Chapter Eight

❧

AUCTIONS AND DEALER CATALOGS

W|ith all the publicity the Internet gets, it's pretty easy to forget that fewer than a third of the houses in the United States are wired. For a new generation, it's getting harder and harder to remember that once upon a time, the world worked just fine without modems.

But while the Net is changing the very way that the book business is conducted—for better or worse—the truth is, for right around 450 years, book dealers have done just fine with the three pillars of book society: the shop, the catalog, and the auction.

Because the truth is, the book world simply isn't one that's entirely adapted to going binary. We can do some marvelous things with computers as far as buying and selling and learning about books, and I hope the previous chapter has pointed some of those things out to you. But at a fundamental level, as book dealers we deal with print, and we deal it for people who love print, not blinking screens.

This chapter should be read in conjunction with the previous one. There is no way to talk about buying and selling books without bringing the Internet into the discussion. It has revolutionized the way books are bought and sold, and every day brings new developments in something that was barely a blip on the horizon when I sat down to write the first edition of this book. However, for reasons that I outlined in the previous chapter, I think it is a dangerous trend for dealers (at any level) and collectors to depend on the Internet as a primary source of information and books—from either the selling or the buying side of things. It's there, so use it and enjoy it, live it up with it. But know that you will never adequately learn about books by staring at a computer screen. You will in all probability never find many bargains on the Internet either.

Books are an intrinsically print-based medium, and the best work is still done by those who are paying attention to print.

This may change, though.

So let's be Luddites for a little while, and hark back to the good old days—four or five years ago—when catalogs ruled the book world.

Why? Well for the book collector, mail order is still where you'll find everything you've ever wanted. No matter how obscure the topic or the author, there is still a catalog-based mail-order dealer out there working that area, somebody who is an expert in the field.

Better yet, the books you never knew you wanted are common in the catalogs. This is the main limitation of the Net: you don't find anything you're not looking for. When you're on-line, you're looking for *something*, and that something is what you'll find. Computer browsers don't browse: they eliminate. You go in looking for a nice copy of Charles Johnson's *Middle Passage*, and that's what you're going to find. You're not going to notice the copy of Roddy Doyle's *The Snapper* that the cataloger mis-priced, because you don't actually browse on the Internet. Think of the Net as a laser beam, pointing at exactly what you want: it's quick, it's efficient, it's bright and shiny. Think of catalogs as the magic cave where you can stumble across treasures; old technology, sure, but still where an awful lot of fun is.

There's also a different market between the Internet and catalogs. Most Internet sales are in the under $200 range; there just aren't that many people out there willing to buy truly high-line items over a modem. This will no doubt change as people get more and more comfortable with the technology; but for the moment, and at least for the next few years, the highest end of the book market is still based on good catalogs, auctions, and personal connections.

So for a broad exposure to the depth and size of the book market, you need to keep up with what's happening at auction and in the dealer catalogs. Even if you have books for sale on the Internet, it's worthwhile keeping up with catalog dealers for making sales. Unlike selling books yourself on the Net, when you work with dealers, you don't have to wait months for someone to stumble across your books on-line before you can cash in on them. Catalogs are specialized, so once you find the people who match your interests, you can very often get better prices than anywhere locally. Catalog dealers know their clientele's wants and budgets, knowledge you can't find on an anonymous search engine. There are certain specialty dealers who regularly have prices 30 percent higher than anyone else; instead of being shunned, these people are considered the best in the business, because they can justify those prices with the best stock in the country and offer flawless copies of very rare books. There are genre dealers who work in very small niches—from private detective novels to the works of the Beats—who know how, when, and where they can sell a particular book. So if you offer that book to them, you're going to get a much better deal than if you just put it into a local shop and the shopkeeper has to hope someone stumbles in looking for it, or than if you put it on-line and hope that somebody is out there looking for it.

In short, auction sales and catalogs are still a vital part of the business.

AUCTIONS

I'm going to start our foray into the world of book catalogs with auctions. Auction houses put out the very best catalogs, bar none. Auction houses—we're talking Christie's, Sotheby's, Pacific Book Auctions here, not eBay or some Internet site with no quality control (for those, see the previous chapter)—are where the very best copies of the very best books appear, and they frequently appear at well below retail cost because most of the people buying from auctions are dealers.

Many would-be buyers, dealers, and collectors are afraid of auctions. Somehow, they've gotten the impression that auctions are for the rich, and that items normally going for a hundred or so will suddenly inflate in a bidding frenzy to three hundred, a thousand, or more.

Sometimes this happens, but usually it doesn't.

People have been buying and selling books at auction since 1676, a sure sign that auctions are working for someone. It's not all that difficult to make them work for you, too.

Auctions are a tool for the savvy buyer and dealer to pick up items that are never going to appear on the open market. As auction houses get their money from a combination buyer/ seller premium, based on the sale price of the books, the auction houses tend to like better-quality items that are sure to move. Because most auctions are attended by dealers, not collectors, prices remain close to the high end of wholesale level for many of these prime pieces. Yes, auctions set records—a

1926 first limited edition of T. E. Lawrence's *The Seven Pillars of Wisdom* fetched over $70,000 at auction, and a signed first edition of Beatrix Potter's *The Tale of Peter Rabbit* sold for £69,700 in London.

But these are the exceptions. More common is for a book to sell at slightly under fair market value. After all, if dealers are buying the stock, they have to plan on a profit margin for themselves. It may not be much—20 percent or so—but if you have a known market for a book, even this can be enough to justify the effort.

Book auctions are held regularly on both coasts (there's not much action in this country outside of New York and California), and bidding can take place either in person, by phone, or by mail. In other words, you need not be present to win, and often at auction, win you do.

The rules for buying sight unseen at auction are slightly different than for buying through a catalog. Sales catalogs offer return policies; most auction houses hold that if you bid, you buy. They don't care if you haven't taken a close look at it first. *Caveat emptor*. That means it's vital, if you're bidding on a truly unusual piece, that you either get a good look at it yourself or have someone you trust examine it.

Auction houses offer viewing hours before the sales. If at all possible, attend. It's the only way to be absolutely sure of what you're bidding on.

However, if you're in another town, or even another continent (don't overlook London as a prime site for book auctions), then viewing becomes difficult, if not impossible. Fortunately, the nature of the book makes this a little easier.

It's fairly safe to say with modern first editions that one looks pretty much like another; or at least it started off that way. If you know the book was issued in brown cloth at a particular trim size, and if you've seen other copies of it, then it's safe to assume that the one offered at the auction house is going to appear much the same. The only details that will differ are matters of condition, and here the auction house takes care of the worries for you.

AUCTION CATALOGS

The catalogs of the better auction houses give very complete and accurate descriptions of the books, more than you'd ever find in a regular sales catalog. All good auction houses will carry a proviso in their catalog that if any item is not as described, they will negate the sale. That means that if you bought a first of Wright Morris's *The Man Who Was There*, and when it arrives you find a tear on the dust jacket that was not mentioned in the catalog description, you're perfectly within your rights to return the book to the auction house. If, however, the book is as described and you simply find out that you paid too much for it, too bad. The book is yours.

Check the small print on all catalogs before undertaking to buy sight unseen. The best auction houses will have catalog notations that include everything down to the smallest fox mark, and this protects you to a large extent, but you still need to know the book you're bidding on.

The best thing about auction catalogs is that because such care is taken in describing the books, they are an invaluable reference source. They can be much more detailed than the best bibliographies on the points of a book's issue, and so a subscription to the catalogs of the main houses is well worth the cost.

You can subscribe to catalogs from the auction houses. General subscriptions to a busy house like Christie's or Sotheby's can run you upwards of $500, but you don't have to sign on for the whole deal, and you can get just the catalogs that interest you: for instance, a travel catalog subscription at Sotheby's London runs around $50. A man who knows more about books than I can ever hope to learn told me that, no matter how poor

I felt, a subscription to the auction catalogs would be something I'd never regret. He was right.

All auction houses will also sell you individual catalogs, if you know what sales are coming up. The houses all have sites on the Net with calendars, or most of them will send you a calendar on request. They also print notices of upcoming sales in book magazines.

Book catalogs are collectible in and of themselves. Dealers do not let go of the catalogs they have gathered, and those for some sales, such as the Garden, Ltd. Sale, or the Streeter Sale or the Siebert Sale of Americana are valuable references.

When you get a sale catalog, read everything. They are marvelous tools for learning, usually well illustrated, and they give you a lot of food for thought. If you're not at the higher end of the market yet, they give you a place to dream, and they give you an idea of what kinds of books hold value, and what those values can be.

There are few better educational tools—outside of hanging out endlessly in good bookshops—than the auction catalog. I have a large shelf of them, and some nights, I'll just pull one down and browse for a while. The sale may be long over, but the books are still out there somewhere. Who knows when I might see one?

BIDDING

If you are attending the auction in person, you will most likely be given a number when you register. Then, if you buy something, the auctioneer's assistant will note that number, and after the sale you can come tally up your purchases. Don't worry about the sitcom cliché of reaching to scratch your nose and having the auctioneer think you just made a huge bid. It doesn't happen.

If you work the auction by absentee bid, you will send the auction house a list of the books you wish to purchase, and your *maximum offer* for each one. They will bid on your behalf up to that maximum. On large sales, they can also take care of "either/or" bids—in which, say, you wanted item 120, but it went too high, so you go for 134 instead. They won't bid on 134 unless you didn't make 120.

This is part of what the auction house does. It doesn't cost you any extra.

SELLING AT AUCTION

Most auction houses tend to be interested in very narrow ranges, and only in the best pieces in those ranges. But let's put up a fair scenario. You've been collecting Gary Snyder books for years. You have the postcard issue of *Go Round*, you have five different versions of the "Smokey the Bear Sutra," you have signed copies of every book he ever wrote, some not just with signatures, but also with doodles. A prime collection.

Now it's time to sell them. You could take them off to a local dealer, but there you'd be looking at the dealer's limited capital, and you've got a pricey collection. Better to offer them up to an auction house, where they will be (eventually) combined with other works of the same caliber into one huge sale, drawing buyers from around the country.

The problem here is that "eventually." If you're in a hurry to turn your books into money, an auction isn't the way to go. By the time you've arranged with the auction house to take the books, by the time the books have worked their way into the sale rotation, by the time the buyer pays the auction house and the house pays you, months and months may have gone by.

But the advantages to selling through an auction are many. Sometimes that feeding frenzy does happen, and you get a nice surprise when the bidding settles down. A friend of mine sold at auction for $28,000 a book he'd bought for $7,000. He'd hoped to get half that.

On a more likely level, auctions let you reach customers

you'd never find on your own, and they relieve you of the pressure of buying and selling.

Most auction houses aren't going to be interested in your run-of-the-mill hypermoderns that appear on the shelves of every bookstore. They're looking for things they can sell quickly and easily, and that usually means things that not everybody else has. Watching the house's catalogs for a few months can teach you the different kinds of materials they're going to handle. When you're ready to go, contact the auction house and tell them what you have to offer. They will refer you to their specialist in that area, and then several calls or faxes will follow, clarifying details. If they want the books, it will be much like sending them to sell to a dealer: they could still refuse them when they open the box. Send everything registered and insured.

RESERVE BIDS

Most auction houses have a *reserve bid*, a price below which they will not sell a particular piece. As seller, it is sometimes your right to set this reserve. If you paid $500 for a piece, you need to make sure you get your profit, so you can set a reserve of, say, $750. If the bidding does not meet or exceed this price, then the sale will be canceled and you'll get your book back. A lot of auction houses have their own scale for reserves: Sotheby's, for example, sets an automatic reserve at 75 percent of the low estimate price. If the piece has an estimate of $1,000–$1,500, they will not sell it below $750.

Reserves are different from *estimates*. Reserves are not announced or published; estimates are simply the range in which the auction house expects a particular piece to sell. You may set a reserve of $250 on your first of Sinclair Lewis's *Elmer Gantry*, while the estimate may be $300–$400. Potential buyers will know the estimate; they will not know your reserve.

Some houses do not allow reserves, and here you can be at

risk. If you paid $500 for it and the hammer falls at $300, you're out of luck. However, this usually only happens when the house is offering a huge collection from a single source, and it's figured that the highs and lows will balance out. Still, it is important to understand all conditions of sale and consignment before doing business with any auction house.

A few auction houses still only charge the purchaser—usually 10 to 20 percent tacked on to the final hammer price. But more houses are also starting to charge the seller, deducting a fee from the final check cut to the consignee. When you want to put an item in an auction, the auction house does not buy it from you; rather, they take it on consignment, agreeing to sell it for you. If they fail, you get your book back. If you get your book back, the auction house usually charges you 10 percent of the reserve price for their trouble. If the book is sold, the commission the auction house takes from you as the seller can vary with the cost of the item. Before you buy or sell anything from an auction house, make sure you understand all their conditions of sale and purchase. These are printed, in vivid legalese, in every catalog.

Only a handful of people do the majority of their buying and selling from auctions; most still go out and find their books the old-fashioned way, combing through catalogs and the shelves of local stores. But if you're looking for a way to supplement your buying and selling, and you have patience, auctions may be for you.

DEALER CATALOGS

Still a lot more common than auction catalogs, even in the days of the Internet, are dealer catalogs, little treasures put out by dealers trying to sell their wares.

The sad thing here is that fewer and fewer dealers are going to the trouble—and it is a lot of trouble and a big expense—to put out catalogs. The Internet is making them less viable as a sales medium, even while it makes them even more important as a medium of the transmission of the art of what we do. That's the hard way of saying that you'll learn more from the time spent with a good catalog—and buy more books—than you would from spending twice as much time on the Net.

While the vast majority of book dealers work out of shops or are turning to the Internet, a significant number also work from the comfort of home by catalog and appointment only. They're a different part of the market, in many ways, looking to sell to a different kind of customer than those who are wired. You'll find more high-line items in catalogs. You'll find more traditional dealers, and because of the expense of putting out a catalog and the effort involved, you'll often find they're more professional than the average Internet-only dealer.

As time goes by, many if not all of these dealers will start to list their wares on the Net; it's questionable how much they'll sell, though. The exclusive dealers rely on personal contact, and on people who can actually see the books they're offering. The Net misses this entirely.

BUYING AND LEARNING FROM CATALOGS

The first step is to get some catalogs and study them. Ads in *Firsts* magazine are a good place to start: a pretty good representation of modern first dealers offer their wares there. You can also check out the ABAA listings or Web site (ABAA.org) to find other dealers who match your interests.

Once you start getting some catalogs, the devil is going to test your resistance to temptation. Even today, when fewer dealers are putting out catalogs, I see ten or fifteen a week. If I hadn't built up some immunity to glowing descriptions and offers of books I'd never seen before, I'd be living under a bridge somewhere by now, trying to figure out where to put the bookcases so they'd get minimal exposure to road dirt.

And those ten or fifteen catalogs I get are the tip of the iceberg. Literally hundreds are available, each catering to specific interests. In the stack by my desk I have a catalog, nearly two hundred pages thick, strictly of books on Arctic and Antarctic exploration; I have half a dozen mystery-only catalogs, another half-dozen of horror and science fiction (many of these split between the "classics"—the pre-1960s writers—and the moderns). Three or four thick catalogs of "modern literature." Want a Saul Bellow? Look in one of these. Here's a catalog with three pages of Eugene O'Neill listings; another devotes nearly forty pages to Philip K. Dick, who if you'd bought just a few years ago, you could practically retire on now. And here's a catalog of fine press material, from Doves to Golden Cockerel to Nonesuch.

All these descriptions of perfect books can seem too good to be true. Many beginners worry about buying from catalogs, but you are protected. Any reputable dealer will have a guaranteed return policy, usually within at least ten days (and before you ever place an order from a catalog or on the Internet, check to see what the dealer's return policy is; if the book is nonreturnable, *don't order it*). Since you're buying the book sight unseen, this is necessary for your own protection. Most dealers who put out catalogs are very careful to describe each item fully, but occasionally you find a bad one. I've only ever had to return one book to a mail-order dealer: while the book I'd bought was described accurately as in "Very Good" condition, there was no mention that it was an ex–library book. With that library stamp, the book was worthless, so I sent it back to the dealer. Experience shows mistakes on the Internet happen rather more frequently; because of the learning curve needed to deal books well, there are simply a lot of people out there listing books who do not have the knowledge necessary to do it right. Check back in the last chapter to learn that lesson again. But remember, for the moment, the rule is this: *if you can't return it, don't order it.*

Most catalogs offer excellent copies of excellent books, and it's perfectly safe to buy from catalogs, sight unseen. If you want to buy, there's almost no reason ever to leave the house.

But catalogs offer more than just temptation; catalogs are on the cutting edge of pricing. Once you learn who prices high and low, catalogs are more useful than any price guide, because they are more current. Particularly on a hypermodern author, whose book could change by a hundred dollars in a matter of weeks, the traditional price guides aren't going to do you much good. *Snow Falling on Cedars* went from cover price to $250 in a matter of weeks; it fell back a bit, but who knows what the long-term effect of the movie will be? While the book was jumping up and down, it hadn't even appeared in the standard price guides, and the Internet prices were swinging to ridiculous highs and lows as the book got priced by the hopeful and the unsure.

When you receive a new catalog, it's imperative that you sit down and study it. Discover the authors you've never heard of—there are bound to be a lot of them. Find out who's soaring in price and who's starting to dive.

Tracking particular authors in catalogs can be a great learning exercise. Take Donna Tartt's *The Secret History*, for example. Soon after the book came out, it skyrocketed in price. Signed firsts were pushing the $150 mark. Everything was rosy, and people were snapping her book up like it was a Fine Steinbeck. But then the bottom dropped out of the market. There was no apparent reason for this—probably just that everybody who wanted one had one, and they were starting to realize that the book succeeded more on hype and style than story. Reality set in and the book plummeted in price. A few months after its peak, it was down in the $75 range, and a year later, you could pick one up for $20. Another example: Don DeLillo's masterful book *Underworld* went up to about $100 on hype that it was going to win the National Book Award; when it didn't, it fell back down to about $40.

Now, if you had not been following its fall, you could have very easily made an expensive mistake, picking up a copy for, say, $75, thinking you could trade it off in a few more months for an extra $50. If you had old information telling you that it was a $100 book heading for the sky—you were in trouble. Same thing when Salman Rushdie's *The Satanic Verses* was up over $500. You can pick it up for an easy $50 now, and often cheaper. Or *The Bridges of Madison County*, which peaked, around the time the movie came out, at around $800; good luck trying to get $200 for it now.

If your information is old, you can't take advantage of the latest trends that are still on the way up. Pick a trend. Have you noticed the recent return to hard-boiled mysteries? A year from now, the names collected will be different, but you can learn who to look for by studying catalogs.

Not only do you learn about who's new and hot from catalogs, but you also learn who's old and eternal. Have you ever heard of Clifford Knight? I hadn't, and had never noticed one of his books, until I saw in a catalog that his novels from the 1940s were selling for upwards of $100. Now I never fail to check the "K" section in a store for him. By truly studying the catalogs, you learn where the money is to be found. And along the way, you just might find a few new favorite authors. The Internet is never going to do that for you, because it only tells you what you're looking for. It never surprises you.

In the stock market, there's something known as *market timing*: this is watching for the first sign of downfall and bailing out. In order to do this successfully, you need timely, current information. Catalogs make market timing possible in the book industry. To keep with the analogy, what keeping an eye on the prices on the Internet does is more like day-trading: looking for minor twitches in price. Catalogs will give you a somewhat longer forecast horizon; the Net will tell you right here, right now. Armed with the information from both sources, you are well prepared to sell your books for the best price you can.

Book dealers are not sending you their catalogs out of the kindness of their hearts. Most dealers will send you regular catalogs for a year; if you don't order anything in that time, either they take you off their mailing list or many dealers offer you a chance to buy their catalogs, to subscribe. Depending on the dealer, this is often well worth the cost.

One final word on catalog buying: if you see something you want in a sale catalog, call and order it right away. Don't wait, don't think about it any longer than you have to. Good dealers are flooded with orders when their catalogs hit the street, and who knows how many other people out there might be after that copy of James Hilton's *Lost Horizon*? Act fast to avoid disappointment. This also holds true if you're putting in a bid at an auction: mail bids are given the priority in which they arrive, so your $50 bid needs to get there before somebody else puts up $50 tomorrow.

SELLING TO CATALOG DEALERS

Because dealers who issue catalogs are so tightly focused, they can often be a prime market for your collection. If you've got a nice assortment of works in a particular genre, start looking through your old catalogs (never throw out a catalog—the one you toss is the one with the reference you'll need next week) and see which dealer offers similar works. Compare the quality and desirability of your stock with what he offers, and then give him a call.

As with buying through the mail, selling through the mail presents certain difficulties. First, the buyer is asking to see your books on the basis of your description. If you don't describe them accurately, the books will be sent right back to you.

You're also having to trust your books to someone you haven't met; the dealer is going to want the books in hand before making an offer, so you've got to trust who you're dealing with. The dealer isn't going to trust you to grade a book correctly. You may be an expert, but he doesn't know that, and he has to protect himself. Later, after you've done a few deals together, this will change, but at first, don't expect to talk about money until after the dealer has the books in hand.

With the Internet, the dealer does have to come up with the cash before you send out the book; this increases dealer risk, but if you're careful about your descriptions, you won't have any problem. For those who are not careful about correctly describing books and treating others fairly, remember that the book world is a very, very small one, and it doesn't take long for a bad reputation to spread.

If you're trying to sell to a catalog dealer, the dealer is not going to offer you a firm price over the phone; you have to be prepared for a little negotiation. Here you are actually dealing from a point of some strength, since by the time this stage arrives, the dealer already has your books, and it would be a nuisance to have to ship them back. After he gets the books, he'll go over them, make sure they fit your description, and offer a price for them. Don't get greedy, but don't think you have to take the first number he comes up with, either. He's got the books in hand; he's already thinking about how to sell them. Keep him interested, and the next time around, you'll find your number and his are going to be closer.

Of course, with selling to catalog dealers, we're talking about getting wholesale prices here. No dealer is going to give you full market value. Allow for his profit—around 40 percent of the final cost of the book—as he has to allow for yours, which means you must have paid less than one-third of the wholesale price of the book.

This business of selling to other dealers is one of the fastest changing areas of the book market, thanks to the Internet. People think, hey, why sell the book for $75 to a dealer when I can put it on-line and get $125 for it myself? The truth is, there's often not a good reason. If you've got time and patience, why not keep it yourself? Do keep in mind your expenses—subscription fee to one of the book markets, and so on—but very often, there's no reason at all to wholesale a book, particularly not a hot book. And sometimes there's a very good reason, such as with *Cold Mountain*, where, although there were a lot of people out looking for copies, there were even more copies for sale. Sometimes you're better off making a reasonable profit and unloading your copy than you are hanging around and hoping to score big. As long as you make your target profit, be happy, not greedy.

Anytime you mail books, be sure to pack them very carefully, send them registered, return receipt requested, and insured for replacement cost, not just face value. Not only can things go wrong between you and the buyer, but shipping services and the mail can't always be trusted. Let's not talk about the day my $2,000 book just kind of disappeared in transit.

As with every other transaction you undertake, keep complete records and receipts.

❧

Chapter Nine

SIGNED EDITIONS, AUTOGRAPHS AND EPHEMERA

T here is nothing as lovely as an autographed book. It has a special feel that cannot be matched by any other copy. This copy was in the author's hand. This copy, unlike the thousands of others that might have been printed, has gone out into the world, then back to the hand that created it, before it finally came to you.

One of the high points of my own career as a scout came fairly early after I became serious. I was going through sale boxes at a store, when I came across a beat-up copy of John F. Kennedy's *Profiles in Courage*. The book was trashed, with the dust jacket torn to ribbons, the spine completely cocked, and a bit of water damage along the top edge. It was also, obviously from its feel, a book club edition. Still, just from habit, I flipped the book open. A piece of paper fell out. It was a letter from Mary Lincoln, saying that the president had been happy to sign the book. And there on the half-title page was the signature of the man himself. I paid two dollars for the book, sent it off to get the signature authenticated—Mary Lincoln signed Kennedy's name a lot more often than JFK did himself—and when it came back real, I quickly wholesaled it off for a profit in the multiple thousands of percent. Although the book was in poor condition, bad enough to be trash, what I was selling was the autograph—in this case, quite a rare autograph. Now, think if that autograph had been attached to a first edition of the book.

SIGNED EDITIONS

Signed copies are always at a premium. Everybody wants a copy of a book that has passed through the hands of a favorite author. There are collectors who only collect signed copies, and there are other collectors who will sell their grandmothers for a fine inscribed book from their literary idol.

If the first edition is the golden currency of the book industry, the signed first is pure platinum.

There are two kinds of signed books. Limited editions, which we've talked about briefly before, were produced to be signed. Signed trade editions are the copies that fans and hopeful dealers have taken up to the author and gotten signed themselves.

Limiteds are usually worth more money than a standard trade edition of the same book. The very fact that they were done in limited quantities puts a premium on them. They should never lose value on a reasonably popular author.

However, a signed trade edition may maintain more value than a limited one in the long run. The author might have signed hundreds of his books, even thousands—I've been to signings where the line to meet the author literally stretched around the block—all to promote the trade edition, but the number still is usually small compared to the total number of copies printed.

Furthermore, the trade edition has actually met the world. It is more numerous, cheaper—the *real* book. Because the trade is out in the world and not locked in a bank vault, it can actually be harder, despite the larger quantity produced, to find a Fine signed trade than a limited.

There is also the distinct possibility that the author never actually handled your copy of a limited edition—in fact, it's nearly a certainty. Publishers send the authors loose sheets; one night, while the author is sitting around watching a movie on cable, he signs a couple hundred pieces of paper and ships them back to the publisher. The publisher then binds these sheets into the book. Its final shape can be as much of a surprise to the author as it is to you.

Therefore, a Fine first trade—particularly with a signature— can easily surpass the limited in price on many volumes.

So never underestimate the allure of a signed trade edition. There are those (like myself) who consider limiteds to be a form of cheating. So many limiteds are being produced now that virtually every popular author has at least half a dozen to his credit. Limiteds are simply not that hard to come by, and worse yet, their runs are being bought primarily by speculators. Most limiteds are no longer, in a sense, fine books (in fact, more and more limiteds are simply trade editions with a limitations page—which shows how many copies were printed and carries the author's signature—bound in), but rather simple objects not really any different from, say, a Hummel figurine. Something one buys to look at, but not touch, and hope it will increase in value.

However, it's a lot easier to find a limited in Very Fine condition than it is to find a trade. Most limiteds are never even opened.

In the favor of limiteds is the fact that many collectors are completists. If there is a limited, they will want it—but they'll also want a copy of the first trade edition. Think how much easier it will be to sell them your first trade if it's been signed.

So both signed limited and signed trade editions have their place in the collector's market. Limiteds are easier to find and are safer investments; trades are cheaper to obtain, particularly if you can get the author's signature yourself. Trades can also rise in value faster, if the author hits or if he tends not to sign (like Cormac McCarthy) or, if after signing freely for years, decides to stop signing (like John Irving), or simply lives somewhere inaccessible, as Paul Bowles did, spending the last 40 years of his life in Tangiers.

ADDING A PREMIUM

When dealing, how much premium can you put on a signed edition? That, of course, depends on the author who signed the book. Dead authors are better than live authors. As for the live authors, some are a lot easier to get than others, and some go through phases in their careers when they're easy. For example, John Irving no longer signs, but he didn't stop until after he hit the big time, so it's not all that difficult to get a signed copy of *The World According to Garp* or even one of his earlier books— but just try and get a signed trade edition of *The Cider House Rules*. Irving has produced a few limited editions since then, but there are almost no signed trades of his later works on the market. So when they do turn up, they're at a premium.

Other authors make themselves readily available. Clive Barker, one of the top horror writers today, signs regularly, rightly believing that the people who line up to get his autograph are the people he owes his success to. A signed Barker is nice to have, and it will sell for more, but it's not a treasure because there are so many of them. The same can be said about James Lee Burke in the mystery field. Burke is almost too nice when it comes to signing. Tony Hillerman and Dean Koontz are examples of authors who signed almost anything early on in their careers, but who now limit themselves to very few signings, and only one book per person at the signings. I've seen Sue Grafton sign books for nine straight hours, though.

And of course between the two extremes are the authors who sign only occasionally. Your first task as an autograph dealer or collector is to learn who falls into what category. You've got a signed Emma Lathen in front of you. How much more is that worth? Only experience and good recordkeeping will tell you just how much.

Signatures and their values also move in fickle trends. An author hot one year will cool off the next. And as with fine art, death always brings on a boom market. As an example of the way market forces work in signatures, the day after Paul Bowles died, in November 1999, a quick check of search engines on the Net showed that the average signed copy had gone up $50—a 30 to 70 percent leap, depending on the title—from the day before.

TYPES OF SIGNATURES

Some of the value depends upon the kind of signature, and here things become even more iffy, because there are two schools of thought on what *kind* of signatures are good on a book. One school believes that any personal markings degrade the value. That is, if the author signs the book to you, or to your aunt Margaret, it's not a good thing—unless you or Aunt Margaret is famous. After all, when you go to sell the book, who wants your aunt Margaret's name right there on the flyleaf? The new owner doesn't know her.

The other, somewhat smaller school believes that all writing is good, and the more the better. It doesn't matter what it says. If the author took the extra time to scribble more than just his name and maybe the date, then the book had more contact with the author, it has more of that special aura. You'll often find these books listed in catalogs as "nicely inscribed."

So there's no pat answer as to which is better—signature only, or inscription to a person. It's going to be a matter of your own preference if you're the one getting the book signed. I always just ask for a signature if the author gives me a choice, but that's me. I can't see asking someone I don't know for a detailed inscription—maybe I'm too shy. Even on books I plan to keep I have a hard time asking for more than just a signature. This person doesn't know me; why should he write something nice for me (although Tim O'Brien looks genuinely hurt if you don't ask him to personalize your books)? Your answer may be different, and you'll find plenty of dealers on either side of the question who will agree with whatever conclusion you reach.

The dating of signed copies is another point of contention. "Signed in the year of publication" as a notation in a book catalog often means you'd better guard your wallet. But then there are authors who find this idea ridiculous, so they'll always date their signature in the year of publication, regardless of when they actually signed it. Edward Abbey was noted for this, and rarely put correct dates on his signings. Since there's no way to know when something was actually signed, those dealers who aren't busy bumping up prices are being skeptical. Again, you just have to figure out where you feel comfortable on the issue.

ASSOCIATION COPIES

One area of the market where there is no contention is in association copies. Association copies are among the most highly sought-after autographed works. Again, if the author has signed the book off to your aunt Margaret, that's not so exciting. But if the author has signed it off to another famous author, his literary agent, editor, or some other notable figure, then *that's* exciting. I've seen copies of otherwise worthless books come out of famous libraries and sell for a fortune, simply because of that magical little touch. This book once sat on the shelves of a favorite author; and it was signed by another famous author.

One of the most commonly found associations is the signing of an author to his or her literary agent. Agents often don't last very long, and when they move on to their next career, they often clean off their shelves. Better than an agent association, though—no matter the fact that without the agent the book probably never would have seen the light of day—is an association with another famous author. These too show up frequently in catalogs, shuffling around from dealer to dealer as much as they do from collector to collector. If you can find, say, a John Steinbeck first signed to William Faulkner, start pricing new cars.

There is another level to association copies, one that particularly shows up with older authors: books signed not by the author himself or herself, but by another famous figure, who was marking territory in the book. I've handled items from H. P. Lovecraft's library, and his bookplate in a worthless book is a guarantee of a couple hundred dollars (there are, actually, people who collect bookplates, and that opens an entirely different market).

VERIFICATION

With all signatures, there is always the question of verification. How do you know the book was really signed by the author? If you're lucky, you stood there and watched the author do it. But if you're buying through a dealer, then verification becomes a little more difficult.

There are many different autograph guides (see chapter 12 for details) that include samples of a few authors' signatures for comparative purposes. These guides can be especially useful on political signatures, presidential or senatorial markings in books. For literary authors, they're likely to have a few big names, but in genres, forget it.

One valuable resource for the serious is Allen and Patricia Ahearn's *Author Price Guides*, available individually or as a set. Each includes a facsimile signature of the author listed. The set covers about 175 popular authors.

When you do see limited editions of works, always look at the signature and make a note of any peculiarities. Then if you see a trade book signed by the same person, you can compare. No two signatures are ever the same, even by the same person, but there are trademark oddities to note. The way an *S* is shaped or the way the *Y* drops down, for example. I once had someone bring in a box with nearly fifty "autographed" books by a couple dozen different authors. Yes, they were all autographed, each and every one by the exact same person—one would assume by the person who brought in the box. The only attempt at subtlety was to use a different pen on a couple of them.

One often-overlooked place to check for verification is on the boards of the book. Many books have a facsimile autograph there on the boards themselves, and you can compare that with the signature.

There are autograph specialists who can verify signatures, but unless it is a particularly valuable autograph, it is generally not worth the expense. If you've got a Millard Fillmore letter signed when he was in office (always worth more than before or after office), then get it authenticated. But for most signatures, the expense is not worth it.

Finally, in and among all this talk of values, it's important not to lose sight of the true value of a signed edition: the association, the closeness with a favorite author. Many authors put a lot of time and effort into getting in touch with their readers, and getting a chance to meet one of these people and talk to them can not only enhance the value of your collection, but more importantly, it can enhance the pleasure you take in their books. Over the years I've met authors who were so utterly gracious and kind that I became an instant fan, even though I may have only gone to the signing out of curiosity or business. I've met others who have failed to reach me and, after a few years of collecting their books, I didn't regret selling the items off and going in search of other, newer authors.

SIGNING ETIQUETTE

When meeting an author at a signing, it's important to obey a few basic rules of courtesy: don't bring a wheelbarrow full of books and expect the author to sign every one. Be reasonable and polite. Don't ask for a full-page inscription. I've actually seen people show up at signings with typed sheets of what they wanted the author to write in their book. Show interest in the author's work and don't make him feel like a commodity. Authors know who's there hoping to wring a few extra bucks from a collection and who's there just as a fan. If the signing is at a store, buy the new book from that store. Shops go to a lot of expense and effort to bring writers in; you have to make the shop feel appreciated, just as you want to make the author feel appreciated.

A casual comment made by an author at a signing can change your whole perspective of a book or its writer. When I met Larry McMurtry the first time, he seemed surly and anxious to be somewhere else. When I commented how much I loved the line "We don't rent pigs" in *Lonesome Dove*, he showed the first smile of the evening and said, "Yes, that was an inspired line." It made me want to go back and read the book again, and ultimately, that's the true value of an autographed copy.

You can also drop authors a note (send it in care of their publisher) to see if they mind signing a book or two for you. If they agree to, your manners must be perfect: do not make this a chore. Wrap the book carefully, include a return envelope with adequate postage, and in short, make things as easy on the author as you possibly can.

A friend got hold of the phone numbers of quite a number of famous authors. He called Ken Kesey at his home. Kesey answered by yelling, "WHAT?" My friend politely asked if Mr. Kesey minded signing a few books. Kesey replied, "Well, no. I sign books pretty well. But it might take me a while."

If the autographed book market seems impossibly complicated, it really isn't. Get the stuff signed, and don't worry about it. It will always appreciate in value.

EPHEMERA

The publishing industry rarely stops at books. Although that's what we've been talking about so far, there is also the cottage industry of ephemera to work in, and it's an industry that can be just as lucrative—if not more so—than books.

Ephemera can be loosely explained as everything about the author that is not a book. I'm going to slightly expand the use of the term *ephemera* for the sake of this chapter, to include what are usually called the B and C list on an author's bibliography. So besides advertisements, posters, catalog appearances, books about the author, or critical studies, I'm also including broadside publications, magazine appearances, videos of TV interviews, or tapes of lectures in the listing of ephemera.

The possibilities are endless, and so are the chances for the avid collector and dealer.

For example, Ernest Hemingway's *The Old Man and the Sea* appeared, in its entirety, in *Life* magazine before its actual book publication. We're calling that ephemera here.

Now, is that magazine appearance more collectible than the first issue of the book? Yes and no. A book collector will only want the book. A Hemingway collector would love to have the magazine on his shelf. There are quite a few authors who had books, or parts of books, first published in magazines. Jack Kerouac published a brief addition to *On the Road* in *Playboy*. Gabriel García Márquez first published *Chronicle of a Death Foretold* in *Vanity Fair*. Even Dr. Seuss's *How the Grinch Stole Christmas* appeared in *Redbook*.

PRINTED MATTER

Many authors publish *broadsides*, single-paged pieces that have not lasted well over the years. This is particularly true among the Beat poets, who turned out hundreds of cheap, mimeographed bits of their work. Allen Ginsberg, in particular, can be tough to find in a good broadside—but they are out there, and they are worth watching for. Other notables who made their mark in broadsides are Richard Brautigan and Charles Bukowski. A personal favorite of mine is Gary Snyder's "Smokey the Bear Sutra," which he wrote the night before a meeting of the Sierra Club Wilderness Conference, in February 1969, got printed up, and passed out at the door. Because the broadside says that it "may be reproduced free forever," there have been literally hundreds of editions of "Smokey," and the main Snyder bibiographer has, supposedly, been working on a "Smokey"-exclusive volume for years. (Fun side note: when I had Snyder sign my copy of the broadside [probable third state], he signed it "Smokey the Bear.")

Broadsides can present a problem of dating and establishing primacy, particularly on the works run off office copying equipment. Little or no attempt was made to distinguish between the first impression or the twentieth. Of course, when the writers were doing these things, they usually weren't well enough known to warrant a fiftieth impression. The first is all there is. But when in doubt, check the specific author's bibliography. This is an area where it's easy to make mistakes.

Because of the inherently limited format, more poets than

fiction writers do broadsides. The equivalent for prose writers is perhaps the magazine article. Virtually all fiction writers get their start in magazines, often in literary magazines with circulations of only a few hundred. The place to start tracking these down is in the library, poring through back issues of the *Reader's Guide to Periodical Literature*, the standard author bibliographies, and the copyright page of any story collection. Magazines, no matter how small, are usually recognized there for first publication of the story in question.

What else counts as ephemera? One of my favorites is appearances in publishers' catalogs. These are very difficult to come by, since you have to get them from a bookstore, but early notice of a particular book—and the publisher's catalog is the first notice—is a wonderful item to have, and you'll be one of the few out there with it. These are not expensive, and perhaps the collectors are more difficult to find, but you can fill a niche with a few catalogs. The hard part will be finding them in reasonable condition; they tend to get heavily marked by salesmen and buyers.

MISCELLANEOUS ITEMS

Publishers also sometimes issue posters to promote books. Another recent trend is T-shirts, which are given away with a purchase of the book. If you've been making friends with the staff at a local bookshop, you should be able to get your hands on a lot of this stuff absolutely free.

Buttons also make good giveaways for publishers, and they make a nice subcategory in the ephemera market. *The Red Couch*, a photo book of, yes, a red couch, with text by William Least Heat Moon, was promoted by a button with, yes, a photo of the red couch. Buttons tend to appear more on nonfiction titles than fiction, but with Least Heat Moon, you're looking at an odd item of which not many have survived since the year of the book's appearance.

TV, radio, and even film appearances are becoming more common for many authors. Beyond the usual interviews on the talk-show circuit, many writers are appearing in the film versions of their own works. Stephen King is becoming as ubiquitous as Alfred Hitchcock. Ann Beattie appeared as a waitress in the film version of her novel *Chilly Scenes of Winter* (the film was titled *Head Over Heels*, as was a paperback reissue of the novel).

Film versions of books usually produce endless items of memorabilia. There are one-sheets (display posters), lobby cards, even dolls and models for some films. For the *Gone With the Wind* collector, there's everything from plates to dolls of Scarlett in her ball gown. These items may only slightly touch the book, but they're eagerly sought after by the true fan. You could fill a couple of houses with *Wizard of Oz* items.

Most of this type of material is only of interest to the extreme collector, rather than to the dealer. This can be useful if you have an extreme collector as a customer. Marilyn Monroe collectors, for example, tend to buy everything. Your scouting trips expose you to a lot of odd stuff that they may not have seen before. This will become second nature to you as you build a network of contacts. Know who is interested in what, but never turn down a fine piece that can tie in to books. Don't limit yourself.

One broad exception to this is items connected with the Kennedy assassination. Everyone and his brother seems to have saved memorial magazines, books, pamphlets, whatever. Socked away in drawers for years, these all make an appearance every November, when a person remembers he's saved these things all these years and thinks they must be worth a fortune. They're not. They're common. Yes, there are serious Kennedy collectors, lots of them. But the amount of available common material is staggering. Same for the first moon landing. World-changing events such as these make for lousy collectible markets. If you see something cheap, grab it and hope, but be prepared to sit on it until you come across a serious collector who maybe doesn't have absolutely everything on Kennedy or Armstrong already. And there are always new collectors born. But don't get too excited or hope to strike it rich here, either.

LETTERS

Letters are a favorite of many collectors. What better thing to own from a favorite writer than a personal letter?

Most writers are surprisingly cooperative about sending you off a quick note when you write to them (the easiest way is in care of their publisher) and say something nice about their books. Writing can be a lonely business, and I have very nice, very charming letters from a number of writers I love.

Better still are letters from authors long gone. I once came across a couple letters from Sir Richard Burton tucked inside one of his books. And a friend of mine once was offered for sale a handwritten poem signed by Robert Louis Stevenson. The woman offering the poem was the great-granddaughter of a woman who was on the ship that brought RLS to the United States when he was trying to chase down Fanny. Great-grandmother was a little girl at the time, and she caught the eye of RLS, who wrote her this little poem.

The lesson here is that my friend has spent the past fifteen years daily cursing himself for not buying the thing. He didn't have the money at the time; given the opportunity again, he'd sell his car before he'd let that get away.

Ephemera in all its many forms is fun. Collecting it gives you a chance to preserve fragile items that otherwise end up in a garbage heap somewhere. I used to keep a *dump* (one of the cardboard display racks bookstores use) from a favorite book in my house; atop the dump was a huge cardboard sign, publicizing the book. The item was worthless, but a lot of fun to own. And isn't having fun with your collection the whole point?

Chapter Ten

❧

BOOK REPAIR, RESTORATION, CLEANING AND CARE

O ne afternoon, while haunting a shop where I'd often found treasures before, I came across a first edition of Graham Greene's *The Quiet American*, one of my all-time favorite books. Although I'd often seen it in catalogs, it was rather more scarce on shop shelves, and I'd never bought a first of this one before. I enjoyed the hunt for it too much (in fact, I've never bought a first of many of my favorite books; I'm trusting fate to toss them in front of me someday, in mint condition and grossly underpriced). But here it was, neatly shelved, the spine in excellent condition with only a trace of fading. Carefully, I pulled the book from the case, opened to the copyright page, and saw that it was, indeed, a first edition.

But there were problems.

Although the spine was in excellent shape, the back of the dust jacket had a long tear in it; on the front of the jacket, someone had actually taken a black Magic Marker and written his name across the cover design. Inside, the hinges were starting to loosen. Although the pages themselves were still clean and tight, there was just a hint of water damage along the top edge.

In short, the book was practically worthless, and I put it back on the shelf, easily deciding to continue my hunt for a clean copy.

Throughout this book, I've told you that condition is everything. One little tear on the dust jacket of a prime book can make a hundred-dollar difference. A previous owner's name on the front paste-down can ruin a book's collectibility.

But can a book be saved? After the abuse, can tears be mended, can patches be laid, hinges repaired, foxing lightened?

It depends on the book, as well as on the value of the book, and on how much effort you're willing to put into improving the book. Some books—like the Greene—are beyond repair. But as a species, books are amazingly resilient. I have books that have endured three hundred years; I have books that have endured the hands of four rambunctious children and who knows how many visiting cousins and friends. You'll be amazed at what a little time and effort can do for a hurt book.

Right up front, let me suggest that after you finish reading this book, you go get a copy of Jane Greenfield's *The Care of Fine Books*. She goes into more detail than I have space for here, and she's an expert in the field of conservation. It's a must-have for your shelves.

HOW TO DAMAGE A BOOK

Let's go about this whole idea of conservation and taking care of books backwards. How can you ruin a book? What can you do to take a collectible volume and turn it into a worthless pile of pulp? You should look at it from this point of view, because often the most damaging things that happen to books are things people do to enhance the book for themselves.

Putting in a bookplate (unless you're somebody famous) is a deadly thing to do. The same with writing your name in a book. Besides simple signatures, inscriptions are also fatal. Most staff at a used bookshop can kill an hour or so of slack time by laughing over mushy inscriptions in books that have been traded in. Who cares that John pledged his undying love to Joyce and that he'd love her forever, or at least until she traded in the copy of *The Little Prince* he gave her for their third-week anniversary? No collector, that's for sure.

Early owners do these things to establish ownership, because it gives many people great pleasure to leave behind their mark. But for the collector, it's a curse.

And that's just the tip of the iceberg. There are many ways to damage a book, and in order to keep your books in collectible condition and at peak value, you must learn to be very careful.

One common and little-thought-of way to damage books is simply to store them wrong. Uneven pressure—if you don't keep your books in a straight, vertical line on the shelf, or if you pack them carelessly in a box when you move—can cause the book's spine to roll, ruining the right angles of a fine book. Other problems of incorrect shelving include putting the books on the shelf too loosely, causing them to lean and start to roll; and shelving the books too tightly, where you risk rubbing the dust jacket every time you take a book off the shelf. Storing books of vastly different sizes together can cause the larger books' boards to warp. Get the wrong kind of shelf, and you can have paint or finisher bleeding onto your books. There are even those who will tell you that untreated wood shelves can damage books by leaking toxic vapors.

Proper shelving will be covered in detail shortly. Just keep in mind what not to do, and if you take this advice seriously, you'll be straightening books in shops, whether you want to buy them or not. The urge to preserve runs deep in book lovers.

Yet even trying to take care of a book can hurt it. Many people repair dust jacket tears with neat little patches of cellophane tape on the jacket's underside. While this is a nearly invisible way to make a rough patch, over time, cellophane tape starts to decay, leaving marks on the book's boards. Tape also leaves a yellow stain where it touches the paper of the jacket. These marks and stains can decrease the value of the book by 20 or 30 percent, if not render it worthless.

If a reader handles a book carelessly, the hinges can weaken, even tear. This is particularly common with children's books and other well-loved volumes that have been read and reread over the years. The binding itself will become loose, noticeable when you open the front board. The gutter between the board and the pages will stretch out, or have little tears in it. This can also be caused by not using proper bookmarks. Tucking a pen into the book to mark your place puts uneven stress on the spine of the book, pulling at the hinges. Or worse, lay a book facedown on a table. You may just have downgraded it from Fine to Very Good. Licking your fingers when you turn the page stains and weakens the fiber of the book, and, as anyone who's read *The Name of the Rose* can tell you, it can also be dangerous.

But more often the signs of degradation are less insidious: dirt, gunk on the dust jacket—the daily wear and tear a book receives over the course of its natural life span. It's not a matter of the book not having been taken care of; it's a matter of time taking its inevitable toll.

Most of these problems are easily avoided. Many can be easily fixed. Jackets can be cleaned, many hinge tears can be repaired. But sometimes you've just got to admit the cause is lost and leave the book on the shelf. I'll find another first of *The Quiet American*. And, hopefully, it will be in better shape.

DUST JACKET RESTORATION AND REPAIR

Now let's take a look at several restoration and repair methods to maximize the value of your books and protect them.

The most common reason for downgrading a book is simply its lack of cleanliness, so first we'll look at methods to restore the original luster to an older volume.

To begin with, remember that the dust jacket is the single most important component of a collectible book. The jacket comprises roughly three-quarters of the value of a modern first edition. This shouldn't be the case—dust jackets have little to do with the authors—but this is the way it is. If a book doesn't have a jacket, it's almost never worth picking up (unless it's something like a Fitzgerald, a Dashiell Hammett, a Jack Kerouac; experience will teach you whose books are especially rare in jackets). And, because the jacket determines such a large part of the book's value, you should concentrate much of your time on cleaning and restoring it.

Before we get into cleaning and restoration techniques, a word of warning: Don't try any of the techniques presented in this chapter on expensive books first. Buy some junk reading copies or old book club editions and practice on these a few times. Cleaning and restoration can be risky. If you're not comfortable with a procedure, *don't do it*. Better to have a bookplate left in than a huge tear in the paper.

CLEANING JACKETS

The easiest thing to do with a dirty dust jacket is to take a little rubbing alcohol on a clean, lint-free rag, and gently wash the outside paper. This will remove 90 percent of the dirt a book gathers over the years, and the alcohol evaporates without staining. Work methodically, in neat lines, as if you were painting a wall. Start at one flap and work back to the other, taking care not to push down too much on the creases in the jacket. WARNING: *This only works on slick jackets!* Using alcohol on a rough jacket of untreated paper is an invitation to disaster.

For a slightly tougher stain, petroleum jelly works wonders. Apply it the same way as the alcohol, and even rubbed-in clumps of dirt will come off. After this, however, go ahead and do the alcohol treatment to get the petroleum jelly residue off the book's jacket.

For the absolutely toughest stains, rubber cement is the answer. If, for example, the book once had a sale sticker placed on it and there's old, dried glue on the jacket, the best way to treat it and get it off is with more glue—specifically, rubber cement. Dab a bit on the affected area, wait for it to half-dry (not quite sticky, but not set either), and gently roll it off with the tip of your finger. This one takes practice to get right. Odd as it may seem, this procedure does not damage the jacket, and the cement will remove almost any type of dirt or grime.

Lighter fluid will work much the same trick as rubber cement: put some on a tissue, dab the tissue onto the affected area, and let the lighter fluid soften the gunk up until it rolls off. The fluid doesn't stain, but it does stink, and personally I've never been happy with the idea of pouring flammable liquid onto my books.

WARNING: *None of these techniques work on rough paper jackets.* You can only treat the jacket this way if it is made of smooth, coated stock. Rough paper will just absorb the solvents and stain worse.

Cleaning a rough paper jacket is rather more difficult. You can start with a good, soft Artgum or Pink Pearl eraser, and see how much dirt comes off. Do not rub hard. There are also some professionally used cleansing compounds that may work. Try

Absorene, available from library supply houses. The stuff looks like Play-Doh; you rub it between your fingers until it's soft, and then use it to brush gunk off the book. It works very well, and since it is dry, you can use it on any kind of paper.

Be very careful with any kind of erasers: they can erase color right off the page if they're used with too much force.

To get stickers off rough paper, aim a blow-dryer at the sticker for a moment; the heat will loosen the glue and you should be able to easily—but gently, so gently—pull the sticker off.

REPAIRING JACKET TEARS

You should now have a nice, clean jacket. What are the other problems that affect jackets? Sun fading is a common problem, but there's nothing you can do about that. Yet more common are little tears, chips, or missing parts of the jacket.

People who give books as gifts like to cut off the price of the book. What's the point in giving a present if you're going to advertise how much the present cost? In catalogs, you see this described as "price-clipped DJ." Most people cut the price out on a diagonal (hopefully minimizing the damage to the jacket), but some square-clip the jackets: neat little right-angle cuts. Although the square cut actually leaves more of the jacket intact, from the collector's point of view, a diagonal cut is better than a square cut (and of course, no cut is best of all). If you've got a square-cut jacket, take a minute to look at it and see if you can, *without taking off much more of the jacket,* change it to a diagonal cut. This is risky, and a matter of personal judgment, and you may not want to try this. A lot of book lovers can't bring themselves to get near a jacket with scissors, and in many ways, they're right: don't alter more than you have to. But from the viewpoint of value, a diagonally cut book will be worth fractionally more than a square-cut book. Or it may not even be a matter of value, but it is easier to find a buyer on a diagonal-cut book than a square cut.

Sometimes you have no choice but to fix a cut. I've come across beautiful books where the price was actually torn off, leaving great rounded, ragged edges. I get a ruler, angle it, looking for the way to neaten the book as much as possible while taking off as little as possible from the remaining flap, take a deep breath, and cut. There is nothing else to be done.

Usually not much can be done about tears or chips in the dust jacket, either. Professional binders can mend tears and small chips on occasion, but this is something best left to the experts. They first match the ends of the tear as perfectly as possible, taking painstaking care and effort to bring the edges back to their original position—on a bad tear, this could mean hours of work, gently trimming loose fibers. Most tears have an overlap, and it's important that this overlap match its original position exactly; this is made all the more difficult by the fact that many paper tears actually start overlapping one direction, and then turn to overlap the other. After matching up the torn edges, a restorer then takes a very thin rice paper patch, and places it on the underside of the jacket, completely covering the tear. Once the rice paper is positioned, it's then very gently placed with only the thinnest layer of rice starch or cornstarch paste. This isn't really something you want to try at home.

Chips are more complicated yet. A chip is an actual piece missing from the jacket. One method of repair is to find another chipped jacket and patch on, much as described above, the missing piece so that instead of having two bad jackets, you have one well-repaired one and one dead one. There are, of course, problems with this. First of all, the volume is no longer original, and it must be advertised as repaired in the affected areas. This brings the price down (although, depending on the size of the chip, not as much as a flawed jacket does; it depends on the collector's feelings about complete structural originality). Second, it can be nearly impossible to match the pieces.

Obviously the two books will have worn differently, and finding a patch with the same amount of fading and similar aging patterns can be nearly impossible—entirely impossible if the book is a rarity to begin with.

Why not just toss an imperfect jacket and replace it with a new one? This happens more than might be suspected. Many jackets are coded and easy to identify as first edition jackets, but many more are not. Further, many books keep their original price through several editions, which can make it nearly impossible to tell when a new jacket has been "married" to an older book. Occasionally you can tell by wear patterns—jackets fit books like gloves over hands, and a loose or too-tight jacket that doesn't match the wear pattern of the book can be a tip-off. But it often takes a trained or lucky eye to see where a new jacket has been used.

Although putting a different first edition jacket on a first edition copy of the book (there are obvious ethical and collectible problems with putting on later jackets) seems perfectly all right—after all, both jacket and book are first editions, it's just that they didn't start off together—this is frowned upon by serious collectors. Again, the whole mythos behind the first edition is to get a copy of the book in as close to its original state as possible. *Any* alterations detract from this. There are collectors who don't care, and who will seek out new jackets for their books, but they are generally frowned upon by the trade. It's an alteration. It's also deceptive.

One final, quite deceptive and quite stupid practice: some people will try to color in faded areas of a jacket with a marker. This rarely if ever works—matching the shade is next to impossible—and it only damages the jacket. It doesn't fool anyone. If you find a book that has been abused this way, and it's a coated-paper jacket, rubbing alcohol may take the ink off.

To sum up the jacket world: cleaning is easy, repairing is hard. Use your own moral judgment on whether or not to replace, but be aware that it's not an entirely kosher thing to do.

Now that we've addressed the jacket, it's time to turn to the book itself.

BOOK RESTORATION AND REPAIR

First, we clean the book; then we take a look at the volume to see that all of the structural parts are intact and tight. As with jackets, you can carefully use rubber cement on the cloth boards of a book without fear of staining. This should remove any residue on the cloth. Simple gum erasers can also remove a fair number of marks and stains. Use a soft artist's brush to wipe off the eraser dust. Again, erasers can seriously damage colored paper and cheap dyes. You must be extremely careful with them.

If the book has been kept in its jacket over the years, the outside of the boards should be in good shape, and you shouldn't have to pay much attention to them.

One of a book's worst enemies is dust. Bookshelves are never dusted very thoroughly, and the top edge of a book—especially if it had uncut pages—can become filthy. Hold the book gently by the spine, the front edge facing you. Take a lint-free, very soft cloth, and very gently brush away the dust in even strokes, bringing the cloth toward you—that is, along the top edge of the book, away from the spine. Repeat this on the bottom edge, then the front edge. Be careful around the book's headband and footband. Again, you can also do this with a soft art brush.

Headbands take considerably more abuse than footbands do. The headband is where a finger is likely to catch when taking the book off the shelf, and missing or loose headbands are common. A good bindery should be able to match your missing headband to the cloth of the footband (again, any such repair has to be advertised), or you can tighten a loose headband with a little binder's glue.

Another structural defect that can be addressed from the

outside is *rolling*. A rolled spine is a serious detriment to the value of a book, and, unfortunately, there's almost no way to return the book to its original square state. One or the other of the hinges has been stretched. But by applying even pressure to the book, you can bring it back closer in line to true. This is most easily done by putting the book on a tightly packed shelf, being sure that the books holding the affected volume in are of the same size, and are squared with the hurt book; also make sure that the front edge of the book is up against something solid to help hold it in place. This is largely a matter of trial and error: you can put too much pressure on the book and end up damaging the hinges even further. It's a good idea to try this technique on some reading copies before trying it on the good stuff. Be aware also that it's a very slow process, and you can't move the book for maybe as long as several months for the treatment to be successful. Even then it might not work. I've seen trued books slowly slip back to their former, rolled ways within days of being taken out of the squeeze.

The one thing on the outside of a book that's very difficult to address is a remainder mark. When a book is taken out of trade circulation and sold off at pennies on the dollar, most publishers mark the books in some way to keep bookshops from returning the volumes at full price. These marks range from a simple black pen slash across one of the book's edges (usually the bottom) to a company stamp, like Simon & Schuster's logo of the man carrying a book, or Alfred A. Knopf's Borzoi hound. Once these marks are on the book, they're going to stay. There are only two possibilities for removing them, and they fall into an ethical gray area. The first, and safer, method is to sand the marks off. Again, this is an alteration of the book; on the other hand, what's the remainder mark but an alteration? Use very, very fine-grained sandpaper, and apply it only with great gentleness, very slowly. If the book's pages were bound tightly, you can probably get most of the mark off. If the book had uncut pages, you're looking at a lost cause; just accept the mark and save yourself some time and frustration.

Or you can try the second method, which is a lot riskier: bleach on a Q-tip. One drop too much, though, and instead of removing the ink, the bleach will bleed onto the inside pages of the book, staining wherever you touched. Bleach also stinks. Although this procedure works, you're probably better off learning to live with remainder marks.

INTERIOR PAGES

Now for the interior of the book. First, check the front paste-down and the front free endpaper for dirt and grime. These pages are handled the most. If the pages are white stock, gently use a gum eraser, which will clean most marks; be sure to brush the eraser dust out of the book before you close the boards. *You cannot do this if the endpaper and flyleaf are of colored stock. The eraser will discolor the paper.*

If a previous owner has written his or her name on the book, or pasted in a bookplate, there is not much to be done. No magic ink remover exists that will take out the name without creating more damage. There's a little bit of hope on the book-plate—many modern plates have such bad glue that they can be gently taken up (work at 45-degree angles to the fiber of the book's page) and removed with little or no trace. However, many more have glue that sticks like an oyster's shell, and any attempt at removal is just going to tear the bookplate, as well as the book page underneath the plate. Write these damages off, and hope later you'll find a copy where the previous owner didn't feel a need to mark territory.

A major problem for the true condition freak is any writing on colored endpapers. Many dealers are guilty of this them-selves, figuring that if they don't mark the price on the first inside page of the book, no one will ever see it. Unfortunately, the first inside page is often colored paper. A pencil mark here does not seem like a problem until you try to erase it. Then you find that not only has the pencil mark come up, but so has the color on the page, leaving behind a little white circle where you rubbed the eraser. You've just taken the book out of contention as a serious collectible.

If you come across a written mark on a colored page, be very, very gentle. Work as lightly as possible with as soft an eraser as you can find, rubbing in very light circles. At the first hint of color coming off, give up. It's better to leave the pencil mark than to make a white spot.

Obviously, this should also warn you never to mark on a colored page yourself. This should be the most obvious rule in the business, but it's alarming how often it's broken.

You can also damage a book by writing on the white pages, even carefully pricing something in pencil. Pressing too hard on a white page when you're penciling in a price can ruin a book. I had to send back a copy of the anniversary issue of *To Kill a Mockingbird* because the shop I bought it from must have been leaning on the pencil when the price was written in. The indentation went through three pages. What were these people thinking of?

There also isn't much that can be done for tears on internal pages; patches can be made with rice paper as described above for jackets, but as with the outside of the book, never use cellophane tape. When patching, make sure to put wax paper or something else nonporous between the patched page and the surrounding pages until the patch is completely dry. Again, be careful to match the overlapping edges exactly, and use as small a patch as possible to cover the tear. Better yet, leave this to a pro.

On antiquarian books entire signatures are often replaced, but one rarely, if ever, sees this with a modern. But because so many antiquarian books are so rare, it is actually acceptable to put in facsimiles of missing sections. Dealers will advertise this alteration, but it's often the only way to get a complete copy of an antiquarian book. Remember that in the old days, books were sold unbound, so the binding is not "original," and the signatures could well have been assembled or reassembled at any time in the book's history. However, you're not going to see this with a modern book.

One of the more common problems with books that have had forty or fifty years of aging is *foxing*. Foxing marks are the little brown splotches that mark the pages—it looks like a fox with muddy feet has run across the book. Foxing is caused by impurities in the paper reacting over time, and the only way to remove it is to unbind the book and then soak the individual leaves in a deacidifier, a sizing solution, and a bleaching agent. Leave this to the professionals, who will know how to put the binding back together. It's an expensive process, and worth the effort only on the rarest of books.

The same holds true for books that are browning heavily. This is the result of the book being printed on cheap, acidic paper. A professional restorer will unbind the book, soak the pages in a deacidifier, and then rebind. Don't try this at home.

Give up on water stains. There's no real hope.

Books that have been improperly stored may have bug tracks in them. There is a remarkable variety of insects that think books are just delicious. Look for not only bodies, but odd colors of dust on the books. Obviously, you're best off not buying a bugged book, but if you've got one, the safest means of treatment is to put the book in a Ziploc bag and stick the bag in the freezer. A day or two will take care of any living creature. Leave the book in the bag for another day after you take it out of the freezer, to allow for any condensation to dry. Then use your artist's brush to remove any animal parts.

You can de-stink a book that's been stored near mothballs by putting the book, along with a box of baking soda, in an ice chest. Leave it alone for a week or two, and most of the stink should disappear.

Occasionally you come across a book that is still good on the interior, but the binding is damaged beyond hope. This is the final repair that can be easily made, but it's very expensive, best done only by professionals, and should be reserved only for the rarest of books.

When rebinding a book, no effort is made to keep the new binding like the old. Usually, a decorative leather binding is chosen, one which will set off the beauty of the text inside. Rebinding can cost $300 and up for a truly fine binding, and it will enhance the value of a book that may otherwise have no hope. For instance, suppose you've got a first edition of *Gone With the Wind*, which would be worth upwards of $3,000 in fine shape. However, on your copy, the boards are actually detached and the printing on the spine is gone. In essence, you have a worthless book in this state. But if you get it rebound, spending, say, $400 fixing it up, you've got a volume that could now be sold in the $600–$700 range, with a little luck. The margins decrease with rebinding, and a rebound book will never have the value or the appeal of an original volume, but there are collectors who, unable to find a fine copy of a favorite book, will settle for one that's been rebound. They can be hard to find, though, and this is the last resort for any book.

While cleaning a book is always a good thing to do, this is not necessarily true with repairs. It's too easy to damage a book if the repair is handled carelessly or by someone not entirely sure of what they're doing.

Also, consider before you repair a book that no matter what the repair, you have to advertise it when you sell the book. If you've fixed a tear in a page, you must say so. If a chip has been repaired in the jacket, you must say so.

CARING FOR YOUR COLLECTION

Now that you've got your acquisitions in the best shape possible, how do you treat them? If you're looking for (and the book is capable of delivering) a fast profit, just turn it around and get it out. But if you're going to age the book awhile, how you take care of it is an important part of the business. Besides, since you've gone through all that trouble to clean the book, you might as well keep it shiny.

I've been in the houses of book dealers who have wall-to-wall bookcases, each filled with neatly squared, perfect volumes. I've also been in the houses of dealers who have piles of books on the floor, piles so high they're starting to teeter. More books are crammed into boxes, and the shelves, if any, have been doubled and tripled so that it's impossible to see what's on them. This goes to show that even the pros get careless. But there's no reason why you should.

Books are made to be kept upright. Piling books on top of each other places unnatural stress on the hinges, makes it difficult to pull a book out when you need it, often causes rubbing on the jacket, and there's always the possibility of disaster should the pile topple. If you must pile books, put the heaviest volumes on the bottom, try to keep the stresses as even as possible, and don't stack more than a couple feet high. If you must box books, don't put them face-edge down in the box. This pushes the spine backwards. Keep them upright, as they'd be on a shelf; use plenty of acid-free packing material to keep everything snug.

SHELVES

If you're taking your books seriously, you need bookcases or shelves. Lots of them.

However, not just any case is going to do. If you use cheap particle-board cases, you run the risk of the rough wood rubbing the bottom edge of the book. Paint the case, and it's entirely possible the paint will come off on the book. As I've said again and again, condition is everything, and no collector is going to smile about paint chips.

A better solution to making rough shelves acceptable is to use shelf paper. It's cleanable, nontoxic, and it shields the books from rough surfaces. Don't put the paper just on the bottom of the shelves—also put it on the sides where the books will come in contact with the case.

If this strikes you as unsightly, go to fully sealed coatings on the wood of the cases, and be sure the coating is completely dried before a book comes anywhere near it. Or use metal shelves with a baked enamel finish. Do not store books on an open-sided bookcase. That open side will put uneven pressure on the book, and the boards will warp. Those metal bookends that you see all the time? Forget them. The prongs that slide under the books will likely damage the bottom edge. If you use bookends, use smooth, nonprotruding ones.

Okay, you've got shelves ready to go, so now you just stuff the books on the fixtures, and you're all set, right? Not quite.

SHELVING BOOKS

There's actually an art to shelving books. This may sound niggling, but it's not. A shelf packed too loosely allows books to lean, thus damaging the boards and the spine. A too tightly packed shelf means you're risking rubbing the jacket every time you take a book off the shelf. Too tight can also warp the spine if the books are not kept in line and pressure is unevenly distributed.

The ideal bookshelf has books on it that are holding each other up, jackets gently touching, nothing leaning, but nothing rubbing either. It should be easy for you to take a book off the shelf, or to put one back on. If you're having to snug the book in, you're too tight and need to readjust. No matter how niggling this point seems, it is vital. A badly shelved book loses value every day.

Books should be arranged on the shelf by size, and the spines should be evenly lined up. As I said before, differences in the sizes of books can cause boards to warp; uneven spines in the lineup cause rolling.

How you take the book on and off the shelf is also important. Put your index finger along the top edge of the book (don't hook the headband), and pull back gently, leaning the book back to fall into the cradle of your hand.

When opening a book, cradle it in your hand, holding the book by the spine, not the boards. Open it as narrowly as you can for inspection. Oftentimes, the only thing that keeps a book from being considered "Very Fine" is how widely it was opened when it was read by the original owner. Never, ever place an open book facedown to mark your place. It stretches the spine and causes the book to fall open to the spot where the pressure was applied. Again, that's the difference between fine and good.

JACKET COVERS

While shelving is important, there is one thing that is even more vital. The absolute best thing you can do for your books is to protect the jackets with a sleeve, such as those made by Brodart or University Products. Virtually any library book you've ever checked out is wrapped in one of these. Sleeves are clear on one side, with opaque paper (make sure the paper is acid-free) on the other. They come in either rolls or single sheets, in varying heights. I prefer rolls because you can cut the jacket to fit the book exactly; the single-sheet jackets are often not quite long enough for a thick volume. As far as height goes, most modern books will fit into either a nine-inch or a ten-inch jacket protector. You'll need the occasional twelve-inch and the very occasional sixteen-inch as well.

To put on a sleeve, take the jacket off the book, measure it, and cut your sheet to size. Open up the paper backing and place the jacket inside, with its face against the clear part of the sleeve. Then simply fold down the top edge of the sleeve to fit the jacket snugly (although you'll get the smoothest results if you pull a little tighter than you think you should, you must be careful not to make it too tight and buckle the paper). Many people then tape the sleeve down, but again, cellophane tape is death to books. A good crease along the new fold will work just as well, without the risk of damage. When I buy books that someone else has wrapped, one of the first things I do is check for tape on the jacket sleeve. If there is any, I put on a whole new sleeve to avoid any risk of residue contamination.

When you're wrapping a book, take care to clean off the white paper dust that sometimes comes off the material. It's not going to hurt anything, but it's unsightly, and it's alarming how many people are too lazy to do this.

Now that the jacket is neatly in its sleeve, lay the book into the center crease, and, smoothing the paper all the way, bring up the end flaps and fold them over the boards. Getting the sleeves on smoothly takes a little practice, but it's worth it. There should not be a single collectible book on your shelves without its dust jacket in a sleeve. The sleeve keeps off dirt and grime, helps prevent rubbing, and forms a barrier between the most valuable part of your book and the rest of the world.

There's also a psychological advantage to putting sleeves on books. The Mylar outside is bright and shiny and adds to the visual appeal of the volume. It also gives the book a strangely special aura, which buyers will pick up on. I've found that buyers will almost invariably value a wrapped book more than an unwrapped copy of the same book. The difference can be as much as 20 or 30 percent, depending on the experience of the buyer. The sleeve tips the buyer off that this book is something special, something worth taking care of, a book that someone already values. And if one person values it, another is sure to, making it easier to sell. Jacket sleeves are not cheap, but they're well worth every penny. I don't even like to touch hardbacks that haven't been wrapped anymore—they feel wrong in my hands, and make me nervous.

The other great advantage to sleeves is that they protect the jacket completely, and yet they can be removed. I once saw someone who had laminated the dust jackets of his collectible books. Yes, the lamination kept the jackets in perfect shape, but he wouldn't be able to give the books away. The jackets were, for all intents and purposes, trash. Good for decoration, lousy for collecting. Never do anything that can't be undone.

One final thing about putting sleeves on jackets: particularly on older books, the endpapers and boards were made of much more acidic paper than the text pages. If you are cutting the sleeves from a roll, it's a good idea to make the sleeve bigger than the jacket—in fact, make it so it neatly fills the inside flap of the book. This puts an acid barrier between the boards and the pages, and will help prevent damage.

A lot of people take the dust jacket off the books they're reading. This seems to make sense—after all, if the jacket is the most valuable part of the book, why risk touching it at all—but while this does save wear and tear on the jacket, it can harm the book itself. The jacket, despite its value, is there to protect the book. The natural oils in your fingers can actually stain the cloth boards of a book, and if the cloth is rough, it's very difficult to clean once dirt and grime have gotten under the jacket. If you want to read your book—and what's the point in owning a fine book if you're not going to take the pleasure of reading it?—take the jacket off, put it in a sleeve, and read it with jacket and sleeve in place.

Finally, there's one other product available, this one specifically for books that never had a dust jacket, like the first issue of the first separate edition of H. P. Lovecraft's *Supernatural Horror in Literature* (look for the typo "elft" on line 1 of page 66). You can buy a wraparound clear Mylar sleeve that fits on the book much as a dust jacket would. This will keep the oils on your hands from touching the cloth boards, and serve to protect the book's exterior. Or you can make a jacket for an unjacketed book from Mylar sheets. It's a good solution for limited editions that are not put in jackets, but it's important that the sleeves be made of chemically inert material.

One of the main enemies of many dust jackets is the sun. Particularly if the jacket was done in deep colors like reds or purples or especially yellows, direct sunlight can cause serious fading. I've seen books that were once a royal purple faded to a kind of sickly puce. Much of the value of a Fine copy of Tony Hillerman's first novel, *The Blessing Way*, is in the difficulty of finding an unfaded spine. The beautiful cover of an Indian wearing a wolf hat fades to a nearly blank background when exposed to the sun for long periods of time. Same with Clark Ashton Smith's *Genius Loci*: the yellow cover is lovely, but just try to find one that hasn't faded beyond the point of pastel on the spine. *Keep all your books out of direct sunlight.*

In addition to sunlight, humidity and temperature can affect books. Keep the books as cool as you possibly can; ideal temperature is between sixty and seventy degrees.

Humidity is a bigger problem. Low humidity can cause pages to crack and become brittle; high humidity can cause mold to grow in books and pages to balloon. You can humidify or dehumidify the air in your house with a variety of machines, most of which are sold for exorbitant prices. Humidity is not such a problem in most modern houses, though, where climate control is fairly regulated.

CASES AND BOXES

Exceptionally valuable books require even more care, and many owners choose to have slipcases or clamshell boxes custom-made for their prizes. Slipcases are quite easy to make yourself, if you're good with materials. Create an open-ended box to the dimensions of the book. Use acid-free materials, and cover the outside of the box with tightly stretched cloth for appearance. A good slipcase should hold the book just as it is held on a well-packed shelf; it should also provide extra support for the book, being strong enough to prevent any sagging or listing.

A clamshell box is a little more complicated. The idea here is to completely cover the book. The bottom of the clamshell is slightly bigger than the book is when it lies flat; the top of the case fits snugly inside the bottom, also snuggling the book into place so it cannot move or shake about. One end of the case is hinged, so the overall look is just like the name describes: a shell, closing down over the book. Again, if you're good with your hands, these are not difficult to make. Library supply houses and fine binderies also sell them, or the bindery can custom-make them for you.

PAPERBACKS AND EPHEMERA

Most of what applies to hardcover, dust-jacketed books can also be applied to paperbacks and ephemera. There are a few other things to consider with these more fragile books, though.

Paperbacks were never meant to last. They were printed with cheap paper, bound with cheap glue, and no one ever expected them to hold up for more than three or four readings. Just finding an old paperback in good shape is an accomplishment, and that explains the prices on early Jim Thompsons ($200 and up) and many other writers who were first published in paperback form (Tim Powers's first book, *The Anubis Gates*, was a paperback original; a lot of Dean Koontz's first books came out as paperback originals, often under a bewildering array of aliases).

A collectible paperback in Very Fine condition is such a rarity that it makes many dealers almost afraid to handle the book when they find one. The cheap paper of early paperbacks falls apart; the glue disintegrates, leaving the pages falling out of the binding; the paper covers tear, rub, fold, and bend.

The easiest way to care for a fine paperback is to go to your nearest comic book specialty store and get some Mylar bags and acid-free backing boards. Comic collectors are experts on the degradations cheap paper is prone to, and they've hit on this solution: bag and back everything. The bags, made of a thin type of Mylar that is nontoxic to paper, come in a variety of sizes and are very cheap. The backing boards will help by adding a little rigidity to the package.

There is one caveat to bagging books: books were meant to breathe. While comic collectors want to keep air out of the bag and completely away from the newsprint comic, books actually need a little air to maintain proper condition. Don't seal the bag, and be sure there's a pinhole or two in it to allow for circulation.

The bag will keep dirt and grime off and protect the book from the daily ravages of time. It is also a good place to start with caring for your ephemera collection. The only drawback is that the Mylar bags aren't made in sizes bigger than old, classic *Life* magazine–size—about ten inches by twelve inches. If you've got posters, you can roll them up into mailing tubes or have them matted and framed (remember to specify acid-free mat board). For smaller pieces, you can get Mylar protective sleeves for notebooks, which allow a nice means of display.

While to the beginning collector much of this may seem to be extreme—after all, a Hemingway has already survived fifty years or so of handling and reading, and there is no shortage of books that have survived centuries—this is where the serious collectors and dealers part company with the dilettantes. Let me say it once more: nothing is more important than condition. Therefore, everything you do to enhance, improve, or maintain condition is worth the effort.

There is also a sense of responsibility to consider. Books are the links in the chain of our civilization. A fine book is, in so many ways, a sacred object, and while it is in your possession it is your responsibility. The book, if it's cared for properly, will be here hundreds of years after you're gone. It may pass through the hands of a thousand more people, touching lives every step of the way. While most people don't see books this way, you should consider them as something like an original oil painting. If you had a Picasso, you'd do everything possible to take care of it, right? Well, doesn't Chester Himes, Kurt Vonnegut, John Fante, or any other fine writer deserve the same consideration? These are the marks of our culture.

Chapter Eleven

❧

THE BUSINESS OF DEALING

I f you don't have any trade credit and yet you still pay full price for a book in a used shop, you've made a costly mistake.

If you are going to approach the buying and selling of books as a business, then you need to get on a business footing, putting yourself on an equal level with the dealers.

That means it's time to start getting a dealer's discount.

When you decide to try to make some money in this business, when you have stepped beyond the boundaries of strictly collecting and are now buying and selling, the first step is to get a business license. This establishes you as a legitimate dealer and as a payer of business taxes. Ironically, this relieves you from paying sales tax on items you buy to resell. Being on the government rolls as a business taxpayer (as opposed to a person paying sales tax) gives you a resale number, which you can then use to claim a dealer's discount at shops—10 percent is standard, but some stores are more generous and offer 20 percent—and it will also enable you to get the items tax-free, saving you another chunk of money.

Check your local laws to find out which apply to you. Besides the business license, you may need a separate resale license; if you're selling to other dealers, you may also need a wholesale license. Check to make sure there are no zoning restrictions, in case you ever have a buyer come to your house. This is not a matter for the federal government; it's a local thing, and it should not be expensive. Don't worry about incorporating unless you find a box full of autographed firsts of *Moby-Dick*.

The strict idea behind the resale number is that only the last person pays tax. Since you're planning on turning the item around, you are not the last person.

But the resale number also means that you are responsible for paying sales tax on any and all items you sell to those who are not buying for tax-exempt purposes. You will be held responsible by the government for the moneys due them, so on any direct, taxable sales, be sure you add on the tax and keep a detailed record of each transaction. Mail orders sent out of state, and thus far Internet orders, are tax-exempt at the moment, but this may change.

Stop in and talk to someone at the state revenue department; they can load you down with all the information and forms you're going to need, because this blessing of a dealer's discount and professional status does not come without paperwork. Obviously, the fact that you are now a licensed business in your state means that the government is going to want to keep track of what you do.

Now, for federal purposes, in order to qualify yourself as a legitimate business, as opposed to someone engaged in an occasionally money-making hobby, the IRS requires that you must show a profit within three years of start-up. How flexible they are on this point may vary, but don't count on any flexibility at all.

Therefore, in order to claim the deductions you deserve, and keep the government happy, you must follow the first rule for every business: *keep the receipt for everything.*

Yes, everything. This book, every book you buy that you're planning to resell (obviously if you are putting a book into your private collection, you should not be claiming it for resale when you buy it; most dealers will still give you the discount, but you should pay tax on the item). Keep receipts for book cleaning supplies, for the papers you need to fill out your paperwork, for business cards and invoices. Keep a mileage log for your car so you can claim appropriate expenses for your scouting trips (a notebook in the car, on which you write date, starting mileage, and finishing mileage for each of your trips specifically to scout should suffice).

In other words, it's important that you keep track of where your money is going and coming from. For this reason, if you're dealing quite a lot, you may want to start a separate bank account just for the dealing. That helps keep your private money away from the business, gives you an extra flair of respectability, and makes it impossible to mistake what an expense was for if you forgot to write it down.

But you'll never do that, will you?

As you scout, you should have your notebook in your car anyway, the one you use to keep track of the stores in your area and what their strengths and weaknesses are. Add a page or two in the back for miscellaneous expenses, and when you walk out of the store, jot down title, price, date purchased—or the same information on books sold for cash—in your notebook on the appropriate page. Now you're not only itemizing for the government, you're establishing a purchasing pattern to look at later and see what percentage of items you're buying and selling at each location. This will help you concentrate your time in the areas where your time gains the greatest return, so here you're killing two birds with one stone.

But that notebook isn't going to be good enough. At home, you'll need a ledger and a large envelope to store receipts. In the ledger, mark down what you've spent and what you've made, on a day-by-day, itemized basis.

Although your license is local, the bulk of your paperwork is going to be federal. In addition to the usual 1040 form, you're going to need to fill out Schedule C ("Profit or Loss from Business") and pay self-employment tax and social security. The IRS maintains a relatively helpful phone line to answer questions, and they have offices in major cities where you can find yourself buried under brochures and forms. Make use of these services.

I am not a tax expert and do not claim to be. I'm just giving you some basic advice. Make sure you consult with a qualified professional before proceeding.

As a book dealer, you'll be spending plenty of time in bookshops, so wander over to the business section and see what's on the shelf about starting and maintaining a small business. There are plenty of good titles out there.

WHAT CAN GO WRONG

One of the main reasons for failure of a small business is overexcitement. A person plunges in, starts spending money that doesn't need to be spent, and before long the money is gone. As a scout/dealer, your expenses are minimal; you're picking up a lot of your stock on trade, trading your way up, and making a profit out of it. Cash outlay is hopefully small. Keep it that way. You don't need a fancy business card (although some sort of card is a must); you don't need fancy stationery. Keep it as cheap as you can while still making it look professional, and leave it at that. Save your money to buy more books.

But there's a caveat there, too, because besides financial overexcitement, the single main reason for failure in the book business is overexcitement about books. Once you start spending a lot of time in shops, you're going to find a lot more books you never knew you had to have until you saw them there on the shelves in front of you. Suddenly, no matter how good your dealing intentions, the shelves of your personal collection are starting to overflow.

And that's okay if you want to emphasize the collection, and if you can afford to handle things that way.

But one of the hardest lessons to learn when you're suddenly faced with a book that you want is that the book will come around again. They all do. You don't need to buy everything the minute you see it. Leave some pleasure—and money—for later. No matter what it is, you will see it again. That even holds true for the very rare and high-line items. Say you just spotted a signed copy of *Treasure Island*, in mint shape. If it's marked $10, grab it and try to keep a straight face until you make it out the door. But if it's at a fair price, no matter how badly you want this book, stop and think first that you will see it again. Fine, high-line items circulate in a very small area, and they show up repeatedly. Many dealers handle the exact same book over and over again. This is where you'll find out if you're a collector or a dealer. Do you buy the book for yourself, or do you grab the book you know you can resell for a profit?

Find which you are, collector or dealer, be happy with it, and learn to what percentage you feel the impulse toward the opposite. There are dealers who consider every book they acquire to be stock—they don't collect a thing. And there are collectors who would never sell a book, even if they were starving. Between them is a wide continuum. You fit on it somewhere, and there's room for everybody.

Just remember that, however you choose to deal, you need paperwork.

Chapter Twelve

❧

REFERENCE SOURCES

T he further into book collecting you go, the more complicated it becomes. Suddenly, where once you were
looking for a nice Jonathan Carroll to read, now you're worrying about the points between the first and second issues of
the first British edition of *Sleeping in Flame*—the difference between as much as a couple hundred dollars or so, and forty or
fifty dollars.

You're only as good as your information.

In other words, to do this well, you're going to need help. It's
said that the wise man is the one who knows where to look
something up. Luckily for all of us, the book market is one
which naturally produces, of all things, books, and there are
plenty of places to look things up. (In fact, collecting and dealing in books on books is a thriving specialty.) Judicious use of
reference sources will make you a better dealer, a better collector, and hopefully help you to avoid expensive mistakes
when you go scouting.

One caveat: Because most reference works are printed in tiny editions, don't expect them to be cheap. A good author bibliography can cost $100; an overview, such as Cox's *A Reference Guide to the Literature of Travel*, can run much, much more. And there is even a first-edition market in reference works: I recently saw a copy of a Sir Richard Burton bibliography, in first edition, selling for $650; a reprint, while still expensive at $65, might be more practical for someone who needs the volume as a working book. Other collectible reference works include the bibliographies put out by small presses of their own works: Doves, Golden Cockerel, and others produce these occasional lists which are a must for the serious, but a serious pain for the wallet.

PRICE GUIDES

The first thing all collectors and dealers need is a good price guide. Three resources are standard in the book industry: Allen and Patricia Ahearn's *Collected Books: The Guide to Values* (Putnam, 1998); *Book Prices: Used and Rare* (Spoon River Books, 2319-C West Rohman, Peoria, IL 61604); and *Mandeville's Used Book Price Guide* (Price Guide Publications, P.O. Box 82525, Kenmore, WA 98028-0525). All of these guides gather their information from offerings in dealer catalogs nationwide.

These three guides will cover a good percentage of the modern book market. They all have their strengths and weaknesses, and their local biases, but each is a very dependable starting point for values. Cross-referencing prices with shops in your area should give you an idea of which most closely matches local trends. Remember that there is no such thing as a standard price in the book world, and that all descriptions of books in the price guides have to be matched with the book actually in your hand. A chipped dust jacket can halve the price of a book printed five years ago, but have little effect on a book printed five decades ago.

In addition to prices, the guides have other uses: Ahearn has the best bibliographic information, which can also aid greatly in assessing value and edition; *Mandeville's* is the most useful for listing points.

The Clique, in England (7 Pullen Dr., York YO2 2DY), publishes the six-volume *Annual Register of Book Values*. These can be bought as a set or individually, in the subjects of Art and Architecture, Children's Books, Modern First Editions, Science and Medicine, Voyages, Travel and Exploration, and Literature. A CD-ROM that covers a several-year range is also available. Individual volumes start at $38, and together they make a useful, wide-ranging set.

One more standard resource, which can vary from being incredibly useful to making you wonder why the authors thought to include a particular book, is the annual *Huxford's Old Book Value Guide* (Collector Books). Huxford's is the best guide for the low end of the market. The other guides concentrate on more unusual items, while Huxford includes the books you're likely to see every day. There are, as I said, some oddities, but they only serve to make the book more useful when you get a hit.

Most of the chain bookstores also sell a variety of pricing guides that are usually parts of series that price everything from baseball cards to Tiffany lamps. Although these are annually updated, where their information comes from is rather difficult to ascertain. While the guides mentioned above are the market standards, prices in these series guides seem to vary widely from what's really happening in the market. If you see one of these on sale, you may want to pick it up, but don't rely on it as your main source of information.

Finally, the other invaluable resource you will want to get as you become a more serious dealer is *American Book Prices Current*. ABPC, put out annually, covers books sold at auction.

While the other price guides mentioned above concentrate on modern books, this takes in the entire spectrum. It is also very expensive—*American Book Prices Current* runs close to $150 (but only about $110 if you have a standing order with the publisher, Bancroft-Parkman, P.O. Box 1236, Washington, CT 06793). However, price aside, once you've devoted yourself to books, you will need to buy these. A good run of these, built up over several years, can answer pricing questions that no other books can. *American Book Prices Current* is also available on CD-ROM.

Check chapter 7 on using the Internet as a price guide before you start trusting the wired world.

If you use any single guide as your only source, you're effectively cutting off your own head. These books all have a production time-lag to contend with, while prices change daily in the book industry. Further, no price guide or standard publication can possibly keep up with the trends in the market. Hot new authors come and go like a summer breeze, and if you only look for authors included in the guides, you'll be missing a lot of the best prospects. That's why you've been saving every dealer catalog you've been able to get your hands on.

DEALER CATALOGS

A lot of the prices in catalogs that aren't set by cribbing off others on the Net are set at book fairs, where dealers can get together and see who's selling what, and some are the result of educated guesswork. But a good supply of dealer catalogs can teach you more about the current book market and current prices than anything else.

The sad thing is, with more and more dealers turning to the Net, those producing catalogs are becoming more scarce. Book dealing, which has thrived for five hundred years on good record keeping, is losing its collective memory.

Still, the wise use of a few letters and a roll of stamps can, at least for a few more years, keep your mailbox stuffed. But before you start to hope that buying from catalogs is going to make your fortune, remember that catalogs are the top of the market. Don't expect to buy any bargains this way. Also remember that, as the top of the market, your actual mileage may vary considerably on any given book. While a dealer can push $200 for *Invisible Cities* in a catalog, you may not find a copy locally for over $150 (if you can find one at all). Catalogs tend to be pricey, because the dealer is doing the hard work for you. But the best catalogs, in addition to being a treasure trove of books that you'll never find elsewhere, can be treated as up-to-the-minute price guides. The currently hot authors are in here, and at the current prices. Looking over the catalogs of specific dealers over a stretch of years can teach you more about the trends of the business than anything else.

AUCTION CATALOGS

Sotheby's, Christie's, Pacific Book Auctions, and several smaller houses have regular catalogs; all the auction houses sell subscriptions, ranging from about $500 or so for a complete subscription to Sotheby's book department offerings, to $20 or less for a small house. With Sotheby's and Christie's, you can subscribe only to the area of catalogs that interests you: for example, travel, or fine printing.

A ten-year run of auction catalogs is perhaps the single most useful tool a high-line dealer is going to have. They're not good if you're never going to stray out of the hypermoderns, but if you're looking to flex your wings in other fields, the auction houses are where the best catalogs come from.

First, you see books that you will never find locally; second, the auction catalog descriptions are the best anywhere.

These are expensive, but, for everything outside the hyper-moderns, well worth the investment.

They're also fun to read late at night, to fuel book dreams.

USING GUIDES AND CATALOGS

Never, ever throw a price guide or a catalog away. Updates do not always have the same books. You may often find yourself scrambling through a stack of material, looking for what year a particular book first showed up. With some practice, it's not that difficult to prorate the market and update material your-self, and the old guides are a valuable source of information. Besides which, watching how the guides change can teach you how the market has changed and whether the prices you're paying or asking are fair.

Pricing a book is an art form in and of itself, and one you can never be entirely sure of. I've seen books priced high fly off the shelf and other books, which should have been highly sought after and collected, sit forever at a fraction of their sup-posed value. Like all markets, it's a matter of supply and de-mand.

As discussed in chapter 7, the Internet has done much to alter the basic forces of supply and demand: supply suddenly vastly outstrips demand on most of the midline items. Keep this in mind when you're trying to assess local value.

Before deciding on whether or not any price is fair, check at least two of the guides if possible, cross-reference the condition of the books, and come to an average price. Then you've got to figure in regional variation and the size of the local book mar-ket. As a rule the Eastern seaboard is higher priced than the South, which is lower priced than the West, which doesn't have nearly as many books available as the Pacific Northwest. An-notate your guides with what you find locally, and only then turn to the Internet to see what's happening out in the broader field. Remember that, while the Net is growing by leaps and bounds, there are still a lot of people out there who have never turned on a computer.

Unless otherwise noted, all price guides show you the high price for a volume in perfect condition. No bumps, no tears, no folds, spindles, or mutilations. That's a *collectible* copy. Once the bumps, tears, etc., start appearing, the book rapidly loses desirability and even more rapidly leaves the realm of the price guides, becoming a simple reading copy. This cannot be stressed enough, and it's a mistake you'll see made all the time. A novice dealer will get a trashed copy of a famous book and price it like it was in mint condition. The Internet is especially bad for this, as there are so many people out there simply trying to clean off their shelves. All descriptions from dealers you do not know (at least by reputation) should be taken with a serious grain of salt. As I mentioned earlier, there is nothing as important as condition, and while there are always exceptions— books impossible to find in perfect condition—most price guides go for the top end (although *Mandeville's* in particular is good about noting grading points, and not always sticking to perfect copies; in *Huxford's*, perfect copies are as rare as they are in real life). In other words, the guides are going for books that are scarce, in conditions that are rarely seen. Keep this in mind when you're comparing for price, and when you're assessing the value of stock you might want to buy. Only experience will teach you what books are seldom, if ever, seen in Fine or better shape, but when starting out, don't fall into the trap of "The price guides list this title at $200, so this must be a $200 book." Very often, it isn't. It's a ten- or fifteen-dollar reading copy.

And remember that in producing a professional catalog, a book dealer has a large financial stake in the outcome, in the process, and in the stock that should at least hopefully (but not always) mean they know what they're doing; whereas a nine-

year-old can put up her copy of *Ramona the Pest* on the Web
with little difficulty.

Editions and Points

Of course, the price of the book can only be found if you know
the book is a first edition. Earlier I went into some detail on
identifying a first, but it is still a tricky task, one in which even
the most experienced dealer can be occasionally stumped. So
in addition to the price guides, you're going to need a first edition guide.

There are two: Edward N. Zempel and Linda A. Verkler's
First Editions (Spoon River Press), which is a lovely and very
complete hardbound volume with virtually any publisher you
could ever dream of looking up, and the much more portable
A Pocket Guide to the Identification of First Editions (McBride/
Publisher, 157 Sisson Ave., Hartford, CT 06105), which con-
denses more publishers (but fewer details) into a handy little
paperback costing a quarter what the Zempel volume does. I
would strongly recommend owning both: the Zempel for home
reference, the *Pocket Guide* to travel with you, innocuously
tucked into a pocket. Overall, *Pocket Guide* features more publishers, but the Zempel is easier to read.

McBride also publishes *Points of Issue*, which bills itself as
"A Compendium of Points of Issue of Books by 19th–20th Century Authors." This, like McBride's first edition guide, is cheap
and pocket-sized, and well worth carrying along with you on
scouting trips. A quick look inside lets you know, for example,
that in Larry McMurtry's *In a Narrow Grave*, the true first issue,
first edition has the word "skyscrapers" misspelled on page 105,
line 12. In the true first, it reads "skycrapers." That's a $2,000
book. If the word is spelled correctly, Ahearn will tell you when
you start to cross-reference your sources, it's a $650 dollar
book. However, a lot of the books listed in McBride's *Points* are

a lot more obscure. Still, it doesn't take up much room in your pocket.

BOOKS AND MAGAZINES ON BOOKS

Now that you are armed with catalogs, price guides, and first edition ID guides, you'll need further sources of more general information to fill gaps in your knowledge or compare what you know with the state of the book-dealing art.

Start with the terminology. *ABC for Book Collectors*, by John Carter (Oak Knoll Publishing, seventh edition produced in 1995), is a wonderful treasury of every imaginable book term, clearly defined and illustrated. Even the cover blurb is identified as a "blurb" in case you weren't sure. Indispensable.

Firsts magazine, issued ten times a year, is a slick magazine entirely devoted to collecting the modern first edition. Since 1991, the magazine has featured everything from collecting movie books to using computers to further your scouting efforts. It also reports on book fairs, signings, and current auction and catalog prices. Best of all, it's a main source for obtaining catalogs. If you spend no other money on references, get *Firsts*. Write to them at 4445 N. Alvernon Way, Tucson, AZ 85718-6139.

Publishers Weekly and the *New York Times* are the place to go to find out what's happening in the new-book world. Get the *Times* at the local newsstand, or direct: *New York Times*, 229 West 43rd St., New York, NY, 10036; phone (800) 631-2580. *Publishers Weekly* can be reached at (800) 278-2991.

As I mentioned above, book collectors love to turn out books on book collecting. Start with Allen Ahearn's *Book Collecting 2000*. Quick and factual, the book trades on the strength of Ahearn's skill as a pricer in the book world. Much of the book is taken up by a price guide.

For a more anecdotal approach, turn to *Modern Book Col-*

lecting, by Robert A. Wilson (Lyons and Burford, 1980). Wilson's book is especially useful for people interested in dealing poetry books. It also has a lengthy, very good section on author bibliographies, listing many prime reference sources; this section alone is worth the cost of the entire book.

Two more excellent books: *Understanding Book Collecting,* by Grant Uden (Antique Collectors' Club, 1982), and *How to Buy Rare Books,* by William Rees-Mogg (Phaidon-Christies, 1985). The first of these is an excellent overall introduction to book collecting; the second, while it concentrates on antiquarian books rather than modern firsts, provides a picture of the book market and its vagaries, as well as good chapters on binding and book decoration.

There are some great books on individual aspects of books and bookmaking. Hartley and Marks Publishers put out a series of books on book minutia; among my favorites are *The Form of the Book,* by Jan Tschichold, subtitled "Essays on the Morality of Good Design"; *Finer Points in the Spacing and Arrangement of Type,* by Geoffrey Dowding, who will ruin your ability to read smoothly for weeks, once he turns you on to the possibilities in the spaces between words and letters; and *Letter Forms,* by the century's premier type designer, Stanley Morison. Dover Publications has a nice reprint of Edith Diehl's *Bookbinding: Its Background and Technique,* which will take you from the earliest wooden bindings up to the modern case. Oak Knoll Press has a list of literally hundreds of lovely titles of books on books. Good places to start are with *Five Hundred Years of Printing,* by S. H. Steinberg, revised by John Trevitt, which will teach you more about books than any other single volume you're ever likely to read, and *Encyclopedia of the Book,* by Geoffrey Ashall Glaister, which is like a very detailed, heavily illustrated version of the *ABC for Book Collectors* (also available through Oak Knoll). The more you know about books, the more you can understand and appreciate what you are doing with them. My entire conception of my life as a book dealer changed when I learned how to hand-set type.

Finally, a couple things just for fun: *A Gentle Madness*, by Nicholas Basbanes (Henry Holt, 1995), is a lovely and loving book about the phenomenon of book collecting, from the absurd—Stephen Blumberg, master book thief—to the sublime, with John Carter Brown. You've probably already read John Dunning's *Booked to Die* (Scribner's, 1992), but if not, go out and grab a copy. While you're there, buy the follow-up, *The Bookman's Wake*. All three of the books noted here will have you out in the car, hunting for books of your own, before you're halfway through.

AUTHOR BIBLIOGRAPHIES

All famous authors have had bibliographies published. The problem is coming up with them. If the Wilson book doesn't list the author you're interested in, you're going to be doing a little more work than you might otherwise.

The first and easiest place to check for a bibliography is on the Net: run "bibliography" and the author's last name as key words and see what shows up. Check out Oak Knoll's Web site (available as a link from the Antiquarian Booksellers Association of America Web site); they specialize in books on books and are likely to have what you're after. Don't forget to look in a good biography of the favorite author. These can be surprisingly complete.

"Bibliography is the geography of the book world," read the cover of an issue of the late and lamented *Antiquarian Bookman*, quoting Pierce Butler. And it is quite true: a good bibliography should be a kind of map, leading you through an author's career from the earliest pamphlets to the final collected works.

There are also bibliographies that cover a publisher's entire output. Usually these are put out by smaller presses, but, for example, the Black Sparrow bibliography is outstanding, and of course, a publisher usually (but not always) knows better what they did with a book than a researcher who comes along later.

Bibliographies are usually divided into three sections, known as A, B, and, not surprisingly, C. The A section lists books by the author; the B section, magazine and anthology appearances; the C section, works on the author. There are bibliographers who don't quite stick to the conventions, but the A list is always books.

According to an article by John Dinsmore in the July 1991 issue of *Firsts*, the first single-author bibliography for an American writer was one on Longfellow, published in 1885. In the hundred-plus years since, virtually every writer who is anyone has had a bibliography published.

Because bibliographies cost big bucks, you're best off if you can use somebody else's when you're beginning. Start your search at the local library: the easiest thing to do is sit at the computer terminal connected to its catalog, run your author's name in as a keyword (not as author), and see what comes up. This should give you not only everything in the library by that author, but also everything about him or her. With the proliferation of computer networks, I can, from my computer here at home, tie into the local university's library catalog, and from there go into other university libraries around the country. This has never failed to turn up the bibliography I need. In other words, if the local library fails you, start working the computer system.

There are numerous other books, not specific to a particular author, which can also help you. *Contemporary Novelists* and *Contemporary Poets* each lists the works of several hundred writers. While not as complete as single-author bibliographies, they can help get your search started.

The Ahearns, noted earlier for their price guide, also produce their own series of publications, *Author Price Guides*, something of a cross between a price guide and a bibliography. They've collected bibliographical information on about 175 authors, and combined this with current prices. Individual author price lists cost from a couple of dollars up to nearly twenty. If you've got their book, you don't need these until you're ready to go full-time in the business. The exception would be for favorite authors, when every extra bit of bibliographical information can be invaluable. The guides are convenient, but, as with most reference material, a little pricey. Still, they're recommended for the very serious, because they can save you a lot of money, noting all exceptions that could otherwise trap you into a mistake. Contact the Ahearns directly for these at their shop, the Quill and Brush, 1137 Sugarloaf Mountain Rd., Dickenson, MD, 20842; phone (301) 874-3200.

If you're narrowing your specialty to a few authors or a single genre, buy every reference you can find in the field. Nothing is too trivial to overlook.

Bibliographies are of the most use for authors who aren't working anymore. To keep on top of those who are still happily typing away, turn to genre publications. Mystery, science fiction, poetry, horror, and mainstream lit all have a wide variety of specialty publications catering to specific niche markets. From *Poetry* magazine, which once featured T. S. Eliot on its pages, to *Cemetery Dance*, where the next Stephen King may appear any issue now, the genre publications can keep you abreast of who is up-and-coming; they're also useful for finding out about small-press works that you'd otherwise never hear about. Don't pass up *Small Press* magazine, which offers reviews of books coming from presses you've never heard of— but often by authors you're more than familiar with.

Within every imaginable specialty, there are reference works to be found and treasured. If you're interested in Antarctic exploration, you can't do without Sidney A. Spence's *Antarctic Miscellany*; if you just want to know who the highlights are in the mystery genre, pick up a copy of *Crime & Mystery: The 100 Best Books*, by H. R. F. Keating. If you love children's books, you can't go wrong with *Children's Book Collecting*, by Carolyn Clugston Michaels. An hour or two on the Internet can lead you to most of these, or to a huge cache of other books, whatever your interests may be. Another good place to check is in the backs of catalogs to see who the cataloger is using for reference.

A quick rundown on some of the better genre references: for mystery, there is the encyclopedic *Crime Fiction II: A Comprehensive Bibliography 1749–1990*, by Allen J. Hubin. If that covers a little too much territory, narrow down to *Twentieth Century Crime and Mystery Writers*, which has come out in three somewhat different editions. The current one is edited by Leslie Henderson. Jon L. Breen wrote *What About Murder? A Guide to Books About Mystery and Detective Fiction*, which can be a great resource.

Horror and science fiction tend to cross over in the references. The sine qua non is L. W. Currey's *Science Fiction and Fantasy Authors: A Bibliography of First Printings of Their Fiction and Selected Nonfiction*. If you've got some money left after picking that up, try Everett F. Bleiler's *The Guide to Supernatural Fiction*. There's also *Horror: Best 100 Books*, edited by Stephen Jones and Kim Newman, which can introduce you to some shouldn't-be-forgotten writers.

For modern lit and poetry, you're best off sticking to the mainstream guides noted above. One exception would be to pick up a copy of *The Norton Anthology of Modern Poetry*. This will not only introduce you to many poets you would otherwise never hear about, but also the back of the book has a complete listing of each author's works. They do not have bibliographical information, but since very few poetry books make it past the first printing, it's an excellent place to start.

RESEARCHING ON THE INTERNET

Thanks to a lot of people with computers and a lot of time on their hands, the Internet can be a great resource in and of itself for bibliographical material. Pretty much any author you can think of has a fan Web site out there somewhere, and a lot of these are amazingly complete. Best of all, because there are no boundaries on the Net, you can find out great information about foreign editions that you otherwise might never have heard of, and be able to link up to other collectors around the world. How else would I get my Polish copies of Jonathan Carroll's stories?

The Internet is also a great place to find out what sells where—take a look at listings for stores around the country—which can help you figure out prices for your own stock, cross-referencing these against the search-engine prices.

In the long run, the Net is going to be the bibliographer's dream. Right now, you can get into the card catalogs of a thousand libraries; while cataloging techniques vary, the simple availability of information on a book can be astounding. Say you have an edition of *The Rubiyat of Omar Khayam* that you want to find something out on. There have been, over the years, thousands of editions of this book. A careful search on the Net can tell you, in not very much time, if there's anything special about yours, when it was first done, and even how common it is.

There are more possibilities. You can tie in to a publisher's Web site to find out what's coming out. You can find Internet book groups for authors you're interested in—maybe you can sell off a couple extra firsts of a book the group is using. You can do newspaper research on books or authors.

Dealers frequently spend a lot of time cataloging their books before listing them on-line, so these listings can be in and of themselves great sources of reference. How many copies were printed? Was the book in the Streeter sale?

One warning about this: because computers have made gathering this sort of information so easy, there are a lot of mistakes getting compounded. Somebody gets a fact wrong on a book, but lists it that way anyhow. A second dealer comes along, thinks, well, that's interesting, I'll put that in my own description of the book—and so on. Never, never simply copy off facts from another dealer's description. Use them as starting points to more research.

Some dealers out there now are actually putting copyright notices in their book descriptions on-line. A lot of work goes into properly describing a book. Feel free to use someone else's description to learn, but not for your own sales purposes.

As more and more gets put on the Web, it is going to become a greater and greater boon for researchers. I do not think the day will ever come when "everything" is on-line, simply because computers have no real memory (more on this in chapter 13); but for the price of a dozen bibliographies, your computer can give you access to ten thousand bibliographies, news groups, publishers, other dealers, libraries, and more.

SCHOOLS

Finally, for the very serious, there are even a couple places you can go to learn books in an academic setting.

Traditionally, bookselling has been passed on from mentor to student; you learn books by working in bookshops. However, not everybody has the time to do that, and some people have a desire to work better than minimum wage jobs (bookstores are fun, but they don't pay) and just do books on the side.

Check your local college's art department for classes in printing or bookbinding. You can learn more about books by hand-setting type for an hour or two than you'll ever imagine. You'll never look at print the same way again.

Book Seminars has an excellent five-day rare book school, held annually in Colorado. They get together a dozen or so experts who give classes in everything from the makeup of a book to the proper use of references to how to price. You get to spend the week hanging out with experts and a hundred or so like-minded students. Besides learning a lot, you get to have a lot of fun, and you're sure to come home seriously charged up and ready to buy. Contact them at (719) 473-6634, or on-line at bookseminars.com. It'll cost you about $700, plus room and board (dorm rooms are available cheap), and it's a great investment in your future.

The University of Virginia also offers classes in books, but their line is more on serious book history. You learn about, say, the British book trade in the 1700s, or do an intensive class on bibliographic descriptions. Contact them at 114 Alderman Library, Charlottesville, VA 22903-2498.

To sum up: never skimp on information-gathering. You're never going to know it all, so it's important to have access to information beyond your stretch. Find your field, buy the best, and be prepared to use the rest. I've had single reference works make me a couple thousand dollars, as they had just what I needed to know. Lou Weinstein, the owner of Heritage Bookshop in Los Angeles, one of the finest bookstores in the country, says a large part of his success is due to the fact that the shop maintains "a reference library of some 13,000 books, and it is used every day."

Finding a good reference work is going to make you more money in the long run than spotting a first of *Winnie-the-Pooh* at a garage sale for five bucks will in the short run.

Chapter Thirteen

❧

THE CHANGING
WORLD OF BOOKS

T hanks, I'd say largely to the *Harry Potter* books, people have caught on to a little fact about the book world: a lot of writers have their books published first in England. Serious collectors, those looking for complete runs of editions, have always known this, and always tried to maintain relations with a dealer in the U.K. who could get them new British books, but with the Internet, this just got a lot easier. Waterstones, the quintessential British bookstore, is as available on the Web from the United States as it is from London. Pick your author, choose your book, pay a fairly ludicrous amount for shipping, and there you go.

This is ultimately going to change the dynamics of publishing in many ways, I think. First, there's the question of rights territories. When an author sells a book, the publisher buys it for certain areas of the world; few publishers, even in this day of consolidation, have a truly worldwide market. Traditionally the United States and the United Kingdom have been separate territories, with a book moving across the ocean to a different publisher. If you look at new book catalogs, sometimes you'll see that a book is "not available in . . ."—choose your country. This means that the rights have not been sold there, or that they are being held by someone who wants to protect those rights by forbidding imports. For this century, British books have been largely protected from U.S. editions, and vice versa.

Let's face it, this isn't going to work anymore. With the Internet, international boundaries to trade are falling left and right. Goods are moving more easily than they ever have before. From a house in the middle of the Wyoming plains, you have access to publishers all over the world.

I think most people caught on to this territorial difference when their kids started screaming for the third *Harry Potter* book. It came out in England months before it came out in the States, a fairly common arrangement. In the old days, you'd just have to wait; now you can get on-line, buy the British edition, and be the first one on your block to know what happens to Harry next.

The U.S. publisher of the Potter books was understandably unhappy about this situation, seeing thousands of sales lost. They had bought U.S. rights, which to them meant that they were going to sell all the copies sold in the United States. They hadn't imagined that there would be this huge near–black market for British editions of *Harry Potter and the Sorcerer's Stone*.

The Internet is breaking down the whole idea of sales territories. And let's face it, the shipping companies have enough to do without looking for contraband books. The United States tried that earlier this century, in a hopeless attempt to keep out *Lady Chatterley's Lover* and *Ulysses*. It didn't work then, and it's not going to work now. All this means the publishers are going to have to change the playing field.

The fourth *Harry Potter* book came out almost simultaneously in both countries. Lessons had been learned.

Over the next decade or so, expect to see more consolidation in the publishing industry. Expect to see more books coming out in identical editions on both sides of the Atlantic. And if we are really unlucky, expect to see severe homogenization in the British publishing industry the way we have in the United States, with the cult of the best-seller and the death of the B-list writer, the guy who writes great books but whose sales can't compete with an instant book on the latest celebrity scandal.

On to the next point, as far as collectors are concerned: England's book market is a fraction the size of that in the United States. A book that has a first hardback printing of fifty thousand here may only have five thousand copies printed there.

Because British editions tend to come in very small runs, for the collector, for the dealer looking for something different, you have to jump on the hot books fast over there, as the first printings run out quick. There's a reason why Bruce Chatwin's *In Patagonia* is a $1,200 book in the British, a $150 book in the U.S. first—and it's not all just following the flag (buying the edition of the author's home country). Or take Paul Bowles, for instance. Checking my bibliography of him—always have your reference books close at hand—I find that the first edition of his first novel, *The Sheltering Sky*, had about equal printings in England and the States, about five thousand copies. However, in the United States, there was a paperback edition that sold an additional quarter of a million copies. So this means when his second novel, *Let It Come Down*, was printed, the print run for the U.S. edition was more than double the size of the British (15,000 vs. 7,000). You don't have to be a genius to figure out which is the more valuable now, which the harder to find.

Conversely, there are authors who do much, much better in the U.K. than they do in the U.S. Lindsey Davis, for example, a mystery writer who sets her books in ancient Rome, does double the sales in England as in the States. Jonathan Carroll has much better sales in England than in the United States, and although Neil Gaiman made a name for himself in the United States with his mythic revisions, in England, he's an object of worship.

We do not have the same tastes as the other side of the ocean.

With the possibility of exceptions in mind, until the publishers figure out what to do, the British edition of a book is almost always going to be more scarce than the U.S. edition. This does not mean that the British edition will always be more valuable—a good deal of the value goes with the question of what country an author is from—but it does mean that a good run of British copies are always a coup to own, and there are always people out there looking for them.

There are some changes in follow-the-flag collecting, too. For most of the history of book collecting, the true first edition a collector wanted was the one that came out in the author's home country. If the author was British, collectors would go for a U.K. copy. Margaret Atwood put a premium on Canadian editions for a little while. But borders are breaking down faster than publishing agreements. In the old days (five years ago or so) you could assume that the flag edition was the true first, the book as it appeared on its very first day in the world. Not anymore. Michael Connelly, for example, a Californian through and through, has published a couple books where the British edition was the true first, appearing before the American edition. There's nothing exactly new about this trend—the British edition of *Huck Finn* is the true first—but it is becoming more and more common.

BOOKS ON DEMAND

An interesting feature in the future of books are books on demand—books that are printed and bound when you want them, while you wait. Pretty much from now on, there need be no such thing as an out-of-print book, ever.

The idea behind books on demand is that it's very cheap to store a computer file of a book, whereas it's very expensive to store a printed copy. Say a publisher does a run of five thousand copies of a book, which sells out in a year or two. The demand for the book is over. However, there are still going to be people out there looking for a copy from time to time. With books on demand, you can go into a bookstore and ask for a book. The shop downloads a file of the book from the publisher's Web site, prints it out on one machine, prints out a cover on another, and binds it all in a third. This technology is already up and functional, on a limited basis, in several bookstores in the United States. The books that result don't look much different from regular paperbacks.

Right now, the equipment needed to put this together is fairly expensive—around $60,000—but as with everything in the computer world, the technology is going to get better and cheaper very quickly.

This is an astounding boon for publishers, who can extend the life of a book forever; for authors, who can rest assured that their books will always be available; and for readers looking for copies of hard-to-find books.

The only limitation of the technology is that the book has to exist in binary form somewhere. This means that the only way older books are going to get into the system is for someone to laboriously put them in there; this isn't all that likely to happen for the vast majority of titles (more on book extinction in a minute). But for books being printed now, the odds of them ever truly, honestly going out of print diminishes by the day.

Someday, surely, this technology will be cheap enough that we can all have it in our houses. Of course, by then, we might have all just moved on to electronic books for daily reading material.

BOOKS ON THE WEB

Some years ago, William Gibson, author of the cyberpunk classics *Neuromancer* and *Mona Lisa Overdrive*, "published" a short story on computer disk only. The disk was created so that the story file would self-destruct as it was read, which meant that, if you had a copy of the story in your collection, you had never read it (at least not until, a few months after the story's release, when a hacker figured out a way around the self-destruct and distributed copies).

The Internet is changing the idea of what print is, what stories are, how we approach books and information (not knowledge; there's never going to be any knowledge on the Web— knowledge requires the filter of an active mind and if anybody tells you otherwise, laugh and turn away). A recent essay in the *New York Times Book Review* suggested that, no matter how much we squawk and yell, eventually, we really will be reading books on computer. Sure, there's no way to replace the perfect technology of the book, but on the other hand, as we spend more and more of our days in front of a computer screen, don't we become more comfortable with the whole idea of reading on a computer? Isn't it possible that, a few years from now, we'll be so acclimated to words on a screen that we can do without books entirely?

Lord, I hope not.

I do believe, however, that certain types of books are already obsolete in printed form. Encyclopedias, dictionaries, almanacs, reference works of all kinds are doomed in print. Why have a five-foot-long shelf full of the *Encyclopedia Brittanica* when you can fit them on a single CD? There's not much good reason—or there is, and I'll get to it in a minute here, but it probably isn't good enough for market forces.

I also tend to believe that best-sellers and books for casual reading are probably going to find more and more happy homes in electronic media. Once the computer has finished weaving its tentacles into the fiber of society and computers are as ubiquitous as TVs or telephones, can we really see a logical reason to go cut down trees for the new Jackie Collins novel? For the new piece of fluff you need to have with you to kill a few hours on the airplane?

As we grow more comfortable with the computer, (you're probably already noticing that I'm highly suspicious of them, yet here I sit typing these words into one) I think we will find ourselves reading more on computer. Finally, we will even read for pleasure on the computer. Isn't most e-mail read for plea-sure? How far of a mental leap is it from there to a story?

Many authors are bypassing print entirely and only publish-ing on the Web. A friend of mine who has six books on the shelves in bookstores, also has three books available only on-line. There are definite advantages to this: as publishing con-solidates (you'd think they'd have to stop sometime, but they keep finding new ways to do it), publishers are less and less willing to take a risk on anything at all. If an author wants to jump out of the box, try something different, it may be that the only way he or she can get the story out is to post it on the Web.

The big problem with this is that, as the Web fills up with more garbage—"My Vacation Site, 1981"—it gets harder and harder to find what's worthwhile. Publishers provided a kind of filter, ensuring at least some degree of readability. The Net can't do that, and a ten-year-old can put up his first attempts at writing horror stories as easily as Stephen King can.

And so a new kind of publisher is now showing up on the Net. They're working much as traditional publishers, letting you know that, at the very least, a few other people have read this book and liked it before they put it out for you to find. So far at least, these are not the big publishers. These are a new wave of publishers, trying something different.

We do, of course, have the 800-pound gorilla exception. In

early 2000, Stephen King published a Web-only book. Hundreds of thousands of people rushed to download it. Single-handedly, he did more to promote the idea of reading a book on a computer screen than anyone else ever could have.

I can see only one real problem with this, and that is the question of memory. Despite the terminology, computers have no memory. I have a book that I wrote on the first computer I owned, about ten years ago, that I will never be able to read again, because modern equipment can't make sense of the files. Technology outdates itself, and I have a fear that, as computers do more and more, they will remember less and less of the old material. I fear that the instruments of minute-by-minute knowledge and advance will disappear. Most science and medical journals now do most of their printing only on-line. What's the shelf life of something like that? Where would we all be now if Copernicus had written *De Revolutionibus* on a Commodore 64?

This doesn't even have to be a matter of outdated technology. Libraries all over the country are getting rid of material (read Nicholson Baker's excellent essay on this, contained in his book *The Size of Thoughts*); old periodicals are just jettisoned outright. I was trying to check something in *Publishers Weekly* at one of the biggest libraries in the country; the librarian told me, "Oh, well, we have that magazine on-line back to 1985." That's lovely, but the magazine started publishing over a hundred years before that.

When Gutenberg started running pages of the Bible off his printing press in Mainz, Germany, scribes and copyists by the thousands cried foul. How could anybody want a book as ugly as what rolls off a press (Gutenberg went to great lengths to make his printed book look as much like a handwritten book as possible, though)? The forces of conservatism never like the new new thing.

Before books become everyday objects in computer form, there will have to be some changes made. First, the reading apparatus will have to get better. You can't have fun reading a book if you're sitting upright at your desk. The first generation of readers, like the very portable Rocket E-book, solve this but bring other problems. When you buy a paperback, you don't have to worry about your batteries dying while you read it. Also, do you really want to take a $200 machine to the beach for your vacation when you could just have a $6 paperback instead?

The second big problem is the screen. Computer screens make your eyes tired. Having light coming straight at you is never a good thing. But a new generation of "video paper" that's coming out may change all this. Instead of using light, the new technology uses incredibly tiny little balls, dark on one side, light on the other. The balls rotate to form letters or illustrations, and it's a lot easier on your eyes than a computer screen.

The new readers do offer wonderful features: for example, the ability to change the size of type in a book. As I get older and closer to bifocals, I appreciate this thought more and more. My ability to read small type isn't what it used to be. The readers also let you bookmark, search, and set up your own notes in the book. They incorporate illustrations so cheaply that production costs for photos (starting at about $500 per for color shots in a book) drop to almost nothing, and so books can become more and more heavily illustrated.

But their long-range effects worry me. I am a book dealer. I deal in print and paper and the dust of hundreds of readers, and I'm happy with that calling. It's all I ever want to do. If it turns out that I'll have to make my living selling computer disks, I'm out of here.

Let's ask one final question: Will an electronic book ever be collectible? I don't see any way that it can be. I can't see a generation in the future looking at a floppy disk—no doubt by then as grossly antiquated in its technology as the ViewMaster is to us—and saying, "Hey, cool, look at the binary code on this."

Books are a tactile thing, and I think we have to make a separation between books as things and books as text. Text is transportable—and will be transported—into new media. But no matter what kind of smart ink the technologists develop, the book as thing will always work better as pages you turn by hand than as something you put batteries into.

And there you have it. It's time to go out and buy yourself some books. There's a whole big world of them waiting just for you.

Chapter Fourteen

❦

1,001 (MORE OR LESS) COLLECTIBLE—AND FINDABLE—BOOKS

W┃hat follows is a highly subjective list of some of the high points of the current collectible market, some first edition books that are now undervalued that will probably appreciate greatly, and, if one reads the list carefully, a picture of the shape of the market as it has existed recently, and how it is likely to change.

I put a similar list in the first edition of this book, and you'll find repeats here. The gratifying thing to me, coming back to the book, was that most of the authors I removed from the original list had to be removed because they'd gotten too big. I only axed one or two for falling off the horizon. This is a good lesson: quality endures.

So here we have a blending of the old list and the new list, a continuation of some trends (serious fiction making a comeback) and a diminution of others (women mystery writers have finally passed their peak).

The list below does not cover the most expensive, most collectible writers. You already know that Faulkner, Fitzgerald, Hemingway, and their ilk are highly collectible. If you see a first edition of one of their books marked at six bucks, grab it and go home laughing. It does happen from time to time. But more often, where the money is to be made, where the collections are to be built, is in the second-level authors, the ones who, perhaps, the people at the friendly local bookstore have never heard of.

Remember the discussion of hypermoderns versus classics. Because, like you, shop owners know that Fitzgerald, etc., are highly collectible and a bookseller is not very likely to miss one on the shelves. It's entirely possible, however, that they'll miss a William Gibson, a Lindsey Davis, a Barbara Kingsolver. It is on these that we concentrate. So while there are some very famous authors noted below—people you may or may not know if they're out of your genre, plus a few A-list writers thrown in for good measure—what follows is primarily a list of what's hot on the B level. If you ever read one of their books in a high school lit class, they're not going to appear below, because you should already know about them. If you've ever seen one of their paperbacks on a drugstore rack, odds are they're not on the list.

For the specialist, there are also quite a few obvious choices, but, I think, some not so obvious ones as well. There are, sadly, no children's books on the list, because the kids' books you already know are really the only ones anybody collects. Milne, Burgess, Potter, Sendak, Cleary, and their ilk are well-known classics.

Hopefully, this list will open your eyes to a lot of authors you've not heard of before. This is good for you both as a dealer and as a reader: just think of what pleasures await you within the covers. You will find titles listed in either alphabetical or chronological order, whichever seemed to me more significant (remember, early books are usually more valuable than later) or easier to remember. There are also some paperback originals mixed into the lot, primarily on the horror and science fiction authors. Many quite collectible authors not on this list—Dean Koontz, John D. MacDonald, Elmore Leonard, and even Stephen King (as Richard Bachman) have written paperback originals. As noted earlier, you should never skip the paperback shelves; there are bargains to be found there, as well, and usually much cheaper ones. Although paperbacks rarely have the value of hardbacks, they can offer some nice surprises.

I have not included any prices. For current prices, check the references listed in chapter 12, and get hold of every dealer catalog you can find. You should have an idea of what these books are going for, but I have chosen to leave off prices for several reasons: first, because they are too changeable; second, because they are largely regional; and third, because it is more important that out of this book you get an idea of the shape of the market than of actual market values. Again, a price guide should be one of your closest friends, something that is in your car on every trip you make to the stores. You'll learn prices as you go, and the ones you learn will be adjusted for the variables mentioned above. Every time you thumb through a price guide, you should be learning more authors you weren't previously acquainted with.

The fact that prices are not included makes it imperative that you know the market value of a book and not grab it simply because it's listed.

Also, don't assume that an author's only worthwhile books are the ones noted here; things change. These are good, solid choices, but every author has other books, too, which can be great buys and even better reads. The list does not in any way cover every book by every author on the list. That would double the length of this book and bog you down with unnecessary detail. More than concentrating on memorizing titles, try to learn names and trends. The market is an ever-changing place.

One last point as far as prices go, a final summation of a point I've been trying to make all through this work: we all have our own idea of what a good price is. Is $1,200 too much for a copy of *"A" Is for Alibi*? Not if you know someone willing to pay $1,300 for it. A quick hundred in turnaround can make for a nice day. On the other hand, if you don't have a customer waiting, and you're going to have to deal it off, a hundred probably isn't going to be enough to ensure that you get your money back out of the volume. Be realistic, or be willing to let the book age on your shelf.

Just about every book on this list is, if nothing else, a fine addition to your library. You're not losing out on anything if the book has to sit awhile, and you might gain a fantastic reading experience and make a new friend for life.

Finally, this list is in no way all-inclusive. You could poll a hundred different booksellers and easily get a hundred different lists (maybe two hundred, because everyone would waffle and mince and qualify). Poll them again in a couple of months, and you'd likely get very different lists. The book market is always changing; it is your job to keep up with it.

Nor are the books listed here absolute guaranteed sales. Local markets can be different, and sometimes you'll find even odd titles overstocked. But chances are, a very high percentage of the books listed here are in high demand at local shops. You just have to find them before the shopkeepers do.

This list is not investment advice in any way. Consider it a nudge, hoping to show you one possible direction to go. But it's only one direction. By no means is it the only one.

Although again and again I've emphasized the importance of specialization, never let that make you pass up a bargain in a field outside your own. Look over all the list. Knowledge is power, and the more you know, the better off you are. As you progress as a buyer, you'll come to find your own natural rhythm and comfort level, and you'll likely find yourself passing up some bargains just because you're not interested in messing with them, while other books, no matter how far from your usual field, will practically leap off the shelf at you and beg to be taken home.

Last but certainly not least, remember this list is about first editions in collectible condition. It's all part of the fun and beauty of the book-buying game. And finally, that's how you're best off looking at this: as a game. A wonderfully pleasant pastime. Yes, you can make a modicum of money doing it; if you work hard and have some luck, you can even make a living. Of course, if you put the same amount of effort and intelligence into another field, you'd probably get rich, while with books about the very best you can ever hope for is the middle class.

But you get to spend all your time with books. And there is no other thing in the world as wonderful as that. If you're not enjoying this, if you're only looking for the quick sale, there are many easier things to do with your time that will probably make you a lot more money.

So head out to the nearest bookshop, scan the shelves, and see what treasures there await you. Enjoy yourself. Some days you'll strike out, some days you'll hit a home run, and practically every day you'll find yourself wondering where in the house you're going to put another bookcase for those lovely items that you can't quite bring yourself to part with.

Now, for all those who find nothing quite as enjoyable as the sensation of putting a book on the cash counter, here are some high points to look for on your next expedition.

ABBEY, EDWARD (literature). Most of his stuff is priced out of reach, but watch for firsts of *Cactus Country* in the Time-Life series, for which he did the text—the only collectible Time-Life book ever.

ACHEBE, CHINUA (literature). *Hopes and Impediments.*

ACKROYD, PETER (literature/SF). *Chatterton, Dickens, First Light, Hawksmoor.*

ADAMS, JANE (literature). *The Greenway, Cast the First Stone, Bird.*

ADAMS, RICHARD (literature). *Watership Down, Shardik.*

ALDISS, BRIAN (SF). Work from the mid-1970s and older. Good titles include *Barefoot in the Head, Dracula Unbound, Frankenstein Unbound, Greybeard, The Moment of Eclipse, Neanderthal Planet, Report on Probability A, The Saliva Tree and Other Strange Growths, Starship.* A very prolific writer.

ALEXIE, SHERMAN (literature). *The Lone Ranger and Tonto Fistfight in Heaven.*

ALLENDE, ISABEL (literature). *The House of the Spirits, Of Love and Shadows.* Her later books were done in much larger print runs and do not have the value of the early titles.

ALLISON, DOROTHY (literature). *Bastard Out of Carolina.*

ALVAREZ, JULIA (literature). *How the García Girls Lost Their Accents.*

AMBLER, ERIC (mystery). *Cause for Alarm, A Coffin for Dimitrios, The Dark Frontier, Epitaph for a Spy, The Intercom Conspiracy, The Levanter, Uncommon Danger.*

AMIS, KINGSLEY (literature/poetry). *The Anti-Death League; Bright November, Colonel Sun, The Evans Country, Girl, 20, The Green Man, Jake's Thing, Lucky Jim, Lucky Jim's Politics, On Drink.* A prolific writer with a long career. This list only scratches the surface. Watch for his pseudonym, Robert Markham.

AMIS, MARTIN (literature). *Dead Babies, Einstein's Monsters, The Rachel Papers, Success.*

AMMONS, A. R. (poetry). *Expressions of Sea Level, Corsons Inlet, Tape for the Turn of the Year, Uplands.*

ANDERSON, KENT (mystery). *Night Dogs, Sympathy for the Devil.*

ANTONIUS, BROTHER (William Everson) (poetry). *A Privacy of Speech, The Waldport Poems, The Blowing of the Seed, In the Fictive Wish, The Masculine Dead, The Poet Is Dead, The Re-*

sidual Years, The Springing of the Blade, War Elegies, The Year's Declension.

ASHBERY, JOHN (poetry). *The Double Dream of Spring, Rivers and Mountains, Some Trees, The Tennis Court Oath, Turandot & Other Poems.*

ATWOOD, MARGARET (literature). *Bodily Harm, Bluebeard's Egg, Dancing Girls and Other Stories, The Edible Woman, The Handmaid's Tale, Lady Oracle, Life Before Man, Surfacing.*

AUSTER, PAUL (literature). *Ghosts, In the Country of Last Things, Leviathan, Moon Palace, Music of Chance.*

BAKER, NICHOLSON (literature). *Room Temperature, The Mezzanine, U and I, Vox.* Baker's stock is still rising.

BALLARD, J. G. (literature/SF). Most of Ballard's highly imaginative titles before 1990 are collectible. *Check for Crash, Concrete Island,* and *Empire of the Sun,* which was made into a film by Steven Spielberg. Also watch for *The Atrocity Exhibition, Chronopolis, The Crystal World, The Drought* (published in the United States as *The Burning World*), *Memories of the Space Age.*

BANKS, IAIN (literature). *The Bridge, Canal Dreams, Consider Phlebas, Espedair Street, The Player of Games, Use of Weapons, Walking on Glass, The Wasp Factory.*

BARNARD, ROBERT (mystery). Titles include *Blood Brotherhood, The Missing Brontë* (also titled *The Case of The Missing Brontë*), *Death of an Old Goat, Death by Sheer Torture, Unruly Son.*

BARNES, JULIAN (literature). *Flaubert's Parrot, A History of the World in 10½ Chapters, Metroland, The Porcupine, Talking It Over.*

BARNES, LINDA (mystery). *Cities of the Dead, Coyote, Dead Heat, The Snake Tattoo, Steel Guitar, A Trouble of Fools.*

BARR, NEVADA (mystery). *Track of the Cat, A Superior Death.*

BARRET, ANDREA (literature). *Lucid Stars, The Middle Kingdom, The Forms of Water, Ship Fever.*

BARTH, JOHN (literature). *Chimera, End of the Road, The Float-*

ing Opera, Giles Goat-Boy, Letters, Lost in the Funhouse, Sabbatical, The Sot-Weed Factor. A classic writer, much collected, but still a hard sell for stores.

BARTHELME, DONALD (literature). Titles include *Amateurs; Come Back, Dr. Caligari; The Dead Father; Guilty Pleasures; The King; Snow White.* The man who reinvented the short story.

BASS, RICK (literature). An especially important nature writer, Bass does wonderful fiction as well. *The Deer Pasture, Oil Notes, The Watch, Wild at Heart, Winter.*

BAXTER, CHARLES (literature). *First Light, Shadow Play.*

BEAGLE, PETER S. (SF). *A Fine and Private Place, The Last Unicorn, Folk of the Air.*

BEAR, GREG (SF). Titles include *Anvil of Stars, Blood Music, Corona, Eon, The Forge of God, Heads, The Infinity Concerto, Sleepside Story, The Wind from a Burning Woman.*

BEATTIE, ANN (literature). *Chilly Scenes of Winter, Distortions, Secrets and Surprises, Falling in Place.* Also watch for her children's book, *Spectacles.*

BENEDICT, PINCKNEY (literature). *Town Smokes, The Wrecking Yard.*

BENFORD, GREGORY (SF). *In the Ocean of Night, The Jupiter Project, Of Space/Time and the River, Time's Rub.*

BERGER, THOMAS (literature). *Arthur Rex, Crazy in Berlin, Killing Time, Little Big Man, Reinhart in Love, Sneaky People, Vital Parts, Who Is Teddy Villanova?* Later titles were done in large runs and can be found cheaply, while early titles, such as his best book, *Little Big Man,* can run into serious money.

BERRIGAN, TED (poetry). *The Sonnets, Many Happy Returns.*

BERRYMAN, JOHN (poetry). *The Dream Songs; His Toy, His Dream, His Rest; His Thoughts Made Pockets & the Plane Buckt; Homage to Mistress Bradstreet, Love & Fame.* A true original, you can't go wrong with Berryman.

BISHOP, ELIZABETH (poetry). *The Ballad of the Burglar of Babylon, The Complete Poems.*

BLAYLOCK, JAMES P. (SF). *Homunculus, Land of Dreams, The Last Coin.*

BOWDEN, CHARLES (literature/nature). *Blue Desert, Frog Mountain Blues, Killing the Hidden Waters, Mezcal.* The book he coauthored on the trial of Charles Keating, *Trust Me,* is the hardest title to find.

BOWLES, PAUL (literature). *In the Red Room, Midnight Mass, The Sheltering Sky, The Thicket of Spring.* One of the often overlooked geniuses of the century. Also check for his books in travel literature sections.

BOWMAN, DAVID (literature). *Let the Dog Drive, Bunny Modern.*

BOX, EDGAR (Gore Vidal) (mystery). *Death Before Bedtime, Death in the Fifth Position, Death Likes It Hot.*

BOYD, WILLIAM (literature). *Brazzaville Beach, A Good Man in Africa, On the Yankee Station: Stories.*

BOYLE, T. COREGHESSAN (literature). *Descent of Man, Budding Prospects, East Is East, If the River Was Whiskey, Water Music.* Other titles are also sought after.

BRACKETT, LEIGH (SF/mystery). Titles include *Shadow Over Mars, The Starmen, The Sword of Rhiannon.*

BRADLEY, MARION ZIMMER (SF). A lot of her earlier books are paperback originals; her title that's always in demand is her retelling of the Arthur legend, *Mists of Avalon.*

BRAUTIGAN, RICHARD (literature). Early titles, such as *A Confederate General from Big Sur, In Watermelon Sugar, Revenge of the Lawn,* and *Trout Fishing in America,* are nearly impossible to find, but worth the effort. It's a good idea to grab more common titles: *Dreaming of Babylon, The Hawkline Monster, So the Wind Won't Blow It All Away, Sombrero Fallout, The Tokyo-Montana Express, Willard and His Bowling Trophies,* whenever the chance arises.

BRIN, DAVID (SF). *Earth, The Postman, The River of Time, The Uplift War.* Even the Kevin Costner movie didn't ruin Brin's reputation.

BRITE, POPPY Z. (horror). Her first novel, *Lost Souls*, is still fairly easy to come by in an unnoticed first. Oddly her second, *Swamp Foetus*, is a bit harder to find.

BUCKLEY, CHRISTOPHER (literature). *Wet Work, Thank You for Smoking.*

BURKE, JAMES LEE (mystery). The Dave Robicheaux books: *The Neon Rain, Heaven's Prisoners, Black Cherry Blues, A Morning for Flamingos, A Stained White Radiance.* Early titles from Burke are very expensive, including *Half of Paradise* and *To the Bright and Shining Sun.* (The biggest thrift store hit I've seen in the past couple years was a copy of *Half of Paradise* for a buck.) *The Convict* was a paperback original released simultaneously with a very small hardback printing that went mostly to libraries.

BUTLER, ROBERT OLEN (literature). *The Alleys of Eden, Countrymen of Bones, The Deuce, On Distant Ground, Sun Dogs, They Whisper.* A writer nowhere near the peak of his talents.

BYATT, A. S. (literature). *The Game, Possession, Shadow of a Sun, Still Life, Sugar and Other Stories.*

CAMPBELL, BEBE MOORE (literature). *Your Blues Ain't Like Mine, Sweet Summer, Brothers and Sisters.*

CAMPBELL, RAMSEY (horror). Early titles, particularly in small press or British editions. By the eighties, his works were done in large enough runs to glut the market. Watch especially for *The Doll Who Ate His Mother*, a classic. Other early classics include *The Face That Must Die, The Height of the Scream, Incarnate, The Nameless.*

CANIN, ETHAN (literature). *Emperor of the Air.*

CARD, ORSON SCOTT (SF). *The Abyss, Ender's Game, The Folk of the Fringe, Lost Boys, Red Prophet, Wyrms.*

CARROLL, JONATHAN (literature/SF/horror). *The Land of Laughs, Voice of Our Shadow, Bones of the Moon, Sleeping in Flame, A Child Across the Sky, Black Cocktail, Outside the Dog Mu-*

seum, After Silence, From the Teeth of Angels. One of the best writers, sentence for sentence, working today, his early books are starting to skyrocket.

CARTER, ANGELA (literature/SF). *Black Venus, The Bloody Chamber, Come Unto These Yellow Sands, Fireworks, Honeybuzzard, The Infernal Desire Machines of Doctor Hoffman* (retitled *The War of Dreams* in the U.S. edition), *Love, The Magic Toyshop, Nights at the Circus, Several Perceptions, Shadow Dance.* Also check for her books in women's studies, mythology/fairy tales, and horror. An undefinable writer, and a true original.

CARVER, RAYMOND (literature). Titles include *Put Yourself in My Shoes, Ultramarine, Where I'm Calling From, Where Water Comes Together with Other Water, Will You Please Be Quiet Please.* Fine prose over a very long career.

CHESBRO, GEORGE C. (mystery). *An Affair of Sorcerers, The Beasts of Valhalla, City of Whispering Stone, The Cold Smell of Sacred Stone, Second Horseman Out of Eden, Shadow of a Broken Man.*

CHILD, LEE (mystery). *Killing Floor, Die Trying, Tripwire.*

CHILDRESS, MARK (literature). *Crazy in Alabama, World Made of Fire.*

CHRISTIAN, PERNELL (literature). *Modern Physics and Other Tales.*

CISNEROS, SANDRA (literature). *The House on Mango Street; Loose Women; My Wicked, Wicked Ways; Woman Hollering Creek.*

COEL, MARGARET (mystery). *Eagle Catcher; Dead End.*

COETZEE, J. M. (literature). *Dusklands, Life & Times of Michael K., Waiting for the Barbarians.*

COHEN, LEONARD (poetry). *Flowers for Hitler, Let Us Compare Mythologies, The Spice-Box of Earth, Parasites of Heaven.*

COLWIN, LAURIE (literature). All of her titles are undervalued, although her final books were done in fairly large runs.

Watch for *Another Marvelous Thing, Family Happiness, Happy All the Time, The Lone Pilgrim.*

CONNELL, EVAN S. (literature). *Mr. Bridge, Son of the Morning Star.*

CONNELLY, MICHAEL (mystery). *The Black Echo, The Black Ice, The Concrete Blonde.*

CONROY, PAT (literature). *The Boo, The Great Santini, The Prince of Tides, The Water Is Wide.*

COOVER, ROBERT (literature). *The Universal Baseball Association, Inc., J. Henry Waugh, Prop.*

CORMIER, ROBERT (literature/SF). *Fade.*

CORNWELL, BERNARD (literature/mystery/adventure). The Sharpe series—*Sharpe's Gold, Sharpe's Eagle,* etc.

CORNWELL, PATRICIA (mystery). *Postmortem, Body of Evidence, All That Remains, Cruel and Unusual.*

CORSO, GREGORY (poetry). *Bomb, Gasoline, The Happy Birthday of Death, The Mutation of the Spirit.* An often-overlooked Beat poet.

CRAIS, ROBERT (mystery). *Voodoo River, Free Fall, Lullaby Town, Stalking the Angel, The Monkey's Raincoat.*

CREELEY, ROBERT (poetry). *As Now It Would Be Snow, The Charm, A Day Book, The Finger, A Form of Women, The Whip.*

CREWS, HARRY (literature). Pre-1980s titles, which include *Car, The Gospel Singer, Naked in Garden Hills, The Gypsy's Curse, The Hawk Is Dying, Karate Is a Thing of the Spirit.*

CROSS, AMANDA (mystery). *In the Last Analysis, The James Joyce Murder, Poetic Justice, The Theban Mysteries, The Question of Max.*

CROWLEY, JOHN (SF/fantasy). All of his titles are eagerly sought. Watch for the paperback of *Little, Big,* which was done concurrent with the very small hardback first printing. Other books are *Aegypt, Beasts, The Deep, Engine Summer, Novelty.*

CRUMLEY, JAMES (mystery). *One to Count Cadence, The Muddy Fork, The Pigeon Shoot, The Wrong Case. The Mexican Tree*

Duck was done in large quantities, but should be a strong title in the future.

Danticat, Edwidge (literature). *Breath, Eyes, Memory; Krik? Krak!; Farming of Bones.*

Davidson, Diane Mott (mystery). *Catering to Nobody, Dying for Chocolate, Cereal Murders.*

Davies, Robertson (literature). Titles include *The Cunning Man, Eros at Breakfast, The Manticore, A Mixture of Frailties, Murther and Walking Spirits, Tempest-Tost, World of Wonders.*

Davis, Lindsey (mystery). *The Iron Hand of Mars, Last Act in Palmyra, Shadows in Bronze, Silver Pigs, Venus in Copper.*

DeLillo, Don (literature). *Americana, End Zone, Ratner's Star.* Later books are also collected, but were done in larger editions.

Dexter, Colin (mystery). Titles include *The Dead of Jericho, The Jewel That Was Ours, The Riddle of the Third Mile, Service of All the Dead, The Silent World of Nicholas Quinn, The Way Through the Woods, The Wench Is Dead.*

Dexter, Pete (literature). *Brotherly Love, Deadwood, God's Pocket, Paris Trout.*

Dickinson, Peter (mystery). *The Lizard in the Cup, The Old English Peep Show, Skin Deep* (published in the United States as *The Glass-Sided Ant's Nest*), *Sleep and His Brother.* A very prolific writer, a key to the mystery genre; this only touches on his collectible titles.

Dillard, Annie (literature/nature). *Pilgrim at Tinker Creek, Tickets for a Prayer Wheel, Teaching a Stone to Talk.*

Doctorow, E. L. (literature). *Big as Life, The Book of Daniel, Lives of the Poets, Ragtime, Welcome to Hard Times.*

Doig, Ivan (literature). *Dancing at the Rascal Fair, Winter Brothers.* A great regional writer.

Dorn, Edward (poetry). *From Gloucester Out, Geography, Hands Up!, Idaho Out, The Newly Fallen, The North Atlantic Turbine, Twenty-four Love Songs.*

DOSS, JAMES (mystery). *Shaman Sings, Shaman Laughs, Shaman's Game.*

DUFRESNE, JOHN (literature). *Louisiana Power & Light; The Way Water Enters Stone.*

DUNCAN, DAVID JAMES (literature). *The River Why.*

DUNN, KATHERINE (literature). *Geek Love.*

EDGERTON, CLYDE (literature). *The Floatplane Notebooks, Killer Diller, Raney, Walking Across Egypt.*

EHRLICH, GRETEL (literature). *The Solace of Open Spaces, Heart Mountain.*

ELKINS, AARON (mystery). *Curses!, The Dark Place, Dead Men's Hearts, A Deceptive Clarity, Fellowship of Fear, A Glancing Light, Icy Clutches, Make No Bones, Murder in the Queen's Armes, Old Bones, A Wicked Slice.*

ELLROY, JAMES (mystery). *The Big Nowhere, The Black Dahlia, L.A. Confidential, Suicide Hill, White Jazz.*

ELTON, BEN (mystery). *Popcorn.*

EMERSON, EARL (mystery). Both of the series Emerson writes are currently undervalued. Buy all of his books, and watch for *The Rainy City, Poverty Bay,* and *Nervous Laughter* in paperback first editions. *Black Hearts and Slow Dancing; Deviant Behavior; Fat Tuesday; Help Wanted: Orphans Preferred; Morons & Madmen; Yellow Dog Party.*

ERDRICH, LOUISE (literature). *Jacklight, Love Medicine, The Beet Queen, Tracks.*

FANTE, JOHN (literature). Everything, both the original editions from the first half of the century and the first edition reprints put out in the past few years by Black Sparrow Press. The main titles to watch for are *Ask the Dust, Wait Until Spring, and Bandini,* but don't miss *The Brotherhood of the Grape, 1933 Was a Bad Year, West of Rome,* and *The Wine of Youth.*

FEIST, RAYMOND E. (SF). *Magician, A Darkness at Sethanon, Silverthorn.*

FINNEY, JACK (literature/SF). *Time and Again, The Woodrow Wilson Dime.*

FISCHER, TIBOR (literature). *The Thought Gang, Under the Frog.*

FORD, RICHARD (literature). *A Piece of My Heart, Rock Springs, The Sportswriter* (a paperback original), *The Ultimate Good Luck.*

FRASER, ANTONIA (mystery). Titles include *Cool Repentance, Oxford Blood, Quiet as a Nun, A Splash of Red, The Wild Island.*

FRASER, GEORGE MACDONALD (literature/mystery). Early titles in the Flashman series: *Flashman, Royal Flash, Flash for Freedom!, Flashman at the Charge, Flashman in the Great Game, Flashman's Lady, Flashman and the Redskins, Flashman and the Dragon, Flashman and the Mountain of Light.*

FURST, ALAN (literature). *Night Soldiers, Dark Star.*

FYFIELD, FRANCES (mystery). *A Question of Guilt, Trial by Fire* (titled *Not That Kind of Place* in the United States), *Shadows on the Mirror.*

GADDIS, WILLIAM (literature). *Carpenter's Gothic, A Frolic of His Own, J R, The Recognitions.*

GAINES, ERNEST (literature). *Bloodline, Catherine Carmier, A Gathering of Old Men, In My Father's House, A Lesson Before Dying, A Long Day in November.*

GALLAGHER, TESS (poetry). *Amplitude, Moon Crossing Bridge, Portable Kisses, Under Stars, Willingly.*

GARTON, RAY (horror). *Crucifax Autumn, Live Girls, Lot Lizards, Methods of Madness, Trade Secrets.* Watch especially for small press volumes.

GASS, WILLIAM H. (literature). *Omensetter's Luck, In the Heart of the Heart of the Country, Willie Master's Lonesome Life, The Tunnel.*

GEORGE, ELIZABETH (mystery). *A Great Deliverance, Payment in Blood, A Suitable Vengeance, Well-Schooled in Murder.*

GIBBONS, KAYE (literature). *Ellen Foster, Cure for Dreams, Virtuous Woman.*

GIBSON, WILLIAM (SF). Everything, even though the more recent titles have been done in large editions. His position as the originator of "cyberpunk" will keep him hot for some time to come. *Neuromancer* (original edition was a U.S. paperback, followed by the British hardback), *Burning Chrome, Count Zero, Mona Lisa Overdrive, The Difference Engine, Virtual Light*.

GILB, DAGOBERTO (literature). *Magic and Blood, Last Known Residence of Mickey Acuna*.

GILCHRIST, ELLEN (literature). *In the Land of Dreamy Dreams, The Land Surveyor's Daughter, Victory over Japan*.

GOLDBERG, BECKIAN FRITZ (poetry). *Body Betrayer, In the Badlands of Desire*.

GRAVES, ROBERT (literature). *Adam's Rib; I, Claudius; Lawrence and the Arabs*.

GRAY, ALASDAIR (literature). *The Fall of Kelvin Walker; Janine; Old Negatives; Unlikely Stories, Mostly*.

GREENLEAF, STEPHEN (mystery). The Tanner series, currently very undervalued. Still not the break-out I expected—a couple of weak books hurt him—but the early titles are climbing up nicely. *Beyond Blame, Blood Type, Book Case, Death Bed, Ditto List, Fatal Obsession, Grave Error, State's Evidence, Toll Call*.

GUNN, THOM (poetry). *A Geography, Fighting Teams, My Sad Captains, The Sense of Movement, Touch*.

HAMILTON, IAN (poetry). *Pretending Not to Sleep*.

HAMILTON, JANE (literature). *A Map of the World, Book of Ruth*.

HAMILTON, STEVE (mystery). *A Cold Day in Paradise*.

HANNAH, BARRY (literature). *Airships, Bats out of Hell, Boomerang*.

HANSEN, RON (literature). *Desperadoes, The Assassination of Jessie James by the Coward Robert Ford, Atticus*.

HARRINGTON, KENT (mystery). *Día de Los Muertos, Dark Ride*.

HARRISON, JIM (literature/poetry). *Farmer, Locations, Natural World, Outlyer and Ghazals, Plain Song, The Woman Lit by Fireflies*. Harrison is on the upswing; watch for all his titles.

HASSLER, JON (literature). *Staggerford, North of Hope*.

HEANEY, SEAMUS (poetry). *A Boy Leading His Father to Confession, Death of a Naturalist, Eleven Poems, Field Work, The Government of the Tongue, Station Island, Sweeney Astray.*

HEGI, URSULA (literature). *Stones from the River.*

HEINEMANN, LARRY (literature). *Close Quarters, Cooler by the Lake, Paco's Story.*

HELPRIN, MARK (literature/SF). *Winter's Tale.*

HEMPEL, AMY (literature). *Reasons to Live, At the Gates of the Animal Kingdom.*

HENRY, SUE (mystery). *Murder on the Iditarod Trail, Termination Dust, Sleeping Lady.*

HINE, DARYL (poetry). *The Devil's Picture Book, Minutes, The Wooden Horse.*

HOAGLAND, EDWARD (literature/western Americana). *African Calliope, The Courage of Turtles, Notes from the Century Before, Red Wolves and Black Bears, Seven Rivers West, Walking the Dead Diamond River.*

HOLLAND, TOM (literature). *Lord of the Dead, Supping with Panthers.*

HORGAN, PAUL (literature/western Americana/history). One of the underrated greats; titles include *Everything to Live For; The Heroic Triad; Lamy of Santa Fe: His Life and Times; Mountain Standard Time; Mexico Bay; Things as They Are; Whitewater.*

HOUSTON, PAM (literature). *Cowboys Are My Weakness.*

HUGHES, TED (poetry). *The Burning of the Brothel, Crow, Hawk in the Rain, Lupercal, Recklings, Scapegoats & Rabies, Wodwo.*

JACKSON, JON A. (mystery). *Blind Pig, Grootka, Hit on the House, Dead Folk, Go by Go, The Die Hard.*

JANCE, J. A. (mystery). *Until Proven Guilty, Injustice for All, Trial by Fury, Taking the Fifth, Improbable Cause, A More Perfect Union, Dismissed with Prejudice, Minor in Possession, Payment in Kind, Desert Heat.*

JARRELL, RANDALL (poetry). *Blood for a Stranger, The Lost World, Pictures from an Institution, Rage for the Lost Penny.*

JOHNSON, DENNIS (literature). *Angels, Jesus Son, Fiskadora.*

JONES, THOM (literature). *The Pugilist at Rest.*

KAMINSKY, STUART M. (mystery). Titles include *Bullet for a Star, A Fine Red Rain, The Howard Hughes Affair, Murder on the Yellow Brick Road, Never Cross a Vampire.*

KAVANAUGH, DAN (mystery). *Duffy, Putting the Boot In.* A pseudonym for Julian Barnes; not to be confused with Paul Kavanaugh, which is a pseudonym for the equally collectible Lawrence Block who is, himself, too big time to make the list.

KENNEDY, WILLIAM (literature). *Billy Phelan's Greatest Game, The Ink Truck, Quinn's Book, Very Old Bones.*

KIDDER, TRACY (literature/history/social issues). *The Road to Yuba City, The Soul of a New Machine.*

KIJEWSKI, KAREN (mystery). *Copy Kat, Katapult, Katwalk, Wild Kat.*

KING, LAURIE (mystery). *Beekeeeper's Apprentice, A Grave Talent, A Monstrous Regiment of Women.*

KINGSOLVER, BARBARA (literature). *The Bean Trees*; later titles had very large printings, but there is a market for them. Watch also for her scarce *Homeland and Other Stories.*

KINSELLA, THOMAS (poetry). *Another September, Downstream, Nightwalker, Poems, Wormwood.*

KINSELLA, W. P. (literature). All before *Box Socials. Dance Me Outside, The Further Adventures of Slugger McBatt, The Iowa Baseball Confederacy, Shoeless Joe,* and *The Thrill of the Grass* rank among his most noteworthy. The best writer to take on baseball fiction.

KOCH, KENNETH (poetry). *Permanently, Sleeping with Women, When the Sun Tries to Go On.*

KOSINSKI, JERZY (literature). All, the earlier the better. Watch for *Cockpit, Being There, Blind Date, The Painted Bird.*

KOTZWINKLE, WILLIAM (literature). *E.T., The Book of the Green Planet; Doctor Rat; Elephant Bangs Train; Fata Morgana; The Hot Jazz Trio.* A truly original writer.

KURZWEIL, ALLEN (literature). *A Case of Curiosities*.

LANSDALE, JOE (mystery/SF). *Mucho Mojo, Savage Season*. Lansdale works fast, in a wide variety of areas. He's an acquired taste, but one more and more people are acquiring.

LEHANE, DENNIS (mystery). *A Drink Before the War; Darkness, Take My Hand; Gone, Baby, Gone; Sacred.* The mystery genre's best hope of a future.

LETHEM, JONATHAN (literature/SF/mystery). *Gun with Occasional Music, Amnesia Moon, The Wall of the Sky.*

LEVERTOV, DENISE (poetry). *The Double Image, Embroideries, Here and Now, Overland to the Islands, To Stay Alive, With Eyes at the Back of Our Heads.*

LOPEZ, BARRY (literature/nature). *Arctic Dreams; Desert Notes: Reflections in the Eye of a Raven; Of Wolves and Men; River Notes: The Dance of Herons; Giving Birth to Thunder, Sleeping with His Daughter; Winter Count.* One of the most passionate writers working today.

MASON, BOBBIE ANN (literature). *In Country, Shiloh and Other Stories.*

McCAMMON, ROBERT R. (horror). *Baal, Bethany's Sin, Blue World, Boy's Life, Mine, The Night Boat, Stinger, Swan Song, They Thirst, Usher's Passing, The Wolf's Hour.*

McCANN, COLUM (mystery/literature). *Songdogs, This Side of Brightness.*

McCORKLE, JILL (literature). *July 7th, The Cheer Leader.*

McCRACKEN, ELIZABETH (literature). *Here's Your Hat, What's Your Hurry; Giant's House.*

McEWAN, IAN (literature). *Black Dogs; The Cement Garden; The Comfort of Strangers; First Love, Last Rites; In Between the Sheets; The Innocent; Or Shall We Die.*

McGUANE, THOMAS (literature). *The Bushwhacked Piano, Keep the Change, The Missouri Breaks, Ninety-two in the Shade, Nothing but Blue Skies, Panama, The Sporting Club, To Skin a Cat.*

McMILLAN, TERRY (literature). *Disappearing Acts, Waiting to Exhale.*

McPHEE, JOHN (literature/history/travel/social issues). All titles are worthwhile; McPhee has never repeated himself. Pre-1980 titles are the hardest to find. *A Sense of Where You Are, Oranges, The Pine Barrens, Levels of the Game, Encounters with the Archdruid, The Deltoid Pumpkin Seed, The Survival of the Bark Canoe, The Crofter and the Laird, Coming into the Country.*

MELLVILLE, JAMES (mystery). *The Wages of Zen; The Chrysanthemum Chain; A Sort of Samurai; The Ninth Netsuke; Death of a Daimyo; The Death Ceremony; Go Gently, Gaijin; Kimono for a Corpse.*

MILLHOUSE, STEVEN (literature). *Edwin Mullhouse, From the Realm of Morpheus, In the Penny Arcade, Little Kingdoms.*

MOMADAY, N. SCOTT (literature). *House Made of Dawn, The Ancient Child.*

MOODY, RICK (literature). *Purple America, Garden State, Ice Storm, Ring of Brightest Angels.*

MOORCOCK, MICHAEL (SF). Everything he wrote is collected; however, there is so much of it, the early titles are the only sure bets. Some of these are *A Cure for Cancer, Elric at the End of Time, Elric of Melnibone, The English Assassin, The Final Programme, The Land Leviathan, The Stealer of Souls, Traps of Time.*

MOORE, LORRIE (literature). *Self-help, Birds of America, Anagrams, Like Life, Who Will Run the Frog Hospital?*

MORRELL, DAVID (adventure/horror). Most famous as the creator of Rambo in his novel *First Blood*, Morrell's book *The Totem* has become very pricey, as has *Testament.*

MORROW, JAMES (literature/SF). *City of Truth, The Continent of Lies, Only Begotten Daughter, This Is the Way the World Ends, Towing Jehovah.*

MOSLEY, WALTER (mystery). *Devil in a Blue Dress, A Red Death, White Butterfly.*

MURAKAMI, HARUKI (literature). The most original writer ever to come out of Japan. Watch for *Dance Dance Dance, Hard Boiled Wonderland, A Wild Sheep Chase.*

NAYLOR, GLORIA (literature). *The Women of Brewster Place.*

NICHOLS, JOHN (literature). *A Ghost in the Music, The Magic Journey, The Milagro Beanfield War, The Nirvana Blues, The Sterile Cuckoo, The Wizard of Loneliness.*

NIVEN, LARRY (SF). *The Barsoom Project, Dream Park, A Gift From Earth, Inconstant Moon, Inferno, Limits, Lucifer's Hammer, The Magic Goes Away, Ringworld, The Ringworld Engineers.* Many of Niven's books are cowritten with Jerry Pournelle.

NORMAN, HOWARD (literature). *The Bird Artist, Kiss in the Hotel Joseph Conrad.*

OATES, JOYCE CAROL (literature). *American Appetites, Angel of Light, The Assassins, Expensive People, Foxfire, I Lock My Door Upon Myself, Lives of the Twins, Night-Side, Solstice, Them, Unholy Loves, Wonderland, You Must Remember This.* One of the fastest writers of quality fiction, Oates could fill up a bookcase by herself. Watch for all her titles.

O'BRIEN, TIM (literature). *If I Die in a Combat Zone, Going After Cacciato, Northern Lights, The Nuclear Age, The Things They Carried, In the Lake of the Woods.* One of the finest writers this country has ever produced.

OFFUT, CHRIS (literature). *Kentucky Straight, The Same River Twice, The Good Brother, Two-Eleven All Around.*

OLDS, SHARON (poetry). *The Dead and the Living, Father, The Gold Cell, Satan Says.*

O'NAN, STEWART (literature). *In the Walled City, Names of the Dead, Speed Queen, Snow Angels.*

ONDAATJE, MICHAEL (literature). *The Collected Works of Billy the Kid, Coming Through Slaughter, The English Patient, In the Skin of a Lion, Running in the Family.*

PAGE, KATHERINE HALL (mystery). Her "body" series: *The Body in the Belfry, The Body in the Vestibule,* etc.

PALEY, GRACE (literature). *The Little Disturbances of Man.*

PARETSKY, SARA (mystery). *Bitter Medicine, Burn Marks, Dead-lock, Indemnity Only, Toxic Shock* (retitled *Blood Shot* in the United States). Her first novels can be good buys; later books had very large print runs.

PARKER, ROBERT B. (mystery). Titles before *Catskill Eagle* are the hardest to find and most valuable; later titles can be a scout's dream; they all had a large print run, but are easy to find for a few dollars and sell higher. These include *Double Deuce, Pastime, Pale Kings and Princes, Playmates, Poodle Springs* (a Raymond Chandler novel finished by Parker; may be found under either author on the shelves), *Stardust, Taming a Sea Horse.*

PELECANOS, GEORGE (mystery). *Shoedog, Nick's Trip, A Firing Offense, Bir Blow Down, King Suckerman.*

PERCY, WALKER (literature). *Lancelot, The Last Gentleman, Lost in the Cosmos, Love Among the Ruins, The Moviegoer, The Second Coming.*

PETERS, ELLIS (mystery). Very prolific, with a very long career. Single titles include *Death Mask, The Will and the Deed, Death and the Joyful Woman.* Peters is better noted for the Brother Cadfael series, all of which are collectible. Some titles include *A Morbid Taste for Bones, One Corpse Too Many, Monk's Hood, St. Peter's Fair, The Sanctuary Sparrow, The Virgin in the Ice.*

PHILLIPS, JAYNE ANNE (literature). *Black Tickets, Fast Lanes, Machine Dreams, Shelter.* Watch especially for the limited editions of her work: *Counting, Fast Lanes, How Mickey Made It, Sweethearts.*

POWERS, RICHARD (literature). *Prisoner's Dilemma, The Gold Bug Variations, Three Farmers on Their Way to a Dance.*

POWERS, TIM (SF). Everything he wrote is collected. The hottest title is *The Anubis Gates.* Also look for *Dinner at Deviant's Palace, The Drawing of the Dead, Epitaph in Rust, Last Call, On Stranger Tides.*

PRICE, REYNOLDS (literature). Everything is worth finding. Watch for *Good Hearts, Kate Vaiden, Mustian, Permanent Errors, The Surface of Earth.*

PROULX, E. ANNIE (literature). *Heart Songs, Postcards, The Shipping News.*

PURDY, A. W. (poetry). *The Cariboo Horses, The Enchanted Echo, North of Summer, Pressed on Sand.*

RANKIN, IAN (mystery). *Hide & Seek, Mortal Causes, Knots & Crosses, Tooth & Nail, Let It Bleed.*

RICH, ADRIENNE (poetry). *Diving into the Wreck, Necessities of Life, A Wild Patience Has Taken Me This Far, The Will to Change.* Books after the mid-1980s have been printed in fairly large editions for poetry; she remains one of the truly original voices in the field.

ROBINSON, LYNDA S. (mystery). *Place of Anubis, Murder at the God's Gate.*

ROZAN, S. J. (mystery). *China Trade, Mandarin Plaid, No Colder Place, Tale about a Tiger.*

RUCKER, GREG (mystery). *Smoker, Whiteout, Shooting at Midnight.*

RUSH, NORMAN (literature). *Mating, Whites.*

RUSSO, RICHARD (literature). *Nobody's Fool, Mohawk, Straight Man, The Risk Pool.*

SALLIS, JAMES (mystery). *Long-legged Fly, Moth, Black Hornet.*

SALTER, JAMES (literature). *Dusk & Other Stories, Light Years, Solo Faces, The Hunters, The Arm of Flesh.*

SALZMAN, MARK (literature/travel). *Iron & Silk.*

SANDFORD, JOHN (mystery). *Rules of Prey.* The rest of his books have had huge printings.

SATTERTHWAIT, WALTER (mystery). *At Ease with the Dead, A Flower in the Desert, The Hanged Man, Wall of Glass.*

SAYLOR, STEVEN (mystery). *Arms of Nemesis, Catalina's Riddle, Roman Blood.*

SELF, WILL (literature). *Cock and Bull, My Idea of Fun, The Quantum Theory of Insanity.*

SERANELLA, BARBARA (mystery). *Unwanted Company, No Offense Intended, No Human Involved.*

SETH, VIKRAM (literature/poetry). *The Golden Gate.*

SHEPARD, LUCIUS (SF). *The Ends of the Earth, The Father of Stones, Green Eyes, Kalimantan, The Jaguar Hunter, Life During Wartime.* A very prolific writer of consistent high quality. Watch for any of his titles.

SHIELDS, CAROL (literature). *Happenstance, The Orange Fish, The Republic of Love, The Stone Diaries, Various Miracles.*

SILKO, LESLIE MARMON (literature/native American). *Ceremony, Laguna Woman, Storyteller.* Her book *Almanac of the Dead* was heavily remaindered.

SIMMONS, DAN (horror). *Carrion Comfort, Entropy's Bed at Midnight, The Fall of Hyperion, Hyperion, The Hollow Man, Lovedeath, Phases of Gravity, Prayers to Broken Stones, Song of Kali, Summer of Night.* Buy Simmons now, before he becomes more expensive than King. The most intelligent writer in horror, Simmons was recently named "Most Collectible Author" by *Locus* magazine.

SMILEY, JANE (literature). *The Age of Grief, Catskill Crafts, Duplicate Keys, The Greenlanders, A Thousand Acres.*

SMITH, JULIE (mystery). *The Axeman's Jazz, Dead in the Water, Death Turns a Trick, Huckleberry Fiend, Jazz Funeral, New Orleans Mourning, Other People's Skeletons.*

STEGNER, WALLACE (literature). Titles include *All the Little Live Things, The Big Rock Candy Mountain.*

STEPHENSON, NEIL (SF). *Snow Crash, The Diamond Age.*

STERLING, BRUCE (SF). *Artificial Kid, Crystal Express.*

STONE, ROBERT (literature). *Children of Light, Dog Soldiers, A Flag for Sunrise, A Hall of Mirrors, Outerbridge Reach.*

STRAIGHT, SUSAN (literature). *I Been in Sorrow's Kitchen and Licked Out All the Pots.*

STRAUB, PETER (horror/mystery). Much of Straub's collectibility depends on his association with Stephen King, but he's a fine writer in his own right—one of the most literate of the genre. Most sought-after is his first book, a volume of poetry called *Ishmael*, printed in an edition of one hundred in London. Other titles to look for: *Floating Dragon, If You Could See Me Now, Julia, Ghost Story*. Later books had very large printings.

TAN, AMY (literature). *The Joy Luck Club, The Kitchen God's Wife*.

TAPPLY, WILLIAM G. (mystery). *Death at Charity's Pond, Dutch Blue Error, Follow the Sharks*.

TATE, JAMES (poetry). *Cages, The Destination, Hints to Pilgrims, The Lost Pilot, Mystics in Chicago, Notes of Woe, Row With Your Hair, The Torches*.

TAYLOR, PETER (literature). *Happy Families Are All Alike, In the Miro District, In the Tennessee Country, Long Fourth, Miss Leonora When Last Seen, The Old Forest and Other Stories, A Stand in the Mountains, A Summons to Memphis, The Widows of Thornton*.

UDALL, BRADY (literature). *Letting Loose the Hounds*.

VAN GIESON, JUDITH (mystery). *North of the Border, Raptor, The Other Side of Death, The Wolf Path*.

VOLLMANN, WILLIAM T. (literature). *Butterfly Stories, The Ice-Shirt, The Rainbow Stories, The Rifles, Thirteen Stories and Thirteen Epitaphs, You Bright and Risen Angels*.

WAKOSKI, DIANE (poetry). Everything is worth seeking. She has published many, many small press works and broadsides. Titles include *Coins & Coffins, The Diamond Merchant, Greed: Parts I & II, Greed: Parts III & IV, Greed: Parts V–VII, The Magellanic Clouds, Smudging*.

WALKER, MARY WILLIS (mystery). *Red Scream, Zero at the Bone*.

WATSON, LARRY (literature). *Montana 1948, In a Dark Time*.

WHITE, RANDY WAYNE (mystery). *Sanibel Flats, The Heat Islands*.

WILHELM, KATE (mystery/SF). Titles include *The Clone, The Downstairs Room, The Infinity Box, Juniper Time, The Killer*

Thing, The Mile-Long Spaceship, More Bitter Than Death, The Nevermore Affair.

WILLEFORD, CHARLES (mystery). *Miami Blues, New Hope for the Dead, Sideswipe.*

WINSLOW, DON (mystery). *A Cool Breeze on the Underground, Way Down on the High Lonely, Life and Death of Bobby Z.*

WINTERSON, JEANETTE (literature). *Art & Lies, Oranges Are Not the Only Fruit, Sexing the Cherry, Written on the Body.*

WINTON, TIM (literature). *The Riders.*

WOLFF, TOBIAS (literature). *Back in the World, The Barracks Thief, In Pharaoh's Army, In the Garden of the North American Martyrs, This Boy's Life.*

ZELAZNY, ROGER (SF). Titles include *Bridge of Ashes, The Hand of Oberon, My Name Is Legion.* One of the masters.

ZUKOFSKY, LOUIS (poetry). *Little, Some Time.*

Appendix

◆

IDENTIFYING FIRST
EDITIONS

A s you well know by now, no factor is more important to
your success than being able to identify first editions
correctly. While you're best off if you keep one of the specialized, detailed guides handy, this appendix describes the publishers' formats you should know without having to look up.
These are the houses that make up the bulk of the books you're
likely to buy.

It is by no means an exhaustive list. There are literally
thousands of publishers in this country alone, and if you are
specializing in one field, you're going to come across many not
listed here. For example, a science fiction and horror specialist
would soon learn the first edition policies of Arkham House
and Dark Harvest; someone dealing in modern literature would
have little need for even knowing what kind of books those
houses produce, but the policies of Graywolf would be of great
interest.

Nobody knows all of these without checking a reference
somewhere.

One quick note on how the list is organized. If an entry says "first editions stated," it means just that. Somewhere on the copyright page of books of that particular publisher, there will be a line reading "First Edition." If the entry says "subsequent editions stated," this means that there is no indication of the first edition, but all later printings will identify themselves in some way—usually by reading "second printing" and a date. Therefore, if an entry reads "subsequent editions stated," the way to identify a first edition is to realize that there is no indication of edition on a first. To see how this works, look at a book from Viking, which probably offers the clearest example of this. Their books read "First published in . . ." on firsts; later printings are clearly indicated.

There are some publishers that have never made any attempt to indicate editions. If a writer you are interested in has worked with one of these houses (such as Johnny Gruelle and Gruelle Co., or the early Oz books with Reily & Lee), then you must turn to specialized bibliographies and learn specific points. Even where no clear primacy of edition has been established, there is usually a hierarchy in the desirability, and this can be determined through points.

ANDREWS & MCMEEL. No identification in first editions; later reprintings are usually identified by stating the printing and the date of the printing.

APPLETON (also Appleton-Century-Crofts). Look for a number "1" surrounded by brackets on the last page of the book on their classic old titles. Since the early 1980s, they have adopted a number line.

ATHENEUM. Prior to 1986, first editions are stated; since then, they have used a number line.

ATLANTIC MONTHLY PRESS. The date at the bottom of the title page should be the same as the date of publication on the copyright page. Prior to 1925, there is no way of knowing for sure.

BANTAM. Number line.

BLACK SPARROW PRESS. Check the colophon page. Many Black Sparrow books have no indication of printing there, but title pages on first editions are in color; on subsequent editions, the title page is in black and white, and there is an indication of printing.

BOBBS-MERRILL. Inconsistent in the early years; check for a bow and arrow at the bottom of the copyright page. After 1936, the books state "First Edition."

BONI & LIVERIGHT. Subsequent printings are identified.

JONATHAN CAPE, LTD. First editions are stated.

CHATTO & WINDUS, LTD. Subsequent printings are identified.

CHRONICLE. Subsequent printings are identified.

CROWN. Before mid-1979, first editions were not identified, but subsequent printings were. After that, there is usually a number line and a statement of printing.

DELACORTE PRESS. Delacorte was originally part of Dell; then, subsequent editions were stated. Afterward, either a statement of first edition or a number line.

DELL. States date of first publication; no indications of other printings.

DIAL PRESS. First editions stated.

DODD, MEAD, & CO. Prior to 1976, no effort was made to indicate printing history. Sporadic efforts were made to either state first edition or to state subsequent printings, but there was no general rule adhered to until post-1976, when the number line was adopted.

DORRANCE & CO. Subsequent printings are identified.

DOUBLEDAY. First editions are stated.

DOUBLEDAY, DORAN & CO. First editions are stated.

DOUBLEDAY, PAGE & CO. First editions are stated.

E. P. DUTTON & CO. Prior to 1976, first editions were not identified, at which point they were stated on the copyright page. Subsequent printings were always identified.

ECCO PRESS. First editions are stated.

FABER & FABER. Subsequent editions are stated.

FARRAR, STRAUS & GIROUX. First editions are stated.

DONALD I. FINE. A number line is used.

DAVID R. GODINE. First editions are stated.

GROVE PRESS. Editions are stated.

JOHNNY GRUELLE CO. Printers of the popular *Raggedy Ann and Andy* books. There is no indication of printing at all.

HAMISH HAMILTON. First editions are stated prior to 1976; afterward, subsequent editions are stated.

HARCOURT, BRACE & CO. Subsequent editions are stated; first editions often, but not always, have a "1" on the copyright page prior to the 1930s; afterward, first editions are stated.

HARCOURT BRACE JOVANOVICH. First editions are stated.

HARPER & BROTHERS. First editions are stated.

HARPER & ROW. A combination of stating first edition and displaying a number line is used. In the mid-1970s, the number line usually appeared on the last page of the book.

GEORGE G. HARRAP & CO. On the copyright page is a line reading "First published." Reprintings are indicated.

WILLIAM HEINEMANN. States "First published" with reprintings indicated as such.

HODDER & STOUGHTON. Prior to the 1940s, no indication of printing was made. After that, printings are dated, and first printings are usually (though not always) stated.

HENRY HOLT & CO. Before 1945, no regular method of indicating printing was used. In general, look for a date of printing, which often indicated first edition; on many titles, subsequent editions were stated. After 1945, first editions are stated. Since 1988, the company has also used a number line.

HOLT, RINEHART, & WINSTON. First editions are stated.

HOUGHTON MIFFLIN CO. Title pages are dated on first editions; afterward, this dating is dropped, and the copyright page indicated which printing. In more recent years, a number line has also been used.

ALFRED A. KNOPF. Up to the mid-1930s, first edition was not indicated, but subsequent printings were. Afterward, first edition is stated.

J. B. LIPPINCOTT. States first edition; often also has a number line.

LITTLE, BROWN & CO. Through the early part of this century, first editions were indicated by a date line on the copyright page, indicating first publication. Subsequent printings added additional date lines. More recently, first editions are stated, and a number line is used.

LIVERIGHT PUBLISHING. Early volumes from this publisher only indicate subsequent printings; more recently, a number line has been used.

MACMILLAN (after 1976, Macmillan Publishing). States "Published" with original date. Subsequent printings are noted below on copyright page. Since 1936, first editions were indicated; since 1979, a number line has been used.

METHUEN. Books state "First published in . . ." Subsequent reprintings are so noted.

WILLIAM MORROW & CO. First printings are usually stated; subsequent printings are always stated. More recently, a number line has also been used, with the number on the far right of the line indicating the year of publication, e.g., "1 2 3 4 5 94 93 92 91 90" to show that the book first appeared in 1990.

MYSTERIOUS PRESS. First editions are stated, and a number line is used.

NEW DIRECTIONS. Before 1970, no indication of printing was made. After that, first printings were stated.

W. W. NORTON & CO. First editions are stated. A number line is also used.

PANTHEON BOOKS. Subsequent printings are identified; first printings are usually, but not always, stated.

PENGUIN. Uses a number line and the statement "First Published."

PETER PAUPER PRESS. Early Peter Pauper books were limited editions; a statement of limitation indicates that the book is a first edition. More recently, there has been no identification used.

PLATT & MUNK. No identification has been used.

PRENTICE-HALL. First editions are stated, either by "First Edition" or by the use of a number line.

PRICE STERN SLOAN. First editions are stated. Prior to the late 1980s, books said "First edition" on the copyright page. More recently, this has been supplanted by the use of a number line.

PUTNAM. Subsequent editions in early Putnam books were usually (not always) stated. First editions should have a date on the title page. More recently, a number line has been used.

RANDOM HOUSE. First editions of Random House books are stated. However, a number line is also frequently used. Random House number lines only go down to "2." Therefore, a statement of "First Edition" combined with a number line stopping at "2" indicates that the book is a true first.

REILY & LEE. After 1937, first editions are stated. Prior to that, there was no regular method used.

ROUTLEDGE & KEGAN PAUL. States "First Published" on copyright page, with the date agreeing with the copyright date.

ST. MARTIN'S PRESS. No indication is given as to the printing of a book.

CHARLES SCRIBNER'S SONS. Prior to 1930, there was no indication of printing given, although on some titles you can check to see if the date on the copyright page matches the one on the title page. After 1930, there was the adoption of the now famous Scribner's *A*. From the 1930s into the 1970s, first editions were identified by the appearance of a capital *A* on the copyright page. After 1972, there is still an *A*, but there is also a number line.

SHEED & WARD. Subsequent editions are stated.

SHEED ANDREWS & MCMEEL. Subsequent editions are stated.

SIMON & SCHUSTER. Subsequent editions are stated on early Simon & Schuster books; also see if the date on the copyright page agrees with the date on the title page. Like so many publishers, a number line was added in the 1970s.

GIBBS SMITH. First editions are stated.

PEREGRINE SMITH. Prior to 1980, there were no indications of edition. Afterward, date on copyright page and title page should match.

STEIN & DAY. Subsequent editions are noted.

VAN NOSTRAND REINHOLD. A number line is used.

VIKING PRESS. Subsequent editions are stated. More recently, a number line has been used on many (but not all) titles.

WARNER BOOKS. First editions are stated.

GLOSSARY

ARC—advance reader's copy. A paperback edition of a book, put out for publicity before the trade edition hits the stands.

association copy—a copy inscribed by the author to another famous or important person; or a copy handled by a famous or important person and including some mark of ownership. An example is Herman Melville's copy of *Paradise Lost*.

boards—the stiff part of a book's bindings; the front and back covers.

broadside—a single-page publication.

chapbook—a small book, often pamphlet-sized. Chapbooks are put out by many small presses, and many poets have their first publications in chapbooks, featuring fifteen or twenty poems.

chip, chipped—a piece of the dust jacket missing.

colophon—the last page of a book, stating printing and type information; many publishers used to use this page for copyright information.

dust jacket (DJ)—the decorative paper covering of a book's binding.

ephemera—nonbook items put out by or about an author, such as magazine articles, broadsides, etc.; also promotional items put out by publishers, and other nonbook items that can be related to a book.

flyleaf—the first loose page of a book, usually a decorative color. Also known as *free endpaper*.

fore-edge—the front edge of the book; where the book opens.

foxed, foxing—a chemical reaction that causes spots on a book's pages to brown; foxing looks like an animal with muddy paws has run across the pages.

half title—a page, set before the title page, with only the book's title printed on it. Also known as the *bastard title*.

headband—a small strip of cloth at the top of the book's spine, used for reinforcement.

hinge—where the binding meets the flyleaf. Also known as *gutter*.

hinged—when the hinge of the book is starting to break apart.

hypermodern—an author whose books first appeared within the last ten years.

leaves—the pages of a book.

number line—a means of identifying edition. Most common is a line on the copyright page that reads "1 2 3 4 5 6 7 8 9 10." The lowest number is the number of the edition.

OP—out of print.

paste-down—the paper covering on the inside of the boards. When you open the cover of a book, this is what's on the left side, attached to the binding; to the right is the flyleaf.

point—a difference between editions of a particular book.

price clip—when the printed price has been cut off the dust jacket.

proofs—an early stage of book production; at this point, the editor and author have made changes to the original typescript, and the manuscript has been typeset; but it is not the final version of the book. Proofs are usually bound in plain paper wrappers.

remainder—a book sold at substantial discount by a publisher who has printed too many copies.

rolled—when the spine is out of alignment, leaning toward one side or the other.

signature—a gathering of pages.

spine—the back edge of a book, what you see when the book is put on a shelf.

state—an edition may have several states. What differentiates states are points, differences in the text or appearance of a book.

trade edition (vs. trade paperback)—the trade edition is the standard edition of a book; a trade paperback is a large-sized paperback.

wrappers—paper covers, as opposed to a hardcover book. Paperbacks are usually described as "in wrappers" in dealer catalogs.

INDEX

◦◦